Presence

Presence
Live Poets' 30 Years at Don Bank
Edited by Danny Gardner

This book is dedicated to all those poets and musicians past and present who have performed at Live Poets – and their observers – and all who read this book and follow our activities in the future in whatever form they may appear.

Special dedication to Live Poets regulars
John Carey and Ed Wilson, who left us in 2022.

Presence: Live Poets' 30 Years at Don Bank
ISBN 978 1 76109 409 5
Copyright © text individual contributors 2022
Cover design: Danny Gardner
Front cover photo: Helen Lu

First published 2022 by
GINNINDERRA PRESS
PO Box 3461 Port Adelaide 5015
www.ginninderrapress.com.au

Contents

Foreword		**9**
Introduction		**11**
2015		**14**
Advice for van-dwelling	Beth Spencer	28
The Mariner	John Egan	29
I'll Mould a Tune	Geoff Yule Smith	30
Weatherboard	Dianne Schultz-Tesmar	31
Live Poets Players Special Performances		**32**
2016		**55**
Life and Death	Enrique Horna	70
The Scream V	Ed Wilson	71
fantasy here at home	Kit Kelen	74
Early Questions	Martin Langford	75
Prologue	Richard James Allen	77
The Spindle Shell	Audrey Molloy	78
Old Tree	Helen Wren	79
Frida: The Red Flag	Lou Steer	81
Ho Ho Heil	Les Wicks	82
Song For Wendy	Kate Maclurcan	84
Other Major Shows Featuring Art and Music at Don Bank		**85**
2017		**115**
letter to frank	Mark Roberts	138
Grand Theft Auto	Philip Hammial	139
Heidelbergian Psyche	Rebecca Kylie Law	140
My Prometheus	Marie Mcmillan	141
Crave Love	Garry McDougall	143
Caribbean Jewel	Wilfred Roach	146
hume and hovell monument	Willem Tibben	147
Day Trips to Dee Why	Cathy Jones	148
Tiger behind those rubber trees	Dona Samson Zappone	150

The empty stage	David Hallett	153
The Year of the Tree	Katherine Gallagher	154
Time Is Memory	George Clark	156
Monumental Care	Mark Mahemoff	157
the other thing	Rob Kennedy	158
The Words Behind the Poems		**159**
2018		**163**
I had a crazy idea to descend into the sewers		
	Ember Flame	184
Intercultural Communication	David Gilbey	187
Teeth and Passport Photos	Clark Gormley	188
These Are a Few of My Least Favourite Words		
	Hamish Danks Brown	189
Couch Adrift	Philip Radmall	190
Jacky Gallipoli	Anthony Scanlon	191
Writer's Block	Dulcie Meddows	192
The Weather Always Wins	Maureen Maguire	193
Float, Ophelia, float	Tatiana Bonch-Osmolovskaya	194
Michael on Darlinghurst Road	Charles Freyberg	196
You Stole My Childhood	Seher Aydinlik	198
I was going to go to Dorothea Lasky's book party in Brooklyn, but instead I stayed on the couch with my depression, not crying		
	Paula Harris	200
How Do You Tame an African Eagle?		
	Dorothy Makasa	202
My Heart Has an Embassy	Jennifer Maiden	203
The First Publishing Decade		**204**
2019		**210**
1937	Emilia Lionetti	229
For Detainees	Susan Bacsi	230

Bamboo	Mary Tang	232
Marcus's Song	Beth O'Driscoll	233
No Friend But the Mountain	Lynne Fairy	236
and my heart crumples like a coke can		
	Ali Whitelock	238
Feline Frolics	Mark Marusic	240
To Do List	Anna Couani	242
The Goddess of Forever	Kari McKern	243
Wildlife Park, Gold Coast	Lesley Synge	244
I Might as well Be from Mars	Nur Alam	245
I Met a Teacher Who Returned from Mars		
	Bhagavadas Sriskanthadas	247
The Little Boy Knocked Off His Bike		
	Jennifer Compton	248
Mont Aigual	Adam Aitken	249
Mohammed in Minnesota	Alastair Spate	250
September 11	Bee Perusco	252
Coming of age	Rozanna Lilley	254
Fatima	Raghid Nahhas	255
So Sleeps the Deer	Ghassan Alameddine	257
Icons of Live Poets		**258**
2020 – The Year We Had to Forget		**269**
In a Sunburnt Country	Anne Casey	275
Untitled	Wil Boag	276
Ode to Nimbyism	Des Maddalena	277
Untitled (Ibis)	Robert Howe	281
I am – i am (trilogy)	Olga Kulanowska	282
The Burn	Jill Carter-Hansen	283
Authorities found in his possession a 'Literary Device' capable of disrupting perception over a wide area		
	Alan Gannaway	285

August 2020	Ann Jarjoura	286
The Lovely Rituals	David Wansbrough	288
Adam	Ten Ch'in Ü	289
Is It Really 2021?		**290**
Matala	Barvara Hush	301
Down	Kerry Jamieson	302
How to Cry in Outer Space	Simon Lenthen	303
King Charles	Devina Bedford	304
Ghost Town	Neera Handa	307
Friendship	Michaela Simoni	308
The Unwelcome Permanency of Implausibility	Trish Jean	309
A Virus Has Escaped!	Yasemin Dolcel	311
Ties	David L Falcon	313
Against the Glass	Roberta Lowing	315
You Get One At Every Meeting…	John Carey	316
Some Sort of Reason	Danny Gardner	317
The Party		**318**
Passing the Baton On		**323**
Acknowledgements		**324**
Thanks		**326**
David Wansbrough		**327**
Sue Hicks		**329**

Foreword

On words, music and keeping an old house alive

Anyone who cares for old buildings, as I do, knows that use is central to their well-being. A structure that is left locked-up, unloved and unvisited, decays. The connection is in part obvious. When people frequent a building, they notice issues that need addressing – leaks, cracks, rot, rust. Visitation guards against unwanted attention – vandalism and break-ins. But there seems also to be an organic relationship between human use and structural well-being. It is as if people breathe life into buildings by being in them – a form of resuscitation perhaps.

Live Poets have quite literally been breathing life into Don Bank – the oldest timber building on the north shore – for thirty years. Having formed in a Neutral Bay café in 1990, they became Live Poets at Don Bank the following year. The vital connection between people and venue has been sustained ever since. I suspect it is symbiotic, for the old house itself speaks of 175 years of change and stasis.

North Sydney Council has long supported creativity within its boundaries but the relationship with Live Poets at Don Bank is one of the most enduring and mutually beneficial. Council is charged with maintaining state heritage-listed Don Bank and the wonderful words and magical music that waft across its boards and through its rooms make that job a little easier.

Congratulations and thank you to Live Poets at Don Bank for thirty years of…well, sheer poetry.

Dr Ian Hoskins
North Sydney Council Historian

Note this use of language in a journal entry of the explorer John Wills (of Burke and Wills fame), 1860: 'I can't see our bodies can last longer than a couple more days. We are in excellent spirits.'

How is that for duality – the ability to be able to recognise and exercise two independent principles at the same time? Duality is largely what makes the arts, and literature particularly, work. It enables us to escape our present circumstances and be inspired by what we can imagine. It's the greatest gift and facility of our greatest invention – our language.

'If you are only concerned about not making a mistake – you will communicate nothing. It is when I am least conscious of what I am doing that I [can] perform at my best – let go – into the moment.' – Yo Yo Ma – Chinese-American cellist

'The whole essence about learning lines is to forget them so you can make them up again…and sound like you thought of them that instant.'– Glenda Jackson, award-winning English actor

Poetry reading is not just acting but it fails when performed rote fashion. You don't just read your poem out loud – you must inhabit it anew each time.

'Poetry and women only lay their last veil aside for their lovers.' – Honoré de Balzac

Introduction

The poet has told you so much about him/herself before he/she have said a word. It's in the way they move to the front of the room or approach a lectern. It's in the manner in which they arrange their merchandise and reading matter. How they drape their excess garments over a chair – flick that scarf or bandanna to one side. The way their eyes address the surroundings – like a sportsman 'radaring' the field of play in order to focus on their next challenge. All that to establish a presence. Posit an identity. Draw attention. Some may be almost apologetic, less imposing than you expected – off-putting even – with awkward gestures or voice tones if seen for the first time shorn of their book. But all an audience can do is wait. And that is the performer's chief weapon. They and they alone – at least initially – can direct the traffic.

The front of the sitting room at Don Bank cottage has seen countless people step forward to deliver over the three decades plus Live Poets has been in residence. Too many people to calculate – in multifarious ways —with as varying levels of effectiveness as there are different types of people. They each have their method, their quest, and their almost unconscious, guiding principles. This book is devoted to them all. The ones we may remember fondly, even fiercely, too – familiarly; as much as those who mystified and/or transported us – as though they were only the shell housing some other-worldly impact and effect. There are those who we never quite worked out. Those who we didn't take to, felt repelled by, but we may still recall what they said, and how they said it.

Some may be more the actor or performer or easy authority,

even. Some may play an instrument or don a character's carapace to promote their case. But most have only one tool they can use to occupy our attention. Words. Language. Certain reconstructions of what and how we've been addressed before. That might seem, on the surface, a limited armoury. But despite these times of conformity and mass control of many by the few as our globe seems to shrink (even as the concomitant cries for 'freedom' and 'the dignity of expression' sound) words are still the most useful and frequently the only, device, we possess. To connect a watcher's mind with our own.

Welcome to Live Poets' 30 Years at Don Bank, focusing particularly on the years 2015 to the present. We do look back to our first decade in publishing. There are special chapters on the Live Poets Players and other events where music and art have featured. We salute the icons of Live Poets past. We look at how the Live Poets interview was initiated. We track our monthly meetings with our annual competitions and atmosphere features like 'Literary Cities', cultural and travel eye-witness responses, historical testaments, and so on. Of course we have poems and stories from many of our guests and our regulars and new found friends in the Open Section or providing conversations over supper in the courtyard. But, as much as individuals have directed traffic with their idiosyncrasies in verse, story and song, our group efforts too have made their mark. We've been louder and more collective more often, it seems. May that continue the more the future and the fortunes of our heirs perhaps become less certain.

But to finish where we began. Over the last decades at Don Bank – particularly from this convenor's perspective – the following have exhibited significant 'identity presence' in their performances if you like: Bogdan Koca (when he spoke to God on the phone, no one had any doubt!), Jess Cook, Ben Ezra, Garry Macdougall, Paula Harris, Amy Bodassian, Kari McKern.

But we must always watch out for that diminutive figure – any night – who comes on late but winds up making our hair stand on end!

There was also the night Kylie Lee Ward began her guest reading. The lights had gone out and there was a brief pause for a figure to come along the hallway at the back of Don Bank. Then she rounded the turn and was moving past the seats to the front – an electronic lantern in her hand. She then began emanating from her words in her opening poem 'My Guest'. She became successively that night a bird parting the flesh of a cadaver in a graveyard, a dame finding goblins in the roots of herbs in a glass of tea; a soldier besieged with unsuspected visions in a journey home from war. All the while maintaining reign over an audience of eyes. Some people I know, who've seen a few things in their time, literally had jaws agape.

I was inescapably back at the café in Live Poets' first year when Daryl Wayne Hall led us to 'Terror Beneath the Sheets', the alcoholic's starkest confession in cold-turkey rehab.

2015

It's April and we are in the crowd that attended the group's twenty-fifth birthday (the February and March meetings were covered in our previous anthology). People are invited to speak of their most vivid experience of Live Poets at Don Bank.

Bee Perusco recalled talking to a friend in Melbourne, Steve Smart, who mentioned he was coming up 'to a gig near you with a good friend soon'. Oh, Bee replied, 'Where?' Steve said, 'Don Bank.' So I have a new saying, Bee added. 'If you want to find out what's going on in your area, go to Melbourne!'

Bee came to Don Bank for the first time shortly after (in 2013) and now they (Bee and husband Alan Gannaway) are virtually the Don Bank house band!

This night they performed 'Mr Politician', 'It's Gonna be All Right' and a nifty little Spanish number.

Philip Radmall was asked what his fondest memory of Don Bank was. 'Mario Cabrera's repeated affirmations of "Oh yeah!" at the show *A Walk Across Spain* (with the work of Lorca and others) in 2013.' Phil then read two poems: 'Rock of Ages' and 'Horrorscope'.

Helen Wren read a poem called 'Letting Go' about a friend of advanced age trying hang-gliding.

George Clark: 'I want to try out a couple of meditative narratives – how religion infuses human behaviour.' He read a poem written at four a.m. on the family farm: 'sensing the expansive grandeur of things'.

Jim Quealey invited us to recognise the hundredth anniversary of surfing in Australia. He cited the concept of the Zen of the Ocean and Surfing with quotes from famous poems about the sea. Such as 'Out of the water I am nothing' as the great Duke Kahanamoku from Hawaii who pioneered the practice in Australia said. Then Jim read 'Sunday Morning' about his own out-of-body experiences while surfing.

On a similar subject, Moree Ward, a Live Poets regular from two decades back, performed the hilarious 'Toes, Starfish and a proud performing Shark' which instructed us, 'toes in your feet have minds of their own / next time you look down you find a star-fish instead!'

Geoff Yule Smith, like Moree Ward, had come out of the woodwork and back from his past associations with Don Bank to join us at the twenty-fifth anniversary night. 'I don't have a weird and wonderful story to tell you. But I have a poem written to a person a thousand years from now. And two short poems about Bali. One, 'Bali', from when I visited there on the way to Europe – it was a reality too beautiful to be true. How it had changed in just twenty months. He then read, 'Something's Gone out of Bali'.

Halee Isil Cosar offered a song of pleasure sung by a beggar: 'see the allure in the connection?'

Mohsen and Jamal from Iraq had a story to share. Jamal: 'Ten years ago we came together and performed as one but today we have divorced! I've left my poem and walked away. But running from words is always good!' Mohsen: 'Now Jamal has started writing in English he doesn't need a translator!' And Mohsen read a poem of his own set on the frontiers of space: 'I walk around the yolk in the egg of this possibility!'

Barvara read her grandfather's poem recalling overlooking 'Dead Man's Gully' (Anzac Cove) to his wife and child at home. In that place, 'children wrapped in innocence are in my waking thoughts. / Darkness now appears.' The combatants used to share things in between the bouts of gunfire, throwing cigarettes to each other, they were so physically close.

Then Willem Tibben came forward. 'I'm going to go back to before Live Poets, from the beginning of 1984. I ran PIE – Poetry, Imagery and Expression – at the Parra town hall with Daryl Wayne Hall. We used to put an ad in the *Parramatta Advertiser* and a journalist there, Sue Hicks, saw the note and she and Danny came along to see us. Afterwards she said, 'Well, if you can do this in Parramatta, we can do it on the North Shore!'

The convenor continued, 'At a time when we thought culture stopped well before we got to Parramatta, it was a dangerous place to go!'

Bill: 'Yeah. No art west of Concord Road!'

Mr Tibben then read his poem from *Litmus Suite*, Live Poets' first anthology, 'Did Bill Shakespeare have to wash the Dishes?' Or, as the poem also avers, did he say, 'I'm working late' and joins the arty crowd at the Mermaid where for the first time he met a Dark Lady?

Doug Nichols, an armchair anecdotist from way back: 'I don't write poetry. I read it every day. I came here for a while some time ago and I felt my talk about the dead poets was excess to requirements. One rule Charles Bukowski had about writing poetry was 'Don't do it! If you don't have the skill, you'll have to pretend. A lot do. But if you write poetry, it's got to come from so deep,' but maybe CB just didn't want too much competition!'

Dianne's story came next. 'I came to Live Poets when it was at the L'Orangerie in Neutral Bay, but I only went once, don't know why. But at Don Bank I never read.' (The convenor broke in at that point. 'You did read one before by Talbot McCarroll – it was in our Literature Olympics in 2016.') 'And I won't read tonight!' Dianne laughed.

And there was Marie Mcmillan's poem for the mother of the (recently) beheaded captor of Isis, James Foley – called 'I am Not Salome and you are not John the Baptist!' A sober epic read off by heart that silence afterwards could not challenge.

The special poetry guest for May was Beth Spencer – reading from her latest book, *Vagabondage*. Beth had forged a bit of notoriety about selling her house and going off to live in a van because, as the poem says, 'I couldn't afford a flat.' I designed the publicity around the idea Beth was going to drop by in the van and declaim from it! I made up a cardboard replica of the interior of a van which would 'background' Beth as she performed at the front of the Don Bank sitting room.

After a brief conversation with the convenor, Beth read the long piece 'Forgetting', which took us in stages through her relationship with her mother's dementia. It was part of how Beth weaned herself off from living in a house. She would park at her mother's care residence and spend the evening, after dinner, with her before going off to a quiet spot a few streets away. As part of the survival tactics of living in a van, you are encouraged to park under a strong streetlight to deter thieves and have a weapon at the ready as you get beneath the covers after lights out.

The best tactic it seems with dementia is to join the other person in their 'perpetual now'. But after swapping stories about their respective childhoods one night, there is the heartbreaking question from her mother Beth then faces: 'So tell me, where did we meet?'

There were many other poignant testaments in Beth's book,

albeit often laced with errant humour, in such poems as 'Free Fall', 'The Pain Body', 'Rescue Me' (which brought a lump to the throat) and, hilariously, 'Lost Woman Looks for Herself' – based on a true story! Later – almost fittingly she thought, once the matter was, thankfully, resolved – Beth lost her car keys and her change purse, momentarily.

Geoff Yule Smith was back for real after the birthday re-union with Live Poets and featured forcefully in the open section with 'Truth – Spare me the Mumbo Jumbo!' Amory Hill offered up a funny telephone call with the US president. Moree Ward delighted with a revisit of 'Java' from *Ten Years Live* and an Ogden Nash poem. Des Pensa's poem started, 'The Worm is Hungry / the Buddha is Meditating.' Newcomer Dominica was very 'out there' with 'Taking My Breath Away' and 'I Want to Keep You!' Marie read an erotic letter from James Joyce to Nora Barnacle.

There was also a session of people reading from Shawn Usher's 'opus' collection, *Letters of Note* – people drew their choices blind from a hat. Vicki McDonald reiterated baseball 'hero' Jacki Robinson's missive to President Eisenhower decrying the great man's call for Negroes to be 'patient' about human rights. Marie read Queen Elizabeth's recipe for drop scones for Dwight. Joanna Jasny intoned Frederic Flom's thank you to Bob Hope for entertaining the troops in Korea. Des Pensa (Maddalena) 're-woke' Mark Twain's fawning, over-written message to Walt Whitman on the Bard's seventieth birthday. The convenor read Bernard Clegg's letter to Oscar Wilde contesting OW's assertion that 'Art is Useless.' Dianne read the marketing manager of Heinz thanking Andy Warhol for his 'recent support'.

In June, Des Pensa (Maddalena) was the guest with the physical launch of the first book in his fantasy fiction trilogy, *Visions of Chaos* (he'd already unveiled it online). Acquitain, a streetwise city merchant wizard, uses a cunning mind replete with charm, coercion, deception and illusion to gain confidence in a dangerous jungle environment. He and his priestess companion, Miranda, join forces to help Acquitain escape a bounty hunter pursuing him into adventures with little people, shamans, spirits, strange rituals, giant ants and a haunted magical mask. The duo come to realise they are only pawns caught up in a mind game between powerful adversaries seeking fulfilment of an ominous prophecy. They decide they are attracted to each other most because they both had strong-willed mothers searching for missing fathers. The quest to discover their roots is a key to unlocking earth's destiny of course. But they must first survive the predations that seek to frustrate them – even as they both use the ability to shape-shift into slimes, jungle cats, snakes, bears and eagles to keep each other off balance. They don't want to find out what their relationship means too early. The startling cover depicts Miranda in half-human, half-jungle cat form.

The complexity of the subject matter would seem to daunt presentation to a 'live' audience *sans* props. But Des's lively rendering of the text and use of voices to render character kept the crowd amused. The lead duo's interactions frequently end in humorous even ridiculous outcomes that they must continually refocus from. The ultimate destinations of their coupling – Miranda's quest for the Moon Mist and Aquitaine's puzzling out of the secret of Astaria – would be played out in the concluding volumes of the trilogy, which Des was still putting together.

This evening also featured the annual Monologue Challenge and a segment called In One Beast.

The challenge this night had a classical bent with Des reading from *Medea*, Geoff from *Lysistrata* and Bob from *Cyrano de Bergerac* – but Bee took the gong by audience vote with her Puck speech from Shakespeare's *Midsummer Night's Dream*.

The In One Beast session was where poets had to present a piece about an animal or a bird. These would be interspersed with comments from naturalists in the field – many of them sourced from the *Bedside Book of Beasts* by Margaret Atwood's partner, Graham Gibson. The convenor read a quote from Ecclesiastes (man vs beast) followed by his poem 'Chapultapec Zoo'. There followed 'A Mirror of my Own Imagination' by naturalist, Ellen Mclay. There was an absorbing description of being taken by a lion by adventurer Dr David Livingstone in 'A Kind of Dreaminess'. Then 'The Conversation of Death' (how wolves hunt) by Barry Lopez. A piece called 'Bears Resemble People and Like to Dance' by a Mewak native. 'What about the Werewolf, the Yeti and the Steppenwolf inside the body of a human?' asked Herman Hesse – and that was all he wrote! There was more on bears – how they are sometimes people with bear heads and brain, a form of theriotype. There were echoes of native symbolism like 'Wearing the bear hat I had access to strange new powers.' Telling echoes from the world of instinct, of savagery and cruelty, of unsublimated raw nature follow – but man is the only animal who kills but does not eat.

This was all good background grist of course to foreshadow Des's sometimes extreme romance in the jungle – preparing our mind for confrontations we could not predict.

In the Open Section this night, Geoff Yule Smith did two

poems, 'Wooden Horse' and 'In My Room'. Alan Gannaway read an original, 'Light Can be Broken', and he and Bee later presented some songs: 'Dream a Little Dream of Me' (ex Mamas and the Papas) and an original, 'Tell the Truth'. The convenor read a J S Harry poem from *Ten Years Live* to honour dear Jan's recent passing. Bob Howe borrowed Wallace Stevens's methodology to produce 'Thirteen Ways of Looking at a Budgie' (not a blackbird!). Remy presented a Tony Abbott poem. In the In One Beast section, Bee produced a piece from 'Homeless: A Sea Creature Speaks', Amory Hill reflected on a pet canary. Kerry performed 'Currawong in the Rain.'

For the August meeting, it was a pleasure to welcome as a special guest Yarrie Bangura, lately from Sierre Leone, who has self-nurtured a distinctive and reactive spoken word style. She's also gone on stage and performed in London in the show *Baulkham Hills African Ladies Troupe* – and performed with Auburn Poets & Writers in the Sydney Festival. She is quite the young lady in a hurry in the performance stakes. I keep encouraging her to get out to Bankstown and the open-mike scene there, but she has a wary, shy side. She could probably do with a good booking manager to secure gigs with appropriate remuneration and to encourage more training in the storytelling art, though it is traditionally part of the family background from where she comes from in Africa.

To actually open proceedings this night – which would include the third annual running of the Short Fiction Cup – there was some discussion on a recent US critic's essay on 'Why Acting Matters' with reference to the performance aspect for poets. Several apparently inexplicable things went on in the background this night. The key to the back shed with the chairs was not in its usual place and Helen removed the door from its hinges with a screwdriver (don't tell anyone!). The people-counter 'alarm' at the front door could not be switched off. Yarrie, nervous of getting home too late, disappeared immediately after her reading and I had to send her a cheque in the mail. After the running of the Short Fiction Cup, I couldn't find the decorated cup to present to George Clark for his second win.

Yarrie was hesitant in interview but shone when her material took flight. Working without notes, she enacted a defiant 'I Want My Innocence Back'. A beautiful lyric followed, linking to 'My Home from Home' (finding peace in Australia). She then segued to a piece called 'The Woman', which included another song and a story her grandmother told her where a pregnant woman becomes as one with animals and birds in similar situations. It had to be seen rather than described but the audience was left mesmerised.

Susan Sleepwriter got things going in the Short Fiction Cup with 'Boils of Billy', which features an uncomfortable realisation. Wil Roach informed us of 'My First Day of School'. Kerry Jamieson read the haunting 'The Willow Tree'. George Clark mined the strange tactics of the 'ESP Peeper'. Then Tatiana Bonch and her son Mikhael inhabited suitably (for this night) strange circs in 'Silence' and 'Night Visitor' respectively. Graham Cameron took us tantalisingly to the brink with 'The Decision' and Marie Mcmillan emanated a night at the Vivid festival. The voting was close. George garnered one more than Mikhael, who was one ahead of Tatiana, Graham and Marie! It was George's second win in three years the Cup comp has been run.

There was also a section this night about the stories behind great artists. For instance, Michelangelo had his nose broken in his teens and had a reputation as a thug. Leonardo was praised for his classless art but why does the *Mona Lisa* not have any eyebrows? Vermeer was typecast as the trapped provider – his wife was always having children. Cézanne could not bear to be touched. But who has asked his supporter-wife about that?

In September, we put out the welcome mat for Ahmad Al-Rady – the co-convenor (with Sarah Saleh) of the infamous Bankstown Poetry Slam. We also had a section, Having Fun with Catullus, with people reading translations of the sassy poet of the late Roman empire, famous for his 'commentary' on its social life. There was also a reading of Judith Wright's work to mark the hundredth anniversary of her birth.

The interview with Ahmad was absorbing. 'Originally, we didn't want to fall back on Rumi or Hafeez's poems that poets in our area knew. We didn't want to travel to the city, an hour travelling and half hour packing, to see at most two hours of poetry, you know? And a lot of the poets we'd go to see we couldn't always relate to their work, so we thought, why not make something, an event here, in the local area, at Bankstown? And so we went around all these places inquiring and the people heard our questions and thought, 'poetry – slam – young people!' and shook their heads. They just weren't wanting to 'get' the idea and we were quite downhearted and resigned. If it hadn't been for one wonderful person who had a contact in the youth centre, we might have given up. Through their help, we were able to establish something. And we got the event started and people came, and kept coming and coming. And we were pulling in all these numbers. It just went a bit crazy. And we thought, wow! We've started something here.'

And word of mouth and people's experiences quickly made the Bankstown Poetry Slam a place of legend.

Ahmad was asked about the Stand Tall/Speak Out initiative with the youth.

'That was something set up with the schools, and we thought, we have to do whole classes, you know. We don't want to use poetry as a therapy for the same group – always in that corner, disconnected – to make this work. We want whole classes and everyone on the same footing and poetry central to everyone's purpose. It's not easy to organise, you know, if you don't have support, because we didn't get any grants for the venue. We had to make our own revenue.'

It's all about giving youth a voice, right?

'Yes, and you know this is talking about the sort of stuff we don't often discuss at home. But with all a person's peers involved, it's making poetry cool, you know? Because you take things from hip hop and music and you're writing about things that are happening in your life (contemporary issues) and then you get to that competitive edge and people see mates doin' things and – it's not sport, you know. It's poetry being cool and people being vulnerable, being prepared to do that and dealing with it. It's not the forms of old but you do read other stuff and someone comes up to you one day and asks, do you know about this guy, Keats? There's so many connections made.'

And it's part of your culture still…

'Where people are talking about what's happening to them and through getting together they find other people who have similar issues and things arising out of them.'

And the street outreach thing I read about?

'It was something I did a while ago. I still do when I get the time – things are a bit busier now! But, yeah, it's helping young people, particularly, who are looking for a way to get respect. And you help make them feel they are being listened to and you can help them get their potential together.'

Make no mistake, Ahmad was an inspirational character. This carried over into his poem presentation, the ladies particularly paying plenty of attention as he unveiled such pieces as 'Grandma', 'Istanbul' and 'Like a Man' with its intimations re family structures in Ahmad's childhood.

In the Reciters of Catullus session, there was a lively 'fireside' conversation among the ladies – Marie, Roberta, Tatiana, Dianne and Kerry particularly – after they read out excerpts from the poet of the Roman era. Marie Mac recalled that some of the rhymes Catullus used were quite focused (at least in translation) – it wasn't all tossed off as cheap criticism or satire. There were questions – whether he was an establishment rake or was he just humoured by the regime, like the film character Mephisto, say, was in Nazi Germany, and accorded latitude to operate. A true portrait of his life – outside the verses – in that time might be revealing. All agreed there was a definite style and panache there. Was he ever threatened or was he a sacred cow? The establishment would certainly not encourage imitation. There are in the verses very knowing observations – even aspersions – about public figures…was his milieu only the select few 'in the know'? Was his attitude a reflection on a culture that used abuse as a common procedure when morals collapsed? Crucial of course was how Catallus was presented to English readers. Was it so free-form in the original – and did that make it more salacious by default? It's established now that you keep hearing about all this bacchanalian behaviour in Roman society and boys being used, Dianne stressed. 'They didn't do it with the young girls. They wanted to keep them pure.'

In the Open Section, Peter Rhodes made his debut northside: 'I've been meaning to for so long!' People were reminded about the Weimar Cabaret coming up and that we were still looking for people who wanted to present.

I had an interesting conversation with Ahmad and his partner, swapping notes about the Bankstown Slam atmosphere compared with Live Poets. 'Here, it was harder to see how the audience reacted, whether they liked my material in the beginning. Later, I was better able to gauge the vibe.' Ahmad added, 'Often with slams, you get process more than content.' But, Sara said, 'You can get a lot of different styles. It doesn't all have to be strutting your stuff. It can be like being told a secret – revealing a character.'

October was the occasion of the Weimar Cabaret and Beyond – poems, stories and poets' songs by and about Berlin in the twentieth century. It was probably the most comprehensive performance yet for the Live Poets Players (see the chapter Live Poets Players).

In the Open Section that preceded it, Bhuppen Thakker presented 'the first and last poems I write', Geoff Yule Smith checked in with 'I'll Mould a Tune' and 'You Get What you Pay For'. Angela presented a piece about North Sydney – grab her, that's rare! Helen Wren read Yeats's 'Byzantium'. Jim Quealey did '4.10 train to Moree' and a preview of the Melbourne Cup, 'Race Day Again'. The irrepressible Peter Cuppidge and his uke was on fire and before he could be stopped had rattled off 'National Alienation' (an anthem), 'Bye Bye Blackbird', 'Anyone for Tennis' and (damn him!) 'Mack the

Knife'! He was unlikely to upstage George Clark's version later, however – he wasn't dressed for the part!

For November it was the Monster Music Muster (see the chapter Other Major Shows) but there was a good open section of poetry. Andrew Vial did a series of sketches: 'Share-traders', 'The Guy Cracked', 'Undressing – a Day at the Beach' (a visit to Hobblers?). Amory presented 'Romeo and Sheilah' (from Steven Herrick's Caboolture poems). Clark Gormley had no guitar but weighed in with 'D-Day' and 'Pirate Cop' and George Clark presented 'Climate and Culture', a piece about Aborigines. Ross Hattaway dropped in with his brother – and we sold a few more copies of *Can I Tell You a Secret?*, which had been launched on a Saturday earlier in the month by Emeritus Professor of English, Elizabeth Webby (see the chapter Live Poets Players).

To end the night, we had the yearly Un-Darwin Awards and the various comps winners announcements – the Monologue Challenge: Bee Perusco; The Orange Wig Award: Kerry Jameson (for her Weimar Cabaret contribution); the Short Fiction Cup: George Clark; and the Open Section poem of the year, which went to Willem Tibben for 'Broome', with an honourable mention for Marie Mcmillan.

Advice for van-dwelling

(surviving the crisis)

Don't tell anyone, especially co-workers.
Kitty litter, buckets and plastic shopping bags
make a good emergency toilet.
Join a gym for the showers.
Get a magnetic sign for the side
saying something like
'Plumbing' with a phone number attached,
so you can park in side streets
and not look suspicious.
No through roads are good.
Park right under street lights to deter car thieves
and mask light coming from inside your van.
Never park in the same spot twice in a row.
Have a pre-bedtime spot and only go
to your overnight spot
when you're ready to crash.
Get good block-out curtains.
Know how to protect yourself
(sleep with a knife
or a good strong piece of dowel
and know how to use it).
Buy lots of books.
(OK, I added that one myself.)
Have good storage for food.
Always dispose of leftovers or anything
that's had food in it as soon as possible.
Have lots of good drinking water.
Be aware of your surroundings and people nearby.
Trust your instincts.

Beth Spencer

The Mariner

Navigate your frail Whitby barque
in the trade winds of the day
and the soft horizons of tomorrow,
across the meridians of months
and the parallels of years.
A cartographer of decades
the ship's log your life's diary, your charts
the scars notched in mind and muscle.
Your bruises sprawl in verse and rhyme
and the white page is stressed with waves
in the wake of your voyages. Wind blown
to the high latitudes of time
where the ice ticks loudly like a clock,
the polestar beckons north
and all directions merge to here.
There is no compass
and then there is no light.

John Egan

I'll Mould a Tune

Like forging steel, I'll mould a tune
that will make you feel like you're over the moon.
If you're good it will make you twist and shout.
If you're bad, ha ha ha ha…watch out!
It will weave within and without your clothes,
it might want to make you strike a pose.
It will weave within and without your love,
so be careful you don't lose a glove.

Come on!
Move your feet and shake your arms
demonstrate your many charms.

Now the frenzied excitement as the music starts,
and the lights and the smoke
and the drinks and tarts,
as guys and girls rush to dance on the floor,
through the buzz and the hum of the band's mighty roar.
And my music weaves its magic within and without,
as the quavers and the crotchets scurry about.
It lifts them and turns them and shakes them and twists.
The heat and the laughter are not to be missed.

And yes – it started alone in my room
when I gave melody and power and life to my tune.
'But why?' you might ask.
'For money and fame?'
Yes, of course
and other reasons more honourable by name.

Geoff Yule Smith

Weatherboard

You stood as a reminder
Of how things were
Made by hand to serve a basic need
Before Council regulations told us
What we could and couldn't build
And greed and advertising told us
What we had to have

Your rusted roof signified your tears
And stood as an icon of memory
Throughout the years

Now you are being replaced by
What's big and cheap
And quick to build
Signifying just how far
We have now come

Dianne Schultz-Tesmar

Live Poets Players Special Performances

The Live Poets Players, a loosely-formed and peripatetic band of Live Poets at Don Bank regulars, first came together in a major way in the Literature Olympics when, as individuals, they were asked to present (three-minute maximum) slices of 'the finest writing history has recorded'. They were first called upon to combine in a performance concept with the 'visit' of *Le Lapin Agil* (Paris, 1906) to Don Bank in 2013.

In the time covered by this anthology, their activities really kicked off with the following event…and has somehow carried on from there.

Poets and Musicians Come to the Farm: a 125th Anniversary Celebration of North Sydney Council's formation, July 2015

The function of this had been set up as an 'idea' by Justin Shiening of North Sydney Council. The plan was hatched to portray it as an invitation to poets and musicians of the 1890s to come to Don Bank cottage, then part of the St Leonards Estate, for a party. The music would actually be performed by the Ceilidh Collective – John Coombs, Di Churchill, Jill Rowston and Penelope Grace.

The throng was welcomed by the (then) owner of Don Bank, (Captain) Benjamin Jenkins, played by the convenor.

'My wife and I extend the warmest welcome to you all. We wish for you to enjoy the entertainments we aim to provide in our humble abode of Don Bank cottage. Not so obviously a farm these days of course and a far cry from some of the grander homes in the St Leonards district, I say. And, on that point, may I say we look forward to being a constituent of the newly formed North Sydney Council after its formal investiture next week. We need to improve the general living standards on the North Shore. I'm sure you'll agree the new entity should enable us to do that more successfully. These are challenging times for our state and our country. We hear increasingly the cry to amalgamate for future strength. Our premier Henry Parkes's speech at Tenterfield still rings insistently for many of us. The boom after the gold rush has come to bust in a general recession. The future must be faced with hope to counter this despair.

'Tonight, we want to celebrate, in our humble way, the culture of our great land, in its music as you've just heard played in the parlour as you came in, and our written culture. The work of men like Henry Kendall and Charles Harpur and Adam Lindsay Gordon. I'd just like to read you a very fine poem by a promising young heir to their tradition. I speak here of Barcroft Boake (in memoriam), and the poem is called 'Where the Dead Men Lie'.'

Afterwards, the party heard from Henry Lawson (played by Edwin Wilson with some aplomb and attitude) with 'Australian Bards and Bush Reviewers' and 'The Uncultured Reviewer to his Cultural Critics'.

A.B (Banjo) Paterson (played by George Clark) followed with 'Saltbush Bill' – 'a long poem this one'. Which he then prefaced with an anecdote: why am I called Banjo?

Captain Jenkins then introduced Victor Daley (played by Mike Richter), who read three poems with something of the manner and approach of his Irish forebears, the emblematic 'When London Calls', 'In Arcady' and 'The Old Bohemian'.

Christopher Brennan (played by Bob Howe) expressed his

disdain of bush poetry: 'I've been to uni. I've studied in Berlin.' And proceeded to inhabit 'The Pangs that Guard the Gates of Joy', 'My Heart was Wandering in the Sands' and 'What of the Battles I would win?'

It was time for a woman's point of view and Mary Gilmore (played by Marie Mcmillan) tendered exquisite proof that 'each word has a weight' with her two pieces, 'The Truest Mate' and 'Child Newsvendors'.

The Ceilidh Collective then returned with several versions of 'Waltzing Matilda' – viz. an old German song, Banjo Paterson's version and a Queensland variant.

Captain Jenkins came back with an intro to the Country vs City debate certain newspapers had made 'quite a lot of hay about' with ref to the respective combatants in this sphere – Lawson and Banjo.

Henry (Ed Wilson) led off with 'Up the Country' then Banjo (George Clark) replied with 'In Defence of the Bush'. The byplay here was quite exemplary, with Lawson stirring and Paterson giving as good as he got. Lawson: 'I feel like a fraud. I was born in a tent in the country but I've spent most of my time in the city.'

The other guests remarked on the adroit costumes the players wore meantime. The ladies in the audience, Kerry and Dianne among them, had come out in their finery, too, with blouses and coats, settings of the time for their hair, and so on.

Willem Tibben then stepped up to present a reflection on John Shaw Neilson with three or four poems of the great man's work. One of his pieces, 'The Orange Tree', refers to a Federation garden.

Mary Gilmore (Marie Mcmillan) came back with 'Men of

Eureka' with its moving tribute to the men who 'made' democracy.

A.B Paterson (George Clark) then rendered from his classic 'Man From Snowy River' – its so-vivid 'moving' chase scene. A bravura performance – the party clapped long and hard for.

Louisa Lawson (played by Barvara Hush) gave us three poems: 'Lonely Crossing', 'The Hour is Come (How did she fight?)' and 'The Reformer'. The opening lines of this last repeated, 'We lead the way, we start the fight, we head the fray.' This formed an impressive plea for women, the new modernity, and also, in Barvara's words, 'an address to you the fifth of my brood, my son, Henry'. Implicit was a wry reflection on Henry's later life as a drunk and 'your love, Mary, going away to Paraguay'. With a beck towards Mary, Barvara added, 'Good to see you again!'

There is an enduring question of what these new movements for women actually meant for such as Louisa. Long after 'The Dawn', her revelatory journal, came on the scene, she ended up in Callan Park mental asylum.

The Ceilidh Collective came back with more music to finish.

Captain Benjamin signed off with this salutary note: 'Long may these tales echo down the streets of what we are – almost a metropolis now!'

The lights came up again on the poster-board ads for 'Federate! Amalgamate! For strength!' and so on.

Over supper of damper and billy tea, the courtyard buzzed. Lawson and Paterson were mock-jousting and laughing, eyes glistening in the light around them. Mike Richter was still high and 'surprised at how it all went. Time became elastic!'

Weimar Cabaret and Beyond: Writings from twentieth-century Berlin

As the program details run-through before 'doors open' was completed, the cast sat around doing last-minute adjustments to costumes. In one corner, Kerry was helping George apply make-up for his role as Mack the Knife. Others nervously went through their pieces again in their head. Marie looked critically over a Berlin tourist's impressions and made marks with her pencil. Musicians plucked instruments – ladies adjusted lashes.

On the walls and various poster-boards around the Don Bank sitting room there were pictures by famous Berlin artists of the day (Weimartime: 1918 to 1933) – Otto Dix, George Grosz, Ernst Ludwig Kirchner and Max Beckmann. There were pictures of performers and quotes from salacious lyrics – all to be revisited once our show got under way.

The Open Section done, the mental drum roll began.

The convenor opened proceedings with the ironic 'Governing in an Ungrateful Time' – was this Tony Abbott, time travelling? Then Alan came to the front with his guitar and Kerry – looking rather magnificent, it had to be said, with her cut skirt and stockings – spread her arms and cleared her throat.

'Strip Petronella Strip' by Karl Tucholsky and 'Dancing Berlin' by Erich Kastner followed – and cameras, with and without flash, clicked.

Four short poems by Bertolt Brecht followed: 'To My Mother', 'The Theatre Communist', 'The Opium Smoker' and 'Mother Beimlin'. These were performed with blank panache by Alastair Spate, whose original postcards from Weimar also occupied the walls resplendently.

Lou Steer stepped forward to take us into the arms of 'Red Melody' by Karl Tucholsky – a tune once immortalised by Rosa Valetti. The convenor then launched into 'Dry Bread Song' by Walter Mehring. But few others could have adequately set the scene from *The Threepenny Opera* – George Clark, backed by Alan Gannaway, performing 'Mack the Knife' in his costume immaculate. More Tucholsky irony followed with 'Shopping', performed by Marie Mcmillan. Mr Clark came back with 'Surabaya Johnny' by Mr Brecht and then Marlene Dietrich emerged with her filmy shift and ornate cigarette holder to escort us – access all areas – as Marie Mcmillan wreathed her way through 'Near You', 'Falling in Love' and 'You do Something to Me'.

Kerry Jamieson returned for Walter Mehring's 'Song of the Stockmarket', an activity scarcely less perilous. Then it was Liza Minnelli time with 'Don't Tell Mama' from *Cabaret* adroitly articulated by Bee and Alan in more costumes to savour. They brought us up to date with two more modern blues: 'Do Right' and 'When I Get Low I get High'.

A break from music then with 'My Books were Burnt' (Erich Kastner) with a more subdued Marie Mcmillan. Lou Steer revisited the present with her raw and raucous 'Love Letter to George Brandis', and Lou then joined the convenor for the sung/spoken *sans* backing 'Aladdin Sane' song by David Bowie.

The creepy 'Train Ride to Berlin' – with soldiers from both armies going up and down the corridor and picking out passengers to check for documents – by Marie Mac was followed by Bee Perusco interrogating 'no-man's-land' and so on by the Wall, the cruelly appropriate ladder to nowhere and the East German high-jump practice area in 'Atmosphere and the Wall'.

Lou Reed's Berlin scene circa 1973 was then enacted with 'Five Foot Ten Inches Tall' and 'Lady Day' with lopsided momentum, like a film alternately slowing down then speeding up, from the convenor, before he segued into David Bowie's 'He Saw from His Window'. The lovers witnessed by Bowie from the Hamsa recording studio had ignited 'Heroes', the hit song Lou Steer now joined the convenor in prosecuting with her edgy chorus.

This finally led to 'Hammer', the cabaret's climax. All the players stood in a row before the audience and, in mime, began striking again and again at an imaginary wall, mouthing, 'Tear it down! Tear it down!' until they were frozen in a last moment of light, then – blackout!

Welcome Back My Friends: Live Poets at the BEAMS street festival, 2015

The theme – with some thanks to Greg Lake (of Emerson, Lake and Palmer) ran as follows:

Welcome back my friends – to the word that never ends,
To promote or to defend – step inside! Step inside!
We can lay the tracks – even if it breaks our backs!
Or just paper all the cracks – step inside! Step inside!
Come inside – the show's about to start!
Come inside – and open up your hearts!
Roll up, roll up, roll up – see the show!

On to the second verse:

We want to open minds – to be cruel or to be kind,
Leave the doubts you have behind – come inside, come inside!
Miracles abound – by the wonders that we've found – just to

have all you around – come inside, come inside!
Roll up! Roll up! Roll up! See the show –oh-oh-oh-oh!

In so doing, the convenor opened the first bracket in Tegg's Lane, Chippendale. It was Live Poets on Holiday in Public, with a difference. After two years at BEAMS with Auburn Poets & Writers, it was time to celebrate the Don Bank venue's twenty-five years in the biz. Danny G invited along some of Live Poets' more out there and loyal performers to do guest spots – folk singer and social activist Kate Maclurcan; Des Pensa (Maddalena), a scientist and businessman and a poet with a sense of humour, now spruiking environmental activisim; flautist and poet Fadeel Kayat originally from Iraq; Benito de Fonzo, one of Sydney's leading performance poets and a playwright to boot; Bhuppen Thakker, an Indian-born livewire poet so good with audiences; diva Lou Steer, who has graced the Live Poets stage under a variety of guises; and Bee and Alan, who have been the musical mainstay of Live Poets over the last couple of years with everything from Edith Piaf torch songs, environmental anthems and Mexican and Italian (and French!) cantina ballads.

'Ay, bee, bee, bee – 1!' repeated again from warm-ups at the mike. Then a cough.

The convenor followed up his siren theme with 'Poem on the Wall' and a summary of Live Poets' beginnings. He then introduced Kate Maclurcan to present 'Our Town' and 'This Land is Our Land' with a distinctly Australian flavour. Des Pensa was next with two of his greatest hits: 'Dirty Dick' and 'Blue Tits'. Fadeel Kayat stepped up to read 'Public Tree' and do two songs on flute before Benito delivered 'Tomorrow – Still

Alive' and 'Sickie' from his latest selected poems. Bhuppen's 'Their Mother Loved Them' was an ironic look at political leaders while 'Sultan's Glass of Water' was an enduring fable on behaviour. Lou Steer raised the temperature with her 'Girl of the Red Heart' and 'A Love Letter (not!) to George Brandis', our esteemed Minister for the Arts. Bee and Alan went electric with 'Mr Politician' but then had to get amongst the crowd that had gathered – a cappella – to deliver a Spanish and French medley after, out of nowhere, the power went off!

Batteries recharged in more ways than one, the group reformed for the second show at Teggs Lane. Danny again led off with a brief reverb of the Welcome Back My Friends theme. Bee and Alan then did a sound check before launching into 'Paradise', then 'Hard Work' and 'It's All Right' and the crowd was now a be-boppin'. Des repeated his first set and Danny G intervened with 'Night Fishing off Don Bank' before Benito came back, followed by Mr Thakker. Danny sang 'Dear One', a torch song from the fifties, and Lou Steer did a reverb of her first set. Benito meantime had found his protégé, Chris Brimo, who set the rap alight with a manic 'Parramatta Road' and 'What I Have Left' in a hip-hop style. The late-night moochers were well and truly aboard the neon streets by this as Kate Maclurcan closed us out with John Prine's 'Speed of the Sound of Loneliness' and a revisit of 'This Land' before there was a combined singing of Stevie Wonder's 'Happy Birthday' (for Martin Luther King) with those immortal lines, 'And I'm sure you would agree / it couldn't fit more perfectly / than to have a world part-ee / on the day you came to be! / Happee Birthday to yah, Happy Birthday to yah – Happy Birth Day!'

The Launch of the Twenty-fifth Anniversary Anthology *Can I Tell You a Secret?*

The convenor led off with 'Hello and welcome to Don Bank on this Saturday afternoon for the launch of this book' – he waves it to the throng. 'It's our twenty-fifth anniversary year – it's ten years since our last anthology – it features the work of over 135 poets. It also contains a forum on presenting poetry to the public by some of our most renowned practitioners of the art.'

He then went on to reflect about how the book was set out and designed to bring the last ten years more alive for more people with a brief resume of every Live Poets monthly meeting during that time. He further explained that he wanted to show glimpses of what happens at a venue 'behind the scenes' – when poets argue or have differences and sometimes don't 'play the game' – and the weird things that happen to the convenor or the organising principle on the night out of nowhere, how circumstances only the organisers know about can throw the game off track.

He also reflected on how the book got its title – and recalled how he 'discovered' Sue Bacsi's perky little figure of the Live Poet for the cover – before going on to consider 'how anyone can turn up at a poetry reading that no one has met before and their minds are a secret before they speak, offering their poems, song, monologues, honed in private and now delivered to perfect strangers. It's often been said anyway that poetry is a sort of secret society unnoticed by so many and yet it can touch them so deeply when they do meet it. And so we called our book *Can I Tell you a Secret?*

The convenor's 'co-conspirator' Willem Tibben was then asked to talk about the venue 'in his experience' of it.

When Elizabeth Webby, Emeritus Professor of English at Sydney University and an enduring friend of the venue, stepped up to do the official launch, she reflected on two poems in its content that struck her particularly: 'On Poetry' by Peter Boyle and 'My Name is Jamal al Hallaq'. And the bottle was then broke against the ship's side.

Ballad of Frida and Diego, July 2016

Diego Riviera is Mexico's best-known painter and a legendary figure in twentieth century art overall. He was particularly revered for his murals and famous for his Communist Party affiliations.

Frida Kahlo, renowned for her uncompromising self-portraits, styled herself as a daughter of the Mexican Revolution, though she had European heritage as well, and began a tempestuous relationship with a wanton Riviera when she was an art student of twenty-two, many years his junior.

The following poems, interspersed with statements from the two protagonists, aim to give some idea of how they related to each other and their life together.

Poems about the couple were called from many people but only Lou Steer and the convenor actively complied. These two would take part in the show alongside the two protagonists – Alan Gannaway as Rivera and Bee Perusco as Frida. There would also be statements about their relationship by the artists.

The first poem was a tribute to Frida from Lou Steer called 'Obsidian Butterfly' which begins with this confronting verse:

'My life is a battlefield / the place where I toast the divine liquor that flows in my veins, / where the jaguar howls to the moon, / where the eagle's talons drip red, / where jewels and plumes adorn every head – / where we are dashed to pieces.'

It then goes on to trace her birth into the human world from the destruction in her mythic past to reach the place where her 'broken body (is) raised above the earth on huge black wings. / They call me Frida / I am Obsidian Butterfly.'

Frida's 'wet nurse' and 'self-portrait' statements are read by Lou before the convenor reads Diego's comments on Frida's 'young' (early) paintings.

Bee then reads Frida's first poem to Diego, 'Delicate Dove and Fat Frog', detailing how they first met and became so entwined 'my brain started the day with your image.'

Diego's's first poem to Frida is then presented by Alan. It ends with an ultimatum from Frida's father: 'You have been a monument to her. / But now you must be human.'

After Frida's poem about 'The Thousand Little Cuts' Diego had given her, which of course she recorded in a portrait, Diego replies with 'When I Love I Also Want to Hurt', which confesses his endemic infidelity complex.

Lou then reads Frida's comments re 'The Divorce', then Danny reads Diego's comment on Frida's place as an artist depicting women's issues.

Bee then reads Frida's third poem to Diego, where she asserts she has other admirers and 'I am still so young in their arms / before their touch' as a way of explaining how she and Diego can no longer have sex again. In his next poem to Frida, Diego (Alan) stresses she – 'my daughter of Mexico' – always more than a comrade, ending with his assertion, 'when the gangsters at home came to me in a restaurant / you stood up and said, 'You'll have to shoot me first!' And, after everything, 'we are the accidents of fate'.

Lou then reads Frida's comments about Diego's character. Bee (Frida) then reads her poem: 'Again, I am Painting on My Back' after the failure of the surgeons to 'heal' her, even though: 'they have amputated toes and now half a leg… / I hope my leaving is peaceful. / And I hope never to return.'

Diego's last poem to Frida is 'Marionette in the Wind', where he describes the bed she died in and the room around it in the Blue House. He tells of how 'in the crematorium the mourners gasped when her body rose to sit / as the flames ate so hungrily'. And now 'the 'skeleton made of papier mâché which moves / as Death, in the form of a breeze / nudges the air'.

Lou reads the last comment – Frida on suicide – and the poem 'Frida's Last Dream', in which, from the family's house in Coyoacan, when she was four years old, Frida watched as a brave Zapatista 'squatting to put on his huaraches / was felled by a bullet'.

Words on the Wall: the Spirits of Sydney in Echo and Ink, Live Poets at the 2016 BEAMS festival

The Live Poets Players returned to the BEAMS street festival for a second year, which turned out to be the last stand of the art under lights event. The LPP set out to represent an oral history of Sydney running from the time the First Fleet landed to the present. Christan Brimo was back for a second gig with the group, along with Des Pensa (Maddalena), Alan Gannaway and Bee Perusco; Fayroze Lutta, who had performed with Danny for Auburn Poets & Writers at the Sydney Writers Festival; Lou Steer; and winner of the Orange Wig award at Live Poets and inveterate Short Fiction Cup entrant, Bob Howe.

A group singing got proceedings going on stage at Henrietta Street with a rendition of 'Botany Bay.' There was then a two-minute pause as a hymn for absent Aboriginal voices. The Colonial Poets were then introduced with Christian performing 'A Coast View' by Charles Harpur. Des inhabited Frank the Poet's 'That Day I will be Free'. And Christian then presented an eye-witness view of 'The Garden Palace Fire' from Danny Gardner's novel, *The Green Diary*.

The Federation era poets then ensued with Danny reading Henry Lawson's 'Sydneyside'. Alan Gannaway interpreted Arthur Adams's 'Sydney' and Des portrayed the bubonic plague in the Rocks, another 'eyewitness' account from *The Green Diary*.

In 'Soapboxers of the Domain', Danny read a poem about 'Arthur Chidley', a sex relations reformer who performed in a Roman toga on the greensward in the early twentieth century, and Fayroze read a declamation by famous character Bea Miles. The witch of Kings Cross, Rosaleen Norton, was depicted in Lou's 'I Put a Spell on You', while Christian presented 'Eternity Man – Arthur Stace', a piece which formed a mad dialogue with the city's streets in Arthur's mind.

A special Kenneth Slessor session followed. There was a fragment of 'Five Bells', ghosted by Lou Steer, and two of Kenneth's poems 'Metempsychosis' and 'William Street' by Bob Howe, bookended by another fragment of 'Five Bells' by Lou.

Bee and Alan read David Campbell's 'Poems on Aboriginal Rock-carvings (a sort of love story in stone)'.

The Poets of the Sydney Push followed. Danny did 'Perfect State' by Harry Hooton and Bob rendered Richard Appleton's 'Sign of the Golden Cabbage'.

The atmo was thick with revellers and window-shoppers of some dancers down the road as it was time for some Modern Protestors: 'Frackin' Gate' by Des Maddalena, 'Parramatta Road' by Christian Brimo, 'Harry' by Fayroze Lutta, several songs by Bee and Alan ending with a riotous 'Mr Politician', and Lou rounded out the rage with 'Mickey Blue Eyes' (ref Mike Baird).

As wrap-up time was nigh, there were poems on Sydney's beauty and the past: the emblematic 'Harbour' by Danny and Judith Beveridge's 'Streets of Chippendale' rendered by Fayroze.

Danny made closing remarks before he reintroduced the players to say goodnight. As always, the inevitable reflections ensued on how difficult it is to get started when there's virtually no one around but you have to get going, compared to the support of individuals and groups who come to stay and even enjoy you as the night-magic strengthened its grip.

Fiftieth Anniversary of the release of Sergeant Pepper, June 2017

The occasion was to be celebrated by inviting Live Poets regulars to present their interpretation of songs from rock's most iconic album by the Beatles. They could do this either by singing cover versions, with or without instruments, reading out the lyrics, or otherwise addressing what the songs were 'about'. The following people signed on for the comp: Mark Marusic and a female friend, Kate Maclurcan, Geoff Yule

Smith, Bee and Alan, Bob Howe and Olga and Megan. A full crowd was in attendance to vote on these performances.

Mark and his female friend led off with an a cappella 'Getting Better'. Kate Maclurcan used all her experience and dexterity to present 'She's Leaving Home' with its double-tone vocals. Geoff Yule Smith invoked 'For the Benefit of Mr K' by spruiking this 'unique' attraction. He was dressed in a natty pink top hat with matching tie and a smart jacket as he did so. Bee and Alan revelled in the twee irony of 'When I'm 64'. Bob Howe presented the quasi-orchestral 'Day in the Life', an insuperable task *sans* instruments one would have thought. He read out the 'notes' of his task and left the rest to our imaginations (!). Lastly, Olga and Megan readied themselves in a back room before the CD backing to their song was 'turned on'. It was there that Olga realised something was wrong. The carefully pinned strawberry cut-outs she had put about her middle were coming adrift and they needed to be further secured. In a flash of creative problem-solving, she asked the man on the door, Willem Tibben, if she could borrow a lace from one of his boots to effect that sinecure.

The strains of 'Strawberry Fields Forever' then proceeded after a thumbs-up signal from down the back. Olga and Megan sang their way to the front, along with John Lennon, scattering baby strawberry cut-outs to all and sundry as they passed. It was a simply impetuous aid to their interpretation and the applause that followed when they were finished was salutary.

Now came the reckoning as people were asked to vote on the performances. The winner would receive a copy of the CD of *Sergeant Pepper*. For some time, it seemed there would be a tie between Kate Mac and Bee and Alan, the practised singers in the pack. But then Olga and Megan secured just one vote more, and the prize was theirs.

Purists of course would raise an immediate concern. On the original LP of *Sergeant Pepper*, neither that song or its cousin, chronologically, 'Penny Lane', appeared. It was on a later compilation CD, released as 'another' *Sergeant Pepper*.

A look at the history of the Beatles also reveals that after the Fab Four had done their last open-air stadium concert at San Francisco's Candlestick Park in August 1966, the Beatles, freed from the madness touring had become at last, scattered to the four winds. When they did come back to London, after several months, to the studio, they recorded 'Strawberry', the first song of their 'next' album. In November, the *Sergeant Pepper* sessions started.

The Trial of Van Gogh: Poems written where his famous paintings in Arles, Provence, were set, September 2017

The germ of this idea actually happened long after my visit to Arles and environs in 2012. Like most Van Gogh tragics, I was keen to visit the actual physical locations of all those frankly 'mad' paintings, as we had been encouraged to think of them at the time, in Arles. It was only after a Facebook exchange with a friend that I decided I'd try to compose poems about those paintings – written from Vincent's point of view, enmeshed as they became in the turmoil of the artist's time there overall. It was a way of him 'answering' his trial by the local populace. I had to set situations around those poems to make a logical story thread and the following Live Poets Players were enrolled to play other characters: Graham Cameron, George Clark, Marie Mcmillan, Olga Kulanowska and Willem Tibben.

As a prelude, Vincent, played by the convenor, reads his poem 'The Second Chair' about the setting and situation of 'A Room in Arles', with the telling line testifying to his isolation: 'there is only one reason for a second chair in this room'.

Graham gives an introduction to Vincent's situation at the time the artist moved to Arles. Vincent is then commenting on his exposure in the locale of his domicile with 'Piercing Eyes of the Pool Room' and their judgemental lights laying bare all character before the habitués of the joint.

There is then a poem about the 'Yellow House' where Vincent hopes to establish a new artistic school of the South and 'Well-lit Café' which expresses a veiled hunger for Arles's fine dining social life and respectability. 'Morning in Japan' has Vincent reliving his arrival by train, his mind peopled by the influence of Japanese painting which had dressed his sensibility in flight from the dire corruption of Paris. Then we have 'River Rhone Roaming', which is a poetic interpretation of the motivations behind his 'Starry Night above the Rhone'.

'My Appearance' segues Vincent's independent mindset with others' comments on his dishevelled state in the street, with George, Olga, and Willem playing respective witnesses, whom Vincent finally refutes with the line, 'Listen. What if I told you – colours have the power to speak to us?'

'Goat-swain' has Vincent roaming the countryside, out of view of the farmer's tractor if he can, following a young girl whom he fashions as a potential conquest almost, in his loneliness, before moving on to the mechanics of the 'Portrait' and a scene on the bridge to another dimension, before 'Blackbird Echo' returns him to the apparent tyranny of crows over a cornfield. 'Boats at Lull-tide' has him seeking escape at the town of

St Marie-on-sea but he's fascinated by the fish smiles on the boats that implore him to 'Go artist and fish for men!'

The central plank of the trial in Arles emerges in 'Hope in a Visitor' one and two. The first is concerned with Gaugin's arrival and the two men settling into their routine with each other, if that is possible. In two, the versions of the explosive events that drive a schism between the artists are reserviced again by Olga and George, then Willem and Marie, and Graham comes back to play the policeman investigating Vincent's severing his ear and presenting it to the prostitute. Vincent has no defence because he has no memory of what took place, did not know 'that man' who did those things. But then Vincent 'reinhabits' that day painting with Gauguin, which results in the only canvas he will ever sell in his lifetime.

'Bandaged Life' is Vincent recovering in hospital, sorry for the trouble he's caused his brother and others, and defiant, but urged, by what acquaintances he still trusts, to go to an asylum. From there, his personality is in recession again through 'Letter Home', 'Iris', 'The Path Knows the Way' and 'The Sower the Reaper', which renders the artist figure as furtive as a Judas waiting to be exposed again. The reader can only think he will ultimately stay in the shelter for the mentally ill but then there are these lines from 'Path': 'finding in my subterfuge / the opening beyond the glades / I had not noticed before – which I shall investigate / when next the starry night above directs me'.

The next thing we see is his brother (Graham) receiving a letter of condolence from Gauguin after Vincent's death – by suicide or murder is not relevant – attesting that Vincent, after everything, 'was an artist, a rare thing in our time… I will see him with my eyes and my heart, in his works.'

Three Faces of Blue, June 2018

This was an ambitious gambit to bring together great jazz music, how it is made, and an attempt to show how it is a product of night in the midday mind as much as it is a chord structure or memory stick to nocturnal preoccupations and behaviour. The piece was a four- parter, or five-parter if you count the music itself: Miles Davis's *Kind of Blue*.

In Face 1, the light comes up on the convenor, shaving and intoning into a mirror, with a troubling observation: 'Distinctions blur. Night becomes your coat. It takes you into a dream while you are still awake. Would people not label us as crazy if these states of mind in sleep we inhabit and exhibit in daytime action?' He continues, 'the point of cross-over always fascinates – feeding art's ambiguity. We are less certain who we are supposed to be. We are less certain, though comfortable in this skin of night, impatient even it might not always augment a sense of expectation.' At this point, the narrator is back in the bar in a club again listening to the music (which is the opening bars of *Blue*'s first track, 'So What') which we hear now in all its glory.

In the next segment, there is 'commentary' on the making of this record with producer Irving Townshend (played by Andrew Vial), sideman Wynton Kelly (Graham Cameron) and Miles Davis (Wil Roach). There is talk of setting up, banter and Miles's instructions, a beginning upset by a technical issue, more banter, then Miles being asked about the origins of the tune: 'church music from my childhood; back on grandfather's farm in Arkansas – playing those bad gospels, walkin' with my cousin along that dark road…'

In Face 2, the man (the convenor) is again talking into the mirror. He muses on the brain's neuron count, how dendrites form filigrees in REM sleep, and dreams expressed in images, for which we need writing to communicate them to others. He thinks what happened that night in the club and on the street is half-dream and half actual event. He recalls seeing a body falling in an instant of violence on the walk back – 'a local character, a person I feel I knew'. But he just ran on, in survival mode, from whatever had happened.

This meditation is broken into by more music from *Kind of Blue* and the production team again discussing how it would happen. It was that crucial passage, 'Freddy Freeloader's' repeated motif, that sparked something in the listener – the breaking of light above in an inexorable dwelling and letting go – that decided his mind. He must go see the authorities - and tell them of what he knew about the man who was struck down. Tell of that body, of that acquaintance, he could not disavow, that he saw fall. (Because) life, in dark or night, in responsibility, must proceed!

That is the essential Face 3 – the role of Art!

The Art of Modern Love (with the Heidelberg flash-mob!), June 2019

Heide is a cottage near Templestowe on Melbourne's outskirts from which, in the 1930s, John and Sunday Reed launched an ambitious quest to welcome and have work together artists and writers in a new spirit of unity. This movement became known as Australian Modernism. It resolved to be free of the country's current 'cultural legacy' largely built on European perceptions. Ironically, in the surrounding area on the Yarra Valley edge,

Australia's 'new impressionists' – Tom Roberts, Arthur Streeton and Charles Conder et al. – had come to capture nature's effects in the open air from the 1880s on. Also, ironically, it was not the art and the literature alone, per se, that came to drive Heide's effectiveness, but the convoluted personal relationships spawned by its constituents in the 'hot house', headed by the 'ménage a trois' of John and Sunday Reed, and the developing artist Sidney Nolan.

The Live Poets Players' 'radio play' – in photographs of the 'action', the cast, in their heavy June coats, look like some Moscow flash mob, gathered around a couple of mikes – aimed to capture this coruscating spirit of Heide over four decades. It used as its chief sources the book *Modern Love* by Heide archivists Lesley Harding and Kendran Morgan, *Australian Gothic – the art of Albert Tucker* by Janine Burke and the art criticism of journalist Janet Hawley. In this hour-long construct of twelve voices and a narrator in four parts – 'Beginning', 'Communication and Conflict', 'What Came After' and 'When it all Gets too Much' – Phillip Radmall was John Reed and Bee Perusco was Sunday Reed, Alan Gannaway was Sidney Nolan and Graham Cameron was Albert Tucker and Sweeney Tucker-Reed. Ember Flame was Joy Hester and Andrew Vial was journalist Michael Keon. Wil Roach was Max Harris (publisher of the infamous literary 'hoax' Ern Malley), Caroline Turner was Cynthia (Reed) Nolan and Robert Howe was Sam Atyeo and Barrie Reid. Danny Gardner was the narrator. Many thanks are due to Alan Gannaway for enabling the show to be recorded.

People looking on seemed struck by the interaction of those various players and the playing out of their circumstances – weird in ken midst the force of ego, artistic impulse and human emotions and convenient amnesia in plotting and counter-plotting. Writing the script was akin to writing a non-fiction book and became an obsessional task.

The courtyard afterwards was redolent with people tending anecdotes. Roger, who was at Don Bank for the first time, was actually raised near Diamond Creek near Templestowe and: 'got some feeling for the area again'. David Wansbrough told of his work with Nolan in exhibitions, as well as Joan Miro and American photographer Ansell Adams. Mark was now keen to study Tucker and the Modernists. Else, my colleague from Customs House Readers Group, was gratified to see the show, being well-versed in the Heide tale herself. Graham was wanting to find out more about Nolan beyond the Ned Kelly paintings. So many people felt for the fate of Sweeney. David W said he felt like hugging Joy,– 'being so misunderstood in her impossible situation'. That is, being told you have only a couple of years to live and yet there is (always) so much more to seek as an artist. But her willingness to leave Albert regardless indicated Sweeney was not his child in fact. Uncertainty over his progeny was part of the reason Sweeney suicided.

2016

Our February debut was a mad night! It was a sell-out, with Geoff Yule Smith and Bhuppen Thakker guesting. It was also the debut at Don Bank for our new resident photographer and publicist, Tony Dushi. He had great fun getting action shots before, during and after the main business of the night, and making it seem like a helluva joint to hang out!

Geoff Yule Smith had reacquainted himself with us the year before and his guest spot was entertainment plus. Two poems to start – one set in AD 3000 – and the pop/rock 'What's the Matter with Me?' Then the synthesiser via keyboard took over with a rendition of 'Australian Rhapsody', which featured on Geoff's latest CD which Helen and I later got to listen to in the car going home. A couple of other less serious scatterings followed, then the R and B toned 'Leaving Zermatt Blues', which had a bit of a story behind it. At the end of his European tour, Geoff got a job at a Swiss ski joint and in his days off he spent his time on the slopes. This extolled the real piano-man qualities of our Geoff, who happened to mention he'd recently scored a new gig at a Circular Quay hotel bar tinkling the ivories. I imagined no better time than sharing a few jars with his peregrinations on a sultry Saturday evening in town.

Sportingly, Geoff also tendered his CD for the raffle and it was won by Willem. Zoe took home *Mosaic*, the Auburn Poets & Writers tenth anniversary antho, and a new attendee won the wine.

In complete contrast to Geoff was our second guest, Bhuppen Thakker. A very engaging and able purveyor of all manners and styles of poetry, from elegy to Slam, with a particular predilection in his subject matter around 'numbers and colours'

– 'tastes and spices' – such as his compelling meditation on the cooking art. In other pieces like 'Spacious' there are social issues to resolve. Bhuppen had caused a stir earlier in his time at Don Bank with his two 'think' pieces, 'Living on five dollars a day' and 'Living on a million dollars a day'. They were parables of conscience in a way – again with that disarming delivery and 'just so' pauses that never wasted an effect. His self-possession was contagious and accessible.

There was lots of music in the Open Section. Bee and Alan presented two songs about domestic violence: 'You Know I Don't Like it' and the searing 'You Burnt Off My Skin'. They then brought us back to better thoughts with 'It's Goin' to be Alright!' Peter Cuppaidge and his uke propelled 'The Orgasmic Waltz' (for Marie, I believe). Joe Flower was there without guitar to spruik his new gig with partner 'Harmony' at the Newtown Community Centre every Saturday and offer up some micro poetry. Jill Carter-Hansen sang the bouncy 'Monkey in my Cupboard' a cappella. Des took on his eco-poet intentions with 'Hawkesbury Pollution Song', Willem read the 'Name' poem. Hamish Danks Brown presented 'My Recent Odyssey'.

The convenor had opened proceedings with a Ted Hughes quote and the poem 'Climactic' about the destruction of Tasmanian alpine forests by wildfires. He closed it with a piece he put together after cleaning out his study over summer and coming across some old editions of *Poetry Australia* edited by Grace Perry and a past mentor of his, Margaret Diesendorf. The result was 'For Margaret D – re Grace who Died at her Farm by Suicide' and included telling lines from Grace's emblematic works, where poetry came to live with her like a sick relative she could not send away. That relative that ultimately lead to her demise.

March saw the next change of pace with Zohab Zee Khan and Edwin Wilson the special guests.

Zohab Zhee Khan (the tallest poet in Australia (!) and current Australian Slam champion) talked about his current project doing a series for the ABC empowering young people to take up poetry, which also involved calling out people on social issues, unemployment, racism, and so on. Re Don Bank, 'I didn't know it existed to be honest but I'm so glad I've found this little cottage between the high-rise. I thank you for your welcome!' Among Zohab's performance pieces was one about a man in his community (in Wagga) putting down immigrants. 'The fact he was saying this to me at all was bad enough in itself but to do it in front of his son – he was effectively setting the tone for the next generation.' Zohab used to have people chant at him, 'Dirty Arab, dirty Arab, dirty Arab', but 'I am from Pakistan, actually – go figure!' Away from controversy was his moving 'Poetry and My Girl'. Zohab apologised afterwards for his stamping (for emphasis): 'I've never said sorry to the floor before!' He'd isolated a weak point in the construction at one juncture. 'Do you like that banter between poems?' he asked the audience. 'I don't really do that!' We were too caught up in the bending and unbending of his body, the sharp intake of his breath, the rapid-fire word release – all compelled attention, magnified intent, magnetised a bond/inquiry. (A regular, Zoe Dobson, said to me over the break, 'I love Zohab because he says, we can do this – discard the whole paradigm. His delivery reminds me of Candy Royalle.') Some people also looked a little bemused, even shocked, during his performance.

Ed Wilson, a Live Poets performer of long-standing, was delighted by Zohab's attitude and antics and cautioned the audience that he couldn't match it. He had his own contrasting effect, of course. After telling us of his coming exhibition in North Sydney, he presented his latest book and then the poems like 'Nancy of the After-glow' (a play on 'Clancy'), 'Modigliani Nude', 'Songman and Didgeridoo', 'The Salt-bush', all laced with the gifts of anecdote that Ed possesses aplenty. Willem later reflected on Mr Wilson's melding of the native singing and imitation of didg sounds: 'He's fearless!'

Ed later added some of his books to the raffle prizes. Ed's coming exhibition would be opened the following week by SMH art critic John Macdonald. Ed cracked us up with 'He's finally decided, I think, that I just won't go away!'

We also had people reading out extracts from 'The Assassin's Cloak' (the power of diaries). There was Brian Eno by Mark Marusic, Alan Bennett by Des Pensa, Samuel Pepys by Willem Tibben, Virginia Woolf by Helen Wren, Queen Victoria by Andrew Vial, Robert Falcon Scott by Hamish Danks Brown, and Joe Orton by Geoff Yule Smith. The convenor read out a piece by Beatrice Webb.

In the actual Open Section presentations, Geoff did a story from his hitchhiking days across Ireland. He was picked up by a man who pulled the car off the quiet road at one point. With one hand in caution on the passenger-side door handle, Geoff asked, 'Why have we stopped?' The man replied, 'I wanted to ask you a very important question.' 'What is it?' Geoff added, warily. 'Have you ever thought about joining Amway?'

Meantime, Mark Marusic read the poem 'Two Tribes'. Jill Hansen sang 'Mirages' a cappella. Andrew did an actor's monologue where an unemployed person presents his case to a potential employer. Des did a poem from the front line of environmental protest, 'Lock-Up', and commented, 'I might even go Greenie – I didn't understand them before but their thoughts and mine have become one.' Helen Wren presented Yeats's 'Easter, 1916'; Hamish Danks Brown, 'All Other Directions'; and our publicist Tony Dushi asked of Malcolm Turnbull – or was it Tony Abbott? – 'Where do we go from Here?'

In April, our birthday month, we unveiled our DVD of last year's twenty-fifth birthday which would be presented to North Sydney Council Leisure Director, Martin Ellis. We also prepared some for general sale. We had Kit Kelen (northern NSW) and Abby Oliveira (from Ireland) booked (Candy Royalle had recommended her!) There were more of Assassin's Cloak tidbits plus there was Jazz Poetry and Shakespeare Moments to keep everyone on their toes. How many minutes in a poetry session? Depends what's in the missile!

Very first up, there was a quote from Allan Ginsberg and a special Irish treat for Abby – the convenor reading Dan Egg's 'The Fridge is Pregnant' from our twenty-fifth anniversary anthology.

Kit Kelen is something of a legend in the poetry book-making trade as head of Flying Island Books, which has presented dozens of Australian poets and counting so far. There was a brief discussion about that, followed by a set which smacked of old fashioned honesty and no-nonsense country caring. It began with 'Let Everything Grow Wild Today', 'Blokes', 'Maygar Idic' (Hungarian 'awakening', a trip to Kit's past), the elegiac 'And Flies all the Way to the Grave' and 'Rome' (bit of travel never hurt anyone!). He veered rural again with 'For Uncles' (bush poet's heaven), 'Macau' (at the university there, Kit had spent years as a professor of English until recently), 'Price of Admission' and the elemental 'Shed'. People lined up to buy his books during the supper break.

We returned with Abby doing tracks from her recent CD: *Cast away your Compass*. The music add-ons were necessarily discarded but rawness took their place after she'd told us of how growing up in poetry performance works in Ireland. 'Fist Police' made her stand up. Then she was further taken in with 'Dandelion', 'Enda', 'I Know Violence', 'The Fly', ricocheting into 'Apocalypse Lil and the Night to Remember'. Abby ended her set at full throttle with 'Instructions for the Book' and 'Gorgeous Boys and Girls of War'.

We were left gobsmacked by the power and yet the vulnerability. Tony Dushi swept in to take Abby in his arms and 'make sure we know where you are!' More people lined up as merchandise was dispensed.

In Jazz Poetry, the convenor got things rolling with 'Bourbon Street' (ref The Birth of Storyville). Then Dianne shone a 'String a Pearls' (ref the Pres – Lester Young). Katherine presented 'Jazzonia' from Langston Hughes, while Willem Tibben enacted 'God Pity Me' from E E Cummings. Bob Howe was awash in 'Jazz Fantasia' from Carl Sandburg ('I meant to go up on the 'toot' part! Shall I do it again? It's very short. Maybe I should sing it!'). Michael A performed 'We Real Cool'. Wil Roach did 'For Our Lady'. Roberta Lowing inhabited 'Charlie Parker 1920–1955'. Jack Peck was the voice of 'The Congo'. Phil Radmall remembered 'February in Sydney' and the convenor took us out again ref Dollar Brand and 'Heaven is…'

The Shakespeare Pieces presented the work and the debate on the Bard. George Clark did the intro to 'Henry Five'. Roberta did Sonnet 35. Two quotes in praise of Shakespeare followed. Olga did a short experience of WS. Willem offered up 'Did Bill Shakespeare Have to Do the Dishes?' Wil Roach remembered 'Doing Shakespeare for a good grade'. Andrew Carter did Sonnet 123 and Catherine Sonnet 18 ('Shall I Compare Thee to a Summer Day?'). Voltaire and George Bernard Shaw reflected on Not Getting Shakespeare. And Kenneth Branagh summed up the Bard issue with gratitude for the raw material. 'That's good for me. I'm an actor. I'm not original!'

Kit Kelen had a parting comment: 'I get more of an idea of how your place works now!' We had been on his shortlist for some time.

Come May and Martin Langford and Richard James Allen were booked and there was the annual Monologue Challenge. Poets were told of the looming Ballad of Frida and Diego project (set for July) because the venue needed people to participate.

The evening started with a quote from Lao Tzu, Chinese poet/philosopher: 'When I let go of what I am, I become what I might be.'

Martin Langford's presentation brought up some interesting points on how we view the land. 'It can seem we haven't moved on much [from colonial times] in how we write to the land and its use: but it's become more complicated.' 'There is a similar process in how the Anzac "myth" is now used.' There was discussion around the current federal government's attitude to the written word – how it compares with how the governments of other places 'appreciate' their literature. Martin made the point re the Australia Council grants, 'The silent act of reading in a room is a hard one to "get",' it seems, for funding bodies to appreciate.' These viewpoints were approached by Martin's poems in his latest book.

Richard's guest spot was more physically active as demonstrated by his energy in execution in such pieces as 'Plan Ahead' and 'Toenails'. There were also paens to the love of another and what tradition 'means' ('Anniversary Umbrella') and 'Kokoda', which featured in our antho *Light on Don Bank* some time back. As always, Richard's enthusiasm and honesty in reaching out to his audience were the things that remained in the mind.

In the annual Monologue Challenge, there was a solid line-up of contenders, including Charles Freyberg, Kelly Connor, Helen Wren, Graham Cameron, George Clark, Olga K, Caroline Turner and a newcomer, 'Jake', but Andrew Vial took the gong by popular vote with his rendition of a speech from Philip Ridley's 'Pitchfork Disney'.

Dianne, Andrew, Charles, Willem and George also presented work in the Open Section.

In June, Clark Gormley presented his wry epic 'Up the Nerdsville Track', when there were also readings from the *Can I Tell You a Secret?* anthology.

The Track was divided up into various sections, which is how the best road trips have to be planned – in stages. It was a mix of poetry, song, unreliable (what else?) yarn stanchioned by a modest powerpoint demonstration. Basically, a journey through Aus Lit and its numerous manifestations and off-the-wall applications. The sections included Erotic Literature, Climatology, Poetry and Wonder, Nerdification Tours – for example, 'A Wide Brown Land' for Dorothy Mackellar and 'Murray, Darling – You're Not the Person You Once Were', 'Me and You and Arthur Dunstal' (remember him?). There was forensic evidence: 'This Slide Looks like a Sea of Dead Kangas'. Place names were vital map grid references – for example,

Tamwish, Four Mile Creek, Dweets River. Also, 'Boots Have Walked Over This Land'. (More to the point, feet against the earth have bashed the saltbush!) There was a lament for John Ashbery, a nerd who's had a tough time of it. The overall message could mean the Nerdsville Track is an information superhighway – Malcom, get on board this holly positive country! But let's not forget how St Paul's Bay made Harold Holt.

As the image on the essential Aussie paperback faded, we were left once again with nostalgia. (A sort of 'We love that essential Anzac morning – as the light rises on the bodies.')

In Reading the Secret, David Falcon, Marie Macmillan, Olga Kulanowska, Helen Wren, Les Wicks, Kerry Jameson, Roberta Lowing, Willem Tibben and Jill Carter-Hansen presented their poems in our twenty-fifth anniversary anthology. Graham Cameron read Ben Hession's '24 Hour News Channel' and the convenor read Randall Stephens's 'Sorry'.

The host asked people to express their opinions on the latest Sydney Biennale, then offered a potted guide based on his customary summary notes (written down *in situ*) of what and when he had seen it. His fullest impression was of the Art Space display with its video of the Mumbai Hotel Massacre and the perpetrators guided by their controllers' mobile phone messages via several surveillance camera positions, and Jumana Manna's exploration of the origins of native music in her country of Palestine at the Art Gallery of NSW.

In the Open Section, Brigitte Staples read a poem for her father. Michael Arlen performed 'A Pun Sleeps on Broadway'. Marie Mcmillan did 'A Gun for Hire', Megan presented 'Man in a Stolen Poncho' and David Falcon read Robert Plinsky's 'Pleasure Bay.'

July was the night of the Ballad of Frida and Diego, featuring Bee Perusco, Alan Gannaway, Lou Steer and Danny Gardner (see Live Poets Players chapter). This was close to a sell-out. The special guest booked could not attend and there was a substitute program where people read from the anthology *Postcards from Planet Earth* (they pulled page numbers out of a hat). Among those participating were Caroline Turner ('If You Call Me'), Roberta Lowing ('Uncertainty is the Poet'), Geoff Yule Smith ('Absent Soul') and Dianne Tesmar ('Cook's Mountain'). The convenor had got things started with the infamous 'Song For People Who Know' by Hans Enzensberger.

In the Open Section, Olga Kulanowska read a three-parter, Helen Wren presented 'My Shakespearean Effort', Geoff performed 'Go Out and Get It', Remy spoke of Doctor Who, Willem read 'Keys', Kerry did 'Sleep' (written on a plane journey) and Marie was very Orstralian in 'Shagging Warnie'.

There were reminders about the (local) Sawmillers Poetry Prize, Readings from the Vault at the Manly Art Gallery and the Live Poets show at the Beams Festival (players wanted!).

August was one of the coldest nights of the year when the special guests were Halee Isil Cosar (originally from Turkey) and her Bedouin Boy accomplice, Mohammed Alenezi. The annual Short Fiction Cup was also on, and a special Palestinian poetry event called A Walk Through Gaza planned.

Halee is a very accomplished poet who has not had a collection released yet. She is a regular performer with Auburn Poets & Writers and has featured at the Bankstown Poetry Slam and also in the pages of *Masque*, a multicultural online magazine edited by Michelle Cahill.

Halee's material is honest and intimate. This evening, she

started in a very powerful way with her poem 'Scapegoat', which reflected on Australia's darker sides. There was reflection on her home in 'Why Turkey' and on the immigration debate with 'Loving a Refugee'. She delighted the audience with her cheeky '8 Reasons why a Poem is Better than a Man'.

Halfway through this set, while suitable Bedouin music ensued, Mohammed did a rousing evocation in full costume of 'Bedouin Boy' with dance movements and an invocation of 'Heaven's Power', where we were metaphorically invited into the court of a desert monarch. It was entertainment A1.

This night also saw the 2016 rendition of the Short Fiction Cup read to and voted on by the audience. Graham Cameron did 'My Best Friend's Secret.' Olga K presented 'Vision.' Defending champ George Clark read a travel tale, 'Paradise'. Des Maddalena presented a dystopian future Sydney with 'In Remembrance'. Kerry Jameson unveiled 'The Book'. Willem Tibben told a jazz anecdote about 'Two Sheds and Rambling Jack' (overheard in the men's restroom at the Basement). Jill Carter-Hansen took us to a farm in New Zealand for 'Revealed'. Jill won her maiden SHC by one vote from Willem Tibben with another vote back to Kerry Jamieson.

It was so cold at half-time that a lot of people could not enjoy supper in the courtyard. We subsequently pulled the pin at nine thirty and cancelled our show A Walk Thru Gaza to another time.

There were two live shows set down for September – 'When London Calls' by Danny Gardner, with music from Dirk Kruithof, and 'Homeless – a Sea Creature Speaks' by Bee Perusco (in a splendid costume) backed by Alan Gannaway (see Other Major Shows chapter). The Open Section featured people reading stark anecdotes about London and its inhabitants over time.

In October, there were two guests, Les Wicks and Michael Alexandratos, and the institution of a new annual competition The Other Archibald, a portrait in words of a famous Australian character living or dead. And there was a performance 'special' called the Novel Cure.

Les Wicks read from his book *Just Getting By – Not Fitting In*, specifically an exchange between two characters, Matt Kovacs and Tess Manning, a poetic narrative of their life in Sydney and their relationship over thirty years. 'It's something I haven't really done at a reading before,' said Les. 'Something Live Poets will get a rather unique taste of.' The result was an absorbing to and fro, with Les playing the two characters.

In his interview, Les 'explained' the concept behind the title. 'None of us fits in. The content is about everything really – men not getting warmth and vice versa.' The convenor mentioned, 'I've been reading you for a number of years and I'm always puzzled by how many personas there are in Les Wicks's poems. Where do they come from?' He replied, 'I think this book is less personal, less political than many others of mine. The poems are like your kids, you know?' Convenor: 'After forty years, what are the main comments you can make about the Sydney – the Australian – poetry scene?' Wicks: 'Taking poetry to new places is fine – but it's got to be more special though no less exotic.' He mentioned a program he was involved with some time ago, Poetry Written on Water, designed to make Parramatta at night more friendly using poetic words outlined on the surface of the river as it flowed past. And poetry on the buses: 'You actually had factory workers arguing over which poet they liked best – the one on the bus this week or the guy the week before. And of course you have relentless engines of the same process at places like Live Poets.' And what was the scene like forty years ago – in pubs I believe, mostly? 'We mostly shared the stage with stand-up comics in the old age. But I see the success of places like Bankstown Poetry Slam and feel the same vibe of the young forging the way forward for the medium. And that frisson attended us and our bolder plans then, when we were making our own place in the game.'

Michael Alexandratos had poems – a translation of anarchist, gay texts from the Greek, gathered from café archives – which were being released in a book, *Forbidden Verses from a Greek Underworld*. He was no less intriguing playing the blagama, a small flute with a haunting tone which those poets would have heard in those cafés serenading their obsessions. The poets were all wanting to make a difference but not get exposed to the authorities. Sometimes, the blagama tones were among the last they would hear outside of captivity. The combination was enchanting and we wait to hear more.

In the Other Archibald Comp, Kate Maclurcan performed 'Song to Wendy' that begins with 'Come to the garden'. It's an ode in tribute to Wendy Whiteley, Brett Whiteley's widow, and what she's achieved in the garden she's made in a local park near the Lavender Bay house where many of his more famous paintings were executed. Andrew Carter performed 'Water Line' about O'Connor's infamous pipeline from Manduring Weir to Kalgoorlie, WA. Bob Howe presented the portrait of a risible prize: 'The Archy Bald of Meaning'. Helen Wren did 'Coping with Age'. Geoffrey Yule Smith presented the case for Howard and Fischer's GST. Mark Marusic did 'Singing the Land' from his book *Iconoclastic Journeys*. Wil Roach performed a tribute to the Empress of Tuna Puna, a portrait of negro pianist Winifred Atwell, who became an Australian citizen after spending many years here. David Altman, who introduced himself at the Sawmiller Poetry Prize, presented 'The Soul of Lloyd Rees.' Kate Mac notched eleven votes from the audience but she was just shaved by Mr Roach.

The Novel Cure session after supper had a subtitle: how to solve your problems by meeting and transcending them through the pages of fiction. People turned this into a theatric, self-help process of zany wit by telling us what they 'learnt'. Mark's problem was 'anger' (as resolved in the wise words of the main character in Hemingway's *Old Man and the Sea*). Marie explored 'claustrophobia', taking cues from *The Little House on the Prairie*, with assistance from Olga, who draped her in a cape for the get-go. Hamish worked on his premature ejaculation with sage phrases from Samuel Richardson's *Pamela*. Barry Sergeant, moreover, 'ate fruit' and eased his constipation through Gregory David Roberts's *Shantaram* and its description of Indian slum-dwellers unselfconsciously relieving themselves as their buttocks hang from a river jetty. Olga protested her innocence at 'Being too Brainy' by referring by contrast to the obnoxiously smart children of Franny in J.D. Salinger's novel. Michael Alexandratos found himself addressing 'Flatulence' through the experience of Ignatius J. Reilly, the hero of John Kennedy Toole's *A Confederacy of Dunces*, while Graham wrestled with his 'Hangover' through the actions of Veronique in Danuta de Rhodes's *Little White Car*. Andrew confronted 'Infatuation' à la Jean Cocteau. Megan had a problem with 'Itchy Teeth' but was mollified as she explored the life experience of millionaire Gene Henderson in Saul Bellow's *Henderson, the Rain King*. There was general hilarity all round as can be imagined. Everyone looked forward to a part two of this exercise at a later date!

A lively Open Section on this night of so many words was opened by Kate Mac and her rendition of 'Blowing in the Wind' and Marie Mcmillan's 'Tango Tilt'.

November was a major theme night – Sydney, My Muse: City of Words, Song and Image – with a special guest appearance of the Diverse group of poets and their verse about pictures painted in Sydney (see Other Major Shows chapter). The Open Section involved people presenting material to fit the theme.

Special guests for the year were remembered in the Un-Darwin Awards. There was the announcement of the various comps winners: Monologue Challenge, Andrew Vial; Short Fiction Cup, Jill Carter-Hansen; Other Archibald Comp, Wil Roach; Orange Wig Award, Bee Perusco (for 'Homeless: A Sea Creature Speaks'). The Open Section (Poem) Piece of the Year was that searing song from Bee and Alan in February. 'You Burnt Off My Skin'. Though Geoff Yule Smith's story 'Amway' ran it close!

Life and Death

A point, a line
Fate is everything and is nothing
It is giving birth to feelings
Of the human soul
Gods whistle without permission
They crush us and make a pilgrimage
On every trail built.

We cry and we laugh
Existence has no age
It is the wheel that turns without hours
The so-called death
Returns us to the starting point
To the mystery of creation.

The understanding has
The wings of heaven
Nothing belongs to us
In this world of demons
And would-be angels
Those who departed
Carry their infinite hope
To open the door
Of the immeasurable.

Enrique Horna

The Scream V

(Stand Little Lass Between Me and the Sun)*

Diogenes was at the beach
replete with sunnies on his nose,
and had not thrown away his towel,
when Olive Cotton came along
(the shadow of a daylight moon)
to hold a lantern to his face,

still searching for an honest man –
and took a photograph of
feigned surprise, the canine
howl of Edvard Munch,
a jetty near unhallowed ground,
as Olive walked across his grave.

'I am Diogenes, the dog,'
he had replied, 'Don't steal
my sun because I bite.'
I've known of goose-flesh
all my life,
and the psychology of 'cold' –
my father's bones in Wardell sand,
a lover's quarrel with the world,
some 'mute inglorious Milton'
of the farm interred –
a new poem brewing
as heartburn.

When doctors say 'I'm here to help'
it's time to run like bloody hell
from orchidectomy –
the first days of my phoney war
with malware coursing in my blood,
and lymph glands part of the chicane.

'I'd rather be myself,' I said,
and not become 'Eileen'
and 'pass' on chemo-cide,
so slip the Harpies
and their raven's call –
FAAAAAAARK!

Ed Wilson

---

* An ekphrastic poem (unsuccessfully submitted to 'The Shadow Catchers' (Red Room Company, 2020)), written on viewing the mock 'scream' on the shaded face of *The Photographer's Shadow*, by Olive Cotton, while thinking about Diogenes (as one does), soon after an aggressive cancer diagnosis (at the end of 2019). When Alexander the Great had sought out Diogenes (on a beach somewhere) and asked what he could do for him, the philosopher is reputed to have replied, 'Stand a little less between me and the sun', thus the slight twist in the subtitle of my poem.

I had been to Melbourne to see the Munch exhibition when it was in Australia, where I had learnt that the jetty (of *The Scream*) was close to a special cemetery for suicides, and Scandinavian angst, that really touched me as my Danish/Irish father had committed suicide before I was born, thus altering the pathway of my life.

Going for 'quality' rather than 'quantity' of life, I had opted against having chemo-cide or a chemical orchidectomy (both horrible choices, and the source of my own 'scream' in the poem, written in full consciousness of Allen Ginsberg's 'Howl' poem, but not in imitation of it in any way), with its 'mute inglorious Milton' reference to my 'tractor driver' father.

At two years off eighty (about the age when Munch had painted *Between the Clock and the Bed*), I am still painting but don't write poetry so much these days as it disrupts my metabolism and biorhythms, but *The Photographer's Shadow* had moved me in unexpected ways. I had suspected and now know the 'scream' (of Olive's subject Max Dupain) was part of a 'staged' composition of feigned surprise (from the Olive Cotton biography by Helen Ennis), and Diogenes certainly would not have worn twee sunnies.

fantasy here at home

it may be the acres keep me at bay
but on them there's always still somewhere to go

I want a burrow, a bird's nest, shoe, straw bales
and turf roof, a caravan rotted in wattle and daub
tin of the wind come through

huff and I'll puff, it all buries, blows down

in the last age a tiny stone cottage
where the bush cosies up

walls lapidary worn
just the one room
in its echo of words
not ever quite fading
and that will be my chosen tomb tardis

big enough for a virtual age
where all there's to know
crowds the head of a pin
so a pin head like me
may still hear the birds
from a tiny stone cottage
the bush elbows in

Kit Kelen

Early Questions

What do you sing?
We sing hauling the ropes to the burden of distance from elsewheres.
We sing, On your knees, Frog, Jack Tar is the best fighting man!
We low-sing the God of sea-burials,
the God of the winds, and of shelter from wind.
We sing to a blankness that never takes shape in our minds.

What are your increase-sites?
Rum makes us big with ourselves if we lean into nothings.
The scratchings at Government Farm.
The Reverend's raised voice is a growth-site:
it troubles each indifferent thing with an infinite shade.
The Governor's oak desk
conjures gentry from goose-quills and lines.

What do you dance?
We dance chain-of-command on parade-grounds –
or raising the flag, which is simpler and taller than men.
Left to ourselves, we dance hornpipes.
Officers have to dance courtesies, bows, and the line
between forthright and rude, on account of their stripes.
Sometimes – to stop us from joking – they dance stripes on us.

What is your dreaming?
It frays. It is no single thing.
It plays the wind's quarters, and won't come ashore.
Some of it's trade-steady progress: high ropes and white-caps,
full sails. Bright eyes from Maidstone are in it,
and love-not-for-us. Jesus, the hands in the tempest.
Hell's embers also, the foundries that made the ship's cannon.
The words in the Book and the printing in books.
The king's gold brocade, and the idea we all might be equal.

And what is your country?

Martin Langford

Prologue

Stop with me now, in this moment.
Here we are, you and I, writer and reader
bound together in an eternal timeless embrace.
It doesn't matter if you are reading this in faded handwriting
on the wall of some historical exhibition about poets long dead
or on a technological device that allows the words
to float like a hologram in the space in front of you.
It doesn't matter how the poem is reaching you –
if it is reaching you, I have you in my arms
and you have me in yours and for this eternal moment
we are dancing together.
                    Only in the distance can we hear
the soft sad music of time reminding us that
this waltz, though timeless, cannot last forever.

Richard James Allen

The Spindle Shell

Love is so short, forgetting is so long – Pablo Neruda

I would carry the shell for years,
pressing the spindle to my fingertip
with the precision of a diabetic
or the sharp truth of Neruda.
I'd since repaired the sleeve of the crane-
print kimono that arrived with his letter,
the one I wore on the day of Great
Undoing. I'd brought him a gift,
a pair of Hyacinth macaws
that knew a bird when they saw one
and settled at once on his shoulders.
He'd brought me a rare *tibia fusus*
from the floor of the Red Sea,
a spirelet housed in a beaded purse.
I knew his soul quite intimately,
but not how he took his tea (white),
or how he laughed like a pirate,
stirring the birds to mild consternation.
We drank *pastis* under trees
where goats played hide-and-seek.
We were perspiring from the journey,
or it could have been from nerves.
We didn't make love, or even kiss,
and, though it was the solstice,
the night was endless, a Möbius strip
that looks, when later cast aside,
a little like the aperture of a precious shell
or a ruptured human heart.

Audrey Molloy

Old Tree

Old tree you are a picture of me
this life I have lived till now.
Your main trunk is solid iron
rising up to the high blue.
Your two side trunks make three.
Like a view of my youthful days:
fearful child, injured teen, fractured mum.
At thirty, my nightmares receded.

Your left branch like my teacher career
nourishing me with its challenge to learn.
Your right branch like my family dear
grandchildren, the vital fruit of new joy.
Your core trunk though mottled and bruised
stands strongly rooted in the desert sand.
Above your grey green tresses shade
this troubadour from the harsh noon sun.

When I stand back from you old tree
to picture you in all your one-ness,
I see my life is not so divided
rather a deep river creates new leaves
and sustains the heart of my song.

Helen Wren

Frida: The Red Flag

The blood of the people dyes the flag red,
which is why we wave it at our enemies – those –
who deny our people the right to be paid a fair day's wage,
who steal food from the mouths of our starving babies
simply to enjoy their mother's tears,
who cheerfully spill our people's blood
in the mad wars of capitalism
which benefit only the global makers of weapons
and their silent investors.

It's why the matador waves the red flag
at the bull in the *corrida,*
for who knows which one will lie bleeding at the end?

When Trotsky came to Mexico,
he was an old worn out bull,
weary of his lifelong struggle,
fearful of the lurking hunters
too cowardly to deal the final blow
in the full glare of the arena.

I – the matador – resplendent in
my suit of lights, my painted corset, my ancient jewels –
I waved our shared red flag
to draw him out
in the sunlight of his final afternoon,
to see him proudly stamp and paw the ground once more,
to feel his hot breath panting against my skin,
to risk all I was, all I had – even Diego's love –
to bring this tired old bull back to his prime.

I saw death in his eyes,
as I cried out in the little death that lovers know.

It was not I – the gaudy matador
who teased and tormented,
whose easy jabs brought the bull to life again –
who dealt his death blow.

When it came –
no music in the arena,
no weeping women throwing him flowers,
no sword of glory for this bull –
a coward's ice pick in the shadows.

The butcher always slaughters the beast trapped on the killing floor.
In the arena, the contest is more evenly balanced –
sun and shade, life and death, human and animal.

Weeping for our fallen bull, robbed of his rightful glory,
we wrapped him tight in the red flag he loved so well
and consigned his ashes to the safety of history.

Lou Steer

Ho Ho Heil

On the station the ageing Nazi skinhead
is just another baldy now, he's
finished his last-minute Xmas shopping.
Poking out from his festive T-shirt
those swastika tattoos on his neck
have paled to a gunmetal grey.

Torn cotton shorts on a multicoloured rail station,
it seems like all his arguments have been fought to exhaustion.
A smiling Moslem woman & her decorated pram pass.
Excuse me.

He carries a fist like some limp Kris Kringle
but there's no party left, his
festive ham sweats on the seat beside him.

Rejoice – like all the other energies, hate fades.
Let it rain, let it sour.
Mistletoe & other plastic celebrations are
relentlessly bright. He didn't say a thing.

But this is valued knowledge.
Children's feuds, the struggles in the queues.
History clutters up summer. This season of giving
hasn't given up. His phone rings,
a loving family reels him in.

Les Wicks

Song For Wendy

Come to the garden and dream – of life how it might yet be
Come to the garden and breathe – the air that floats through the trees
Come to the garden and be whole
Come to the garden and feed your soul
Come to the garden and be uplifted
This garden of beauty that we've been gifted

It was a junkyard choked with vine and weeds
but her creative eye could see the seeds
derelict railway siding, full of danger, dense and dark
time had forgotten this tumbledown park.

But Wendy never shied from danger.
She'd lived her life on the edge.
She saw the beauty, with her artist's vision
she started the clean-up; and made it her mission.

Come to the garden and dream – of life how it might yet be
Come to the garden and breathe – the air that floats through the trees
Come to the garden and be whole
Come to the garden and feed your soul
Come to the garden and be uplifted
This garden of beauty that we've been gifted

The jungle tried to repel her – but grief and loss propelled her.
With Corrado by her side, bit by bit they turned the tide
with passion they've worked all these years.

Come to the garden and dream – of life how it might yet be
Come to the garden and breathe – the air that floats through the trees
Come to the garden and be whole
Come to the garden and feed your soul
Come to the garden and be uplifted
This garden of beauty that we've been gifted

Kate Maclurcan

Other Major Shows Featuring Art and Music at Don Bank

November 2015: The Monster Music Mash!

To round off the year in a suitably dynamic fashion, the visit of the Paul Buckberry-led Faraway Eyes ensemble was augmented by other music supports from evergreen Kate Maclurcan, Penelope Grace and Fadeel Kayat, who have delighted us so much with past appearances.

The basis of Faraway Eyes, beyond Paul's lead guitar and the bass and banjo of Nigel Lever, was the sublime harmony of the three girl singers: Deanne Dale, Meredith Osbourne and Heather Johnstone. This was made manifest in such a classic as Paul McCartney's 'My Love'. Thusly, 'Let Your Love Shine Down' and the shimmering beauty of Crosby Stills and Nash's 'Helplessly Hoping'. There was surprise and wit too in 'Standing in the Eye' and 'Hit in the Dark Side by a Rainbow!' plus 'good ol' gal' nostalgia in 'What Are you Doing Now?' The beginning of Neil Young's 'The Loadout' in low light was haunting – crowned with the lament, 'look at mother nature on the run'. And 'I was thinking what a friend had said and I was hoping it was a lie.' The eery daymare of the final sequence was palpable as our life force was sent 'to a new home in the sun'. We just wanted to take one more photo in our mind of those ladies' tones!

Kate Maclurcan's set began with John Prine's 'What in the World' followed by the aching 'The Speed at the Sound of Loneliness'. Kate indulged 'Blowin' in the Wind' with all her love for

Dylan. There was 'New Day' from her latest CD and Phil Och's searing 'Joe Hill'. She finished with another standard, 'This Land is Your Land', with a distinctly Antipodean twist.

Penelope Grace's 'Rookwood Raid' saw the fiddle as weapon in a session of furious execution, which recalled her evocation of the fervour of the Eureka Stockade in an earlier appearance. We were gobsmacked by our transport!

Fadeel meantime tendered delicate but direct sonorous tones from a prone Chinese harp under the play of his various hammers. This was interspersed with quite a deal of supplementary 'coaching', vocally, by the Iraqi, now something of a busking legend around the Parramatta area.

September 2016: When London Calls

The convenor retraces his trip to London to seek fame, fortune and fellowship in the UK poetry scene – with Dirk Kruithof playing rock hits from the times.

It begins with Danny musing in his mind on that journey on Flight 745 via Singapore and Bahrain – possibly mouthing the opening monologue by Jon Anderson from Yes's 'Tales from Topographic Oceans' en route.

Then, in the cold morning air kerbside in the Strand, he reads Arthur Daley's salutary poem from the 1890s, 'When London Calls'. This is followed by one of Danny's early London efforts, 'Scarecrow', ending with 'one fell on me and almost frightened me to death'.

Dirk segues into the first bars of 'Can't Stand Losing You' by the Police before Danny joins him in the first verse and chorus. Part of the East End anthem 'Squatting' is next, where our poet's lover is about to introduce him to her friend Joe. This is followed up as the lights darken with the Floyd's 'Brick in the Wall', thence the poem 'End of Form', the first 'single' from Danny's book *Hope in Progress*. With quasi-Nazi artwork, this piece would later feature in Michael Horowitz's *New Departures* magazine.

More Floyd then from Dirk as Danny joins him for 'Young Lust' – 'need a dirty woman / to show me round!' This leads to the poem 'The Hunt' – for example, the loneliness of mattress-hopping. The Police then make a return with 'Bed's Too Big Without You'.

Bethnal Green and Hackney's 'Funk Thatcher' atmo is then forsaken for Camden and 'Option', picking over a second-hand life, while 'Keats and Shelley argued on Hampstead Heath'.

As more opportunities pass by, Pete Gabriel bobs up with 'Don't Give Up', where Danny and Dirk are joined by Jill Carter-Hansen, who does the 'Kate Bush' on that signal single: 'I can't take anymore…!'

But Danny finds a new love and a room where the words of poets and musicians will flow on up to the ghosts in the rafters – treat it like home! Was this the fellowship he'd been searching for?

We are then in a sequence in a Monument pub where the hero, washing up, hears on the radio about John Lennon's death. This is subsumed by 'Roxanne' from Dirk and Danny's vocal – 'got to go new York!' before the new book is launched and is reviewed in *Time Out* and the Kangaroo Kid is signing up a storm at the Recovers Bookshop.

It's time for Floyd again and 'mother do you think they'll drop the bomb?' The finale is a patched-together 'National Address' which ends in 'everything is under control / everything is under control / everything is under!'

The last London gig for Danny before the plane to Sri Lanka on the way home is at the Atomic Energy Authority, where his girlfriend works.

'We're banned! The film of the gig has been confiscated! Lights out!'

Just off in the distance are the bars to 'Nice day for a white wedding!' a mad chorus and a final flourish from Dirk.

After the hubbub of supper conversation, Alan began making 'sea sounds' to a backbeat on a playback at the front of the room. Then, by degrees as it seemed, Bee Perusco 'materialised' from behind a screen in her elaborate make-up and costume before immersing herself into the swirl of Alan's now echoey guitar tones. It was transfixing.

Bee and Alan's 'Homeless: a Sea Creature Speaks' aims to awaken us to the challenges faced by refugees in a world we are making increasingly uninhabitable. For we are all, ultimately, that sea creature without shelter. We are forced to ask the 'people in power', is this the only way to go? Will fantasy be the only outlet of expression we will ultimately have left? What price for the natural wonders of our world held to ransom? Is this the fate society deserves – giving up so much to the entitled few and their greed? Are we still human without expressing humanity to fellow beings?

Bee's sinuous movements in her dance/spoken word expression reflected our dilemma over the future. And another question of this onlooker: 'did the allure we create to express ourselves only stanchion our final fragility?'

It was twenty minutes of a journey in performance – music and words joining forces in a synthesis carried off in seamless execution.

It was hard to return to normal programming. We broke

for the raffle while Bee and Alan got all their equipment out and the nightclub became a sitting room again for the second time that night.

Olga K and David Olsen offered up their entries in the recent Sawmillers Poetry Prize, Maggie Mason did a very expressive piece about her girlhood. Andrew Carter did a brush turkey ditty – the first time we'd seen him perform at Live Poets.

There were also earlier – to continue the London theme – several items of Literata Eccentria. Just four samples will suffice here.

James Boswell, 9 May 1763

'At the bottom of the Haymarket I picked up a strong, jolly, young damsel, and taking her under the Westminster Bridge I conducted her and then – in armour complete [is he saying he wore a condom?] – I engaged her upon this noble edifice. The whim of doing it there with the Thames rolling beneath us – amused me much!'

Nina Hamnet, 1930s, Fitzrovia

In her youth, she had been the model and lover of Modigliani – but now she was a fixture at the Wheatsheaf pub. 'Modi said I had the best breasts in Europe,' she would drawl in her booze-roughened Carmarthen accent, often hauling up her sweater to reveal the evidence. 'Go on! Feel them! They're good as new!' Constantly broke, she worked the bar for free drinks and donations which she carried around in a tin box. She later wrote a racy autobio called *The Laughing Torso*.

Dylan Thomas at play

He had a favourite pub game called 'cats and dogs' which

he developed at home in Swansea. It involved crawling around the bar on his hands and knees biting women's ankles. Once he snapped a front tooth when he bit a lamp post by mistake. On 12 April 1936, at a pub in Soho, he walked over to Caitlin Macnamara, put his head in her lap and said he was going to marry her. Caitlin was then having an affair with the painter Augustus John. But she agreed to spend the night with Thomas at the Eiffel Tower hotel in Percy Street – John later picked up the tab.

T.S. Eliot, an austere gentleman in 1923

He rented rooms at the Burleigh Mansions on Charing Cross Road. Here he hosted a series of bizarre dinner parties. He once told Osbert and Sacchavel Sitwell to 'ask the porter for the Captain when you arrive' though Eliot had never been in the armed forces. During a meal, the guests noticed that Eliot was wearing pale green face powder in order to look more like the 'tragic poet'. At another gathering where he invited various members of the famous Bloomsbury literary group, Eliot became paralytically drunk, threw up, then passed out, leaving guests to see themselves out. Next morning, he spent an eternity on the phone trying to apologise to Virginia Woolf.

Our thanks for these gems to the book *Writer's London*, compiled by Ian Cunningham.

November 2016: Sydney – My Muse. City of Words, Song and Image

DiVerse was the catalyst of this evening. This evolving ensemble of wordsmiths go to galleries around Sydney and environs and practice 'ekphrasis' – write poems responding to the art on display. 'Though painters weren't always so keen on the idea!' joked their 'boss', Rob Kennedy. Five of their number presented work about their favourite Sydney paintings for our theme night.

Open Section readers were invited to read a poem about Sydney, whether by themselves or by somebody else that inspired them.

There was a special 'appearance' by Sydney's poet of poets, Kenneth Slessor, his work performed by George Clark and Jennifer Thurstun.

Additionally, pieces from the book *Limericks of Sydney*, chosen and introduced by ABC 702 announcer Ray Taylor (Live Poets' co-founder Sue Hicks had helped research the book in the 1990s) would be sprinkled throughout the evening.

As the evening's curtain came up, the convenor read a passage from James Cook's *Endeavour* journal about the English sailors' initial contact with the natives of Botany Bay, which ended with these fateful two lines, 'we thought they were motioning us to shore, but in that we were mistaken'.

There were then David Marr's comments about modern Sydney, 'which keeps growing and looks to the East, but only as far as the breakers out there'.

The first limerick of the night was about a young man who lived in the Rocks.

First reader in the Open Section was John Egan from Poets at the Petersham Bowlo with a reflection about Slessor's friend in his poem 'Five Bells', Joe Lynch. Ed Wilson followed with 'Catholics Kissing at the Opera House'. Another limerick followed before Helen Wren's 'Sydney – when Spring is Here!' and Marie's witty 'Place in Sydney (Centennial Park)'. Robert Kennerley read John Forbes's 'Stunned Mullet', which painted a rather acerbic vision of the Harbour under the watch of Alan Bond's blimp. Another limerick about a Razorhurst 'floozy' ensued. Willem Tibben reflected on two instances when he viewed that modern jewel of art's democracy, 'Sculpture By the Sea'. Brigitte Staples read Judith Beveridge's 'Streets of Chippendale', which glistened with other voices. Caroline Turner channelled Clive James being 'In Town for the March' and made us realise the poet's final, diminished perspective, holding his mother's hand in fright. There was another limerick about a scene in a Redfern flophouse. Graham Cameron offered up a very personal impression of Sydney – his love and him seeking romance in the moonlight on Balmoral Beach – only to meet a flasher on the loose! Geoff Yule Smith rendered his song penned for the 2000 Olympics, but the committee had already decided on another tune for their theme. Geoff also read his poem 'I love Mosman on a Summer's Day'. Another limerick about a Strathfield 'woman of the night' followed. Dianne Schultz-Tesmar invoked Dorothea Mackellar's 'Dusk in the Domain' and Mark Marusic tendered two poems from his latest book, 'Time for Tea' and 'Theatre'. The final limerick in this section was about 'a lady from Umina who gave her husband a frightful shiner. 'She's heard someone say, while she'd been away, that he's been found in bed with Anngina!'

Rob Kennedy then introduced 'Diverse'. The paintings the poets read poems about were displayed on storyboards at the front of the Don Bank sitting room. Louise Wakeling wrote of a painting of Patrick White by Brett Whiteley – the poem was called 'Whiteley, White, Whitest'. It was included in the Live Poets' 25th Anniversary Anthology, *Can I Tell You a Secret?* and centred on the tactical relationship between Golliwog Brett and

Australia's only Nobel Prize winner for Literature. Brenda Saunders spoke of Margaret Preston's 'Banksia Men' and the fury of a Sydney fire which spared her bush studio and meant she could now see the river beyond the blackened scrub. Marcelle Freiman's poems sought the bigger picture in the work of Grace Cossington Smith, and Margaret Bradstock pitched insights gleaned from Whiteley's portrait of rain on the Harbour and views of the Opera House expressed by Reg Mombasa and Peter Kingston. Garry Macdougall, the only guy in the paintbox, was on last and didn't want to talk about paintings until he'd explored the history of French towns named after saints with us (relevance to Sydney?) He then took up his wrestling with a portrait of a hoya, a plant that has marched from the tropics to Sydney's backyards in the train of the eastern seaboard's changing climate (and our vulnerability to that other dubious import, the cane toad!). The plant – in a decanter – had been painted by Cressida Campbell, and Garry employed a novel method of evincing its protuberant, fervent shape by running terms together after the Scandinavian fashion. Not content with that, he decided he would sing – not say – his poem. This was an unsuspected masterstroke! Something like a musical Scrabble board 'painted' on the air – complete with complementary body movements. You probably had to be there.

Garry shrugged about it sometime later. 'It was wonderfully silly. I based it on a kind of Gilbert and Sullivan treatment of the work. Very HMAS *Pinafore*!'

After that, it was time for the esteemed, adroitly attired (particularly after he'd discarded his pre-emptory bandanna!) Mr Slessor (aka George Clark) and his 'assistant', as she said,

Jennifer Thurstun. KS began with 'Out of Time' – one of his celebrated preoccupations along with water and memory. Jenny then rendered the equally enigmatic 'Sleep'. Sydney urban was evinced in 'Thieves Kitchen'. There was a foray into the maritime wiles of Captain Dobbin and then part of 'Five Visions of Captain Cook'. One thought KS must have had an excess of salt in his veins. 'Kenneth' then wanted to demonstrate some of the lesser known parts of his ouvre, he and Jennifer pronouncing his two-hander 'Man of Sentiment', which was rather a to and fro struggle over a walk in the garden – 'just one more step, a bee's foot to the corner' – with KS never less than a gentleman and his consort never less than wise. George then came back for the last verse of the emblematic 'Five Bells', which, in 1975, had this convenor avowing, 'He's the best poet I will ever read!' – this decided in his downtime from trying to sell short, erotic fiction (I will pen the centre-fold!) to *Cleo* and it's unsurprisingly 'remote' editor, Ita Buttrose. Here, finally, KS (that is, George) had swum into his element with an unerring delivery that stopped all clocks (and the breath of some of us!). Thus Slessor, with grace, departed the stage – very much alive.

We adjourned to a very late supper – and fellowship – in a quite chilly courtyard, until warmed by the raffle, a poem about Sydney's tentacles from Jill Carter-Hansen and some decidedly X-rated verselets from Kerry. The hubbub rose again. There was still apparently some time before we could say goodbye to 2016.

June 2017: With Andy Upstairs At Max's

Max's Kansas City was an infamous rock club in Manhattan established in the 1960s. But it was much more than that. As legendary owner Mickey Ruskin put it, 'Max's was the place where Pop Art and Pop life came together in New York!' There was a rock stage at the end of a tunnel upstairs. But at the front of Max's, under pictures of famous visitors over the years, the art establishment and the art explosions underneath it came to mingle and cross-pollinate. This was principally under the stewardship of Andy Warhol and his set, originally. Max's, though, soon came to be the place where an artist or gallery owner from any one of so many disciplines – Op Art, Earth Art, Conceptual Art, Minimal Art, Post-minimal Art, much less Abstract Expressionist and its many offshoots still – needed to be seen in the cigarette haze of Max's bars among the stars or otherwise lounging, pose-ready, in the banquette seats.

Two of those artists were Robert Mapplethorpe and Patti Smith and any cursory trawl of their early-career diaries reveals the slavishness of their pursuit of Warhol through many hopeful evenings and early mornings that he didn't show.

Before pictures from Max's, and the many luminaries it hosted – from David Johanssen of the Dolls to David Bowie, to Iggy Pop and Lou Reed to Nico and Bruce Springsteen to Alice Cooper and Tim Buckley to Janis Joplin, William de Kooning and Johnny Thunders – the convenor read out those diaries of vain hope and stark despair, until that night fame's fire was lighted.

He began the sequence with David Bowie's 'Andy Warhol silver screen – hang him on my wall hey, hey' from Hunky Dory – and ended with Lou Reed's monotone hymn upon Andy's passing with the 'the last of the great temptations. A Dime Store Mystery.'

July 2018: Homage To Darlo

There could scarcely have been a more integrated evening around a central theme than the one somehow concocted in Homage to Darlo. It would feature instalments from the convenor's Green Diary m/s, Open Section contributions interspersed with snippets of Darlinghurst literary history, a mini-show by the mercurial Vashti Hughes, TAP Gallery history and anecdotes from Lesley Dimmick, the wit and whimsy of Slessor's 'Darlinghurst Nights' and Charles Freyberg's KX characters from his recently released book *Dining at the Edge*.

There were text and images re Darlo on poster-boards around the sitting room including the 'Rock 'n' Roll Walk of Fame 'n' Shame' vividly tracing the area's 1970s-80s-90s night life – from Frenchs Wine Bar to the Albury and the Paddo Town Hall.

Cathy Bray had got us started in the short Open Section, however, with an explosive complaint. She wrote a review for *Five Bells* online magazine that the editors bannered, 'You Should Have Gone'. It was a performance re Kenneth Slessor's 'Darlinghurst Nights' that had to be renamed for legal reasons. It was a sublime showcase of KS's work attended by pitifully few spectators. Cathy entitled her piece 'How Do You People Sleep at Night?' and went on with the following: 'If you haven't been to see this show, you should go outside now and kick yourself – really hard. You're an idiot! Your partner who agreed with you not to go is also an idiot!' It was in Cathy's eyes, and those of so many other people who are interested and know, 'a world-class production' and everyone should be promoting it like mad.

The 'Green Diary' sections 'Rebirth in Taylor Square' and 'Windmills' told of a gormless young man taught the error of his ways in a Wooloomooloo squat and banished to the outlaw edge of town – survival, if it could be found, in a darlo flophouse. There – in the endless streetlight that was like moonlight – the lad dreams about the windmills that once threshed grain for the colony. He followed Old South Head Road in his mind through a covey of convict pirates, before being rudely 'parachuted' back to Bourke Street at rush hour in the 1970s.

Literary Sydney – a Walking Guide (Peter Kirkpatrick and Jill Diamond) supplied the official history bits. Darlo, though, was principally the past haunt of novelists rather than poets. People such as Xavier Herbert, Mandy Sayer, M. Barnard Eldershaw, Dymphna Cusack, Christopher Koch, David Ireland, Patrick White and Peter Corris. Kenneth Slessor lived most of his life around Elizabeth Bay. Christopher Brennan and Harry Houton at different times obviously, lived in Kellett Street, Kings Cross – and Steele Rudd in Roslyn Street. Merv Lilley and Dorothy Hewett ('Alice in Wormland') domiciled in Bourke Street in the 1980s. Henry Lawson spent time in Darlinghurst Gaol in 1908–1910. Peter Boyle lived in Clapton Place in 1997, as did William Dobell, the painter, in the 1940s. A lot of other people set their poems and stories in Darlo – ref Grant Caldwell's description of spruickers on Darlinghurst Road: 'ferret-faced men in suits hand you cards'. And there is this Nancy Keesing quote from her time at SCEGGS private school: 'As we walked home from class today past Darlinghurst fire station one lady broke off her high-heeled shoe – and ripped another's cheek right through. Gee, ladies fight like children too!'

Vashti Hughes is the daughter of jazz supremo Dick Hughes, and has a passion for history and personal stories delivered through theatre and music. Her 'Mum's In – Stories from Razorhurst' is a dark, one-woman cabaret which explores the characters of Sydney's inner-city underworld in the 1930s – namely Kate Leigh, Tilly Devine, Nellie Cameron, Guido Caletti and Frank Green. Vashti opened her show at Don Bank with songs from this opus: 'Getting' F - - - - up the Cross!', 'Never Let People Say – crime doesn't pay!', 'Bish, Bash, Kapow!' (featuring Caletti the tough man), the Nellie (a North Shore girl) Cameron song 'Take it Out on Me'. These vivid, noir ballads basically turned the air blue, rounding off with the classic 'Do Yourself a Favour' and the immortal couplet from 'Stick My Head': 'I'd rather put my head in an oven / than to be stuck at home with you!'

Lesley Dimmick presented memories of TAP Gallery, Darlinghurst – a companion venue to Live Poets over the years (audiences migrated between the two). TAP apparently featured poetry with host Robert Balas long before 'the bum paintings that were done at our annual parties!' Lesley has always considered art and poetry a natural fit – it was partly the genesis behind Balas's Open All Hours featuring his poems and the artworks on TAP's walls over the years. But to go back to when TAP first started, said Lesley, 'I was going to art school in Darlo and I heard of a space (in Palmer Street) being available. I was living above the Piccolo like Vashti was – and I decided to get something started. It's been a long battle over the years to keep a space for artists going!' Keeping closures by Council at bay has been a recurring struggle. Lesley will never forget a friend discovering some of Rosaleen Norton's paintings being thrown into a skip. (Norton is a KX legend certified by many as a practising witch.) But TAP anniversaries have always been legend.

'This is the last party of yours I'm coming to!' was the response verbally when Lesley told a trans, who'd peed on the floor upstairs, to 'Get a mop and clean it up!'

And Lesley told of almost dropping the crockery when a client of the madam upstairs at the Piccolo hinted at a threesome: 'with YOU, the redhead!'

After that hoot, it was time for more literary history and Clark and Eades being Mr Slessor. 'Darlinghurst Nights' details, in descriptive doggerel, the lives of young starlets who, in the 1920s and 30s, are slaves to the apparent glamour of the entertainment hub's social whirl. George and Janet delighted in inhabiting such gems in verse as 'Choker's Lane', 'Kimono Cora', 'Ticket in Tatts', 'Goodbye Ice Man', 'Gunman's Girl' and 'Green Rolls Royce' and several others, the duo adroitly swapping voices back and forth.

Charles Freyberg is a Kings Cross poet and playwright – and a chauffeur in a tux in his spare time. His book *Dining at the Edge* had been recently, lavishly launched at the El Rocco Cavern below Bar Me in William Street, with a violinist of renown and back-up singers, et cetera. His set at Don Bank ran the gamut of the book's riches, tracing the various experiences of characters – or were they extrapolations of Charles' experiences? The busker in 'Buddha with Koto', listening to Maria Callas – in bed and out – with a friend, 'pursuing' strangers in St Mark's Park, Tony and the Boss in the Venus Room, Louise in a cafe in Roslyn Street, Helen at the Goldfish Bowl, Martin and his paintings in a shadowed room, Michael and Louise at deadlock – and Vanessa doing a car job at the Wall in 'KX Fantasia'. As the back cover says, 'Angel boys wrestle with gargoyles while lovers and eccentrics twist the language to find their truths.'

Charles opens the door to East Sydney's demi-monde of infamy and spent momentum, which is exactly what our night of tribute sought to explore!

A few more snippets from notorious addresses in the quarter and we came again to the 'Windmills' scene in the 'Green Diary' a set piece ending with William Street's indomitable Coca Cola sign silently summoning mammon.

It was fitting to finish with Graham's story of the young boy in the car with his parents – driving back from beaches down south via Darlo and Taylor Square – passing ladies outside expensive car sales windows on William; waving at people in traffic light halts. As Graham put it, 'I went back there when I was a student in the city and stood myself on those same street corners. But those ladies I wanted to see again never showed up.'

There, by the red light, hangs a tail.

September 2018: Feel Like I'm Fixin' To Die, Rag – Mad US Politics In 1968

This forty-five-minute show was designed to remind us that Donald Trump seems to inhabit a mad hatter's reign now – but the US is no stranger to craziness in administration. For instance, look at 1968. In that calamitous year, the US slid further into the bog of Vietnam, Martin Luther King and Bobby Kennedy were shot down in cold blood and the New Left yippies wanted acid – a drug that causes erotomania – put in the water coolers in the Pentagon and 'Lace' piped through the aircon system. This rolling miniseries of potential mayhem built up steadily to the Democratic Convention in Chicago which protesters vowed to storm despite knowing Mayor Dailey would unleash his stormtroopers to crack their heads in response.

Central to the show was Country Joe Macdonald's sleeper hit song, the 'Feel Like I'm Fixin' to Die' rag, with lyrics that suddenly caught fire in a people's rebellistic consciousness.

Viz: 'And it's one two three / What are we fighting for? / Don't ask me, I don't give a damn / Next stop is Vietnam! / And it's five, six, seven / Open up those pearly gates. / Well there ain't no time to wonder why / Whoopee! We're all gonna die!

Just days before the convention hit full stride, Country Joe got an idea what his song had also unleashed. He got into a city lift to be confronted by a man who screamed, 'I fought in Vietnam for guys like you!' And he broke Country Joe's nose in a single blow.

In darkness, in the show's beginning, there were these plaintive questions to the US president about Vietnam repeated: 'LBJ, LBJ, how many kids did you kill today? LBJ, LBJ, how many mothers have only grief to say?'

The convenor did the background commentary of events of that time and Bee and Alan sang a selection of the songs (including 'Fixin') – like 'Ballad of the Green Beret' (Barry Sadler), 'Fortunate Son' (Tom Fogarty), 'Love Me I'm a Liberal' (Phil Ochs) 'Bringing Them Home' (Pete Seeger), 'We Shall Overcome' (standard) – right through to the call 'We Gotta Get out of This Place' (The Animals).

The show came to an end with a repeat of 'For What It's Worth' (Buffalo Springfield) and those ricocheting lines, 'Stop people. What's that sound? Everybody look what's goin' down. Stop!'

The trio later repeated this show at 'Poets at the Petersham Bowlo' with the addition of the song 'Last Train to Clarkesville', an apparently bubbly song by the Monkees but about a recruitment station that became emblematic of the Vietnam War's dragnet.

March 2019: Geoff and Jade Hit the High Lights

Before a sell-out crowd and with mum watching proudly on, Jade Yee-Smith made her debut at Live Poets, backed by her dad on vocal and keyboard in a show that had the audience craning for a better view of 'who is behind that startling voice?'

At just fourteen years old, Jade was a semi-finalist in the City of Sydney Eistedfford and that event's Junior Singer of the Year. Later this year (2019) Jade will sing, act and dance the lead role of Roxy in the Willoughby Girls High's production of *Chicago: the Musical*.

This night at Don Bank, Geoff was on familiar ground but there was undoubtedly a lift in his performing. After a lusty opening of 'Keep on Rockin'' and 'OK, by me' (intermittently with Jade), Geoff addressed how his pursuits feed off each other with his poem 'I'll Mould a Tune'. A lovely palm tree atmosphere pervaded the couple's come and go duet in 'Paradise Island'. The lights were dimmed for Jade's story 'Grandpa Garry's Graveyard', acted out by Geoff, which ended with the protagonist emerging spookily with knife erect (the crowd shrank back in suitable alarm!).

The lights then came up again for Jade's finale: the contemporary torch classic, 'You're the Best Part'. The final soaring pearls of this song are what properly magnetised the crowd's attention and a foot-stomping stand up and clap applause followed. A girl with a future on the boards, there can't be much doubt.

May 2019: Three Ways To Crack a Nut! – Ali, James and Lynda

The performing arts in their startling variety were certainly on rampant display this evening. Special poet guest Ali Whitelock was heralded by a great strapline on the PR leaflet from Mark Tredinnick describing Ali as 'Charles Bukowski with better dress sense!' Two things quickly stand out about Ali. The attitude: does it matter what you've heard about me before? And: I have no use for the higher case! There is also a blanket approach to the white page – cram it dense with all that you can! (check the pages of her latest book, *And I Crumpled Like a Coke Can*). And then there is the matter of poem titles. Aside from that aforementioned 'leader', try on these for size (lower case) – 'the time it takes to boil an egg', 'please do not pee in the sink!' and 'the shit we are in'. And what temporal status can possibly be afforded 'fridge poetry'?

The last thing is the brevity of set comparatively. She must memorise it all the night before. The book is really no more than a prop you might wear like a T-shirt, part of the poet in view. But there is little escape from the wry eyes and the deadpan, almost a put-down, unravelling. The lead poem from this collection is about the death of her father. It's a dense page of driven images and correlations – only about three lines from the end, she props and all but loses it. But isn't the misstep what indelibly endears us to the poet?

About three weeks before this Live Poets date, I had heard

Melbourne-based James Griffin would be in town for some gigs in Newtown or wherever and I got onto him through Facebook to ask, would there be a chance – our gig is just a few days after that?

Here at Don Bank this night, Griffin unpacked in an interview about his past times in Sydney, in the pubs that dotted the metro area in the early 80s – when James headlined a rock band with 'The Agents' and 'The Subterraneans'. The convenor asked him to talk about the best parts and the drawbacks of that time.

Griffin: 'Well, I played everywhere then at places like the Darlo and Newtown pubs, the Windsor, the Stagedoor, the Sydney Cove Tavern et cetera. It was a good time to get a band together – it was all happening. People, young people, were telling their story then. Genuine Australian stories. Before things went all hip-hop and internationalised and we heard all those ghetto echoes from other places. When the internet and the cheap plane flights came in. I say that from a geographical fact rather than judgementally, musically. But drawbacks? What are they?'

'So how did poetry rather than songwriting originally come to you?'

'Well,' he replied, 'it was probably from my father walking around, singing jingles of the day – and sayings, quotes out of nowhere.'

When asked to do that old chesnut – compare poetry and song lyrics, James replied, 'They both have their place. Poetry doesn't always have to be direct – there's more depth there – whereas a lyric message is designed to be hypnotic in effect.'

James certainly had some great lines in the songs he so generously presented in his extended set – before and after supper

– tracks from his recently reprocessed CD, *New and Selected* (it sounds like a poetry title!). Included here was the sly 'I Don't Think I drink Enough' and 'I Might Have Drunk at French's' (loaded with local colour) and the caustic ozpic, 'Take it From the Top'. Then there was the ironic 'Australia's Just a Suburb of the USA'. The dreamy melancholy of 'Another Country from Sundown to Dusk'. 'Midnight in the Graveyard of Lost Guitars' at ghost-town ridge. There was the engaging way James used by-the-way conversation seguing one track to another. 'Where's the Party?' (was there ever a more 1980s question?) may have been in there as well. As we rolled effortlessly to the cynical-becoming-sinister 'Suburbs of the Heart', the finally aching 'Sacred Things', before the close-out, 'A Song is Not a Song', set off to paint the darkness. This was a remarkable, down-home, generous enjoyment of our space the crowd will scarcely forget.

People had come up to get merch before supper. Now, more shuffled up, notes in hand. Bless the guy – he stayed then to hear the rest of what else might be in store. James Griffin, please carve your name in the Don Bank stone in the courtyard!

Finally, we had another star this night. There was plenty else happening in the courtyard while people were accessing supper and 'another cup of red, thanks!' Lynda Lovechild and her irrepressible resistance. She set up her stall to raise funds for a Sydney refugee centre. She had done this also the Saturday before when Australia voted amidst an atmosphere of ground zero in Warringah – bolstered by the Get Up campaign to 'vote Tony (Abbott) out!'

As people crowded round now in the courtyard, Lynda repeated those too-typical ditties to the 'Liberal' electorate – based on famous songs of the past. Thus, 'Blowing in the Wind' by Bob Dylan became 'the answer, my friends, is don't vote for them!' And there was the reworked country classic 'Pauline, Pauline – Porleen!' 'Why don't you give up politics? Go back to cooking fish and chips!' There was also the piece dedicated to Behroush Barooshi – author of *No Friends but the Mountains*, written via text from Manus island – when Bob Dylan's 'With God on My side' was morphed (for BB) into 'no Libs on his side!' This was all filmed by husband Leigh for posterity.

July 2019: Why Art Is Good For the Brain! (Plus My Sauce Good)

This address starts with a quote from writer David Malouf to Trent Dalton: 'If a piece of art engages you, then it puzzles you.' Ipso facto, if a painting or an artwork makes you stop and look at it, then you have to know why that is so.

What is it about art that makes people stop to look at it, and what do they feel inside when they do? Why, they ask themselves, do I feel it as good for my brain?

We all know there are many types of artworks, many styles and disciplines of paintings, that we are seeing when we go to a gallery. Some undoubtedly engage us more than others. And the type and style of painting that makes me stop and look and feel good about seeing it is different from what may attract every other person in this room. Also we know there are many types of art that we all like together.

Alain de Botton and John Armstrong have nominated seven main functions of art: in helping us to remember, in helping us appreciate sorrow, in rebalancing our attitude to existence, in understanding ourselves, in growing us as people with new information about the world, and in promoting empathy.

So the authors think the majority of paintings we see are covered by their rubric – of doing one or the other of those things to our consciousness – sometimes several at the same time. But what else is involved when we look at a picture? What is going on chemically in our brain? Behavioural studies have shown that the paintings we feel most deeply about when we see them allow us to focus inward to our most personal thoughts and feelings – in a 'unique brain state'. The art elicits increased activity in the hippocampus and humans draw on their own experiences when processing complex art – and we do it instantly. As Picasso has said, 'the picture lives only through the man/woman who is looking at it'.

There is also the idea that looking at art gives us a 'special' pleasure – in a way, looking at art is better than sex! Or a substitute for sex. A former partner of mine and I found our physical feelings for each other reactivated by going to a gallery – it made us feel sexy.

The possibilities of art as entertainment have made curators fix on new ways to present art. Digital manipulations of the work of Van Gogh, Klimt, Monet and many others have been made to create spaces where the spectator can effectively walk through, surrounded by those emblematic works, rather than merely looking at them from a fixed point. Spectators' intellectual engagement is enhanced by art happening as an event with audio/visual and other technical aids so that we absorb the overall mental experience rather than just the art's pictorial effects. In Holland, you can go to a Van Gogh exhibition, for instance, and actually 'sit' in his room in Arles, or at his café under the starry starry night.

Yet most of us still access most art in books as illustrations, et cetera and on social media – in our ordinary day to day rather than going to a gallery. So what does art do for you?

Is there a painting or an artwork that may not be good for the brain – that, arguably, should not be seen, that may be considered too violent or morally antisocial? The crowd was shown a sketched picture by George Grosz depicting the headless corpse of a woman on a bed in a tatty room backgrounded by a man looking up guiltily from washing his hands at a sink in an en suite.

Is art always a question we should not shirk from answering?

Other artists were looked at, like performance 'fiend' Mark McGowan, who has enacted numerous bizarre feats like sitting in a bath of beans with two chips stuck up his nose and forty-eight sausages strapped to his head for two weeks. Or Marcus Clarke with a stuffed stoat on his head drinking Guinness and channelling spirits from the underworld. What are they hoping to achieve – for our education?

There are always other ways that Art can help you – like how it got John Olsen over heartbreak or how making art significantly reduces stress-related hormones in your body. Art calms and uplifts the spirits, according to Live Poet regular Kate Maclurcan. Laura Jane Smith spent nearly twenty years of her life detained in various psychiatric hospitals in the UK with doctors offering conflicting diagnoses until she just decided, 'I would paint how I was feeling as words weren't really helping – I splashed paint on long pieces of paper in my room. When I showed the results to a consultant, he was able to diagnose and treat me and my condition began to improve.'

The buzz around the room when the lecture was done showed what effect the audience was expressing.

The lead guitarist in 'My Sauce Good' – Dirk Kruithof – actually had several of his paintings on display around the Don Bank sitting room while the trio that included his wife, singer Laura Brodsky, and percussionist Tim Bradley swung into its set. 'Wake the World' got things started then tunes sung by Laura in other languages like 'An Anti-Colonial Lullaby' and 'Nunca Mas' (in Spanish). There was Dirk at play in the grunge 'Walkamile Blues', finally forming an anthem that didn't want to quit. Laura was then back with the torch song 'At ZZ'. At the beginning of 'The Silences' there is a scream.

This combo kept you on your toes and the rhythms were infectious. The fade out became a rhumba. Dirk proffered a CD for the raffle but not a painting. They were uncomfortably urban in tone but there was one serene terrace house!

September 2019: News – What Is It For?

Where do you get info about the world outside of the company of family and close friends? Is it from newspapers, TV, magazines, books? Online via websites? Social media?

Is it a combination of all these? What is your personal test for the veracity of this info? How can you trust what you are perceiving as genuine news? Has media become impossibly corrupted in your view? Do you believe in the term fake news? Are you even conscious of it? How sure of his/her facts can today's journalist be when they sit down to write a story for public consumption?

I read out a Heckler column from the *Sydney Morning Herald* which had a headline 'Basically, TV news is absolutely grating'. That person did not think the media was doing its proper job. But in this complex and confusing world, what constitutes news? And what is it for?

There was a counter to the apparent gloom about free press emanating from Trump America with reports of people paying for subscriptions for news outlets as a revulsion against the administration declaring, the press is our enemy. I pointed out local journalists in 'free' magazines in Sydney doing responsible, community-minded articles.

How did newspapers start in the modern world and what did they look like? I then displayed and read from a copy of *The Daily Universal Register* – a precursor of *The Times* of London. A facsimile edition of it from Saturday 1 January 1785. Price: twopence halfpenny. The leading article told of the challenges of setting up a newspaper today. That took up half of the first page. The rest consisted of theatre alerts, some shipping notices, other public announcements and plans for the Chamber of Commerce, et cetera. There were other articles inside and births and deaths. Rudimentary real estate notices informed the back page along with the price of stocks and other financial information – some shipping info and London's weather forecast.

Not that much different to today, yeah?

Later, Alastair Spate in his guest spot read several poems prompted by current affairs – surreptitiously asserting that if our traditional media is corrupt, only interested in keyboard clicks and failing their 'jobs' – there is a role for poetry to play.

I reflected too how news, and how it is being spun, has now become a target for producers of television dramas.

I also read parts of articles from an old edition of *Granta* magazine which featured famous news stories like the madness (in pics and text) surrounding the trial of UK serial killer Fred West and his wife Rose in November 1995, and a husband and wife in Canada watching a CNN update of the Kobe earthquake in Japan in the mid-90s and suddenly feeling the awful truth about their daughter, Angela – half a world away.

As a companion feature to the above, Open Section readers and regulars picked out poems at random to read from an anthology called *News that Stays News* (a play on the famous Ezra Pound quote re the art). There was one poem for one day of every year over the course of the twentieth century.

October 2019: Literary Cities – A Tribute To Venice, Voices of Visitors To the Ethereal Metropolis, featuring Bee And Alan, Songs of Old Italia, and the Masked Bard Ball

After a quick opening by the convenor, the main theme of the night was previewed and then we had Andrew Bukenya interviewing Wil Roach about his London memoir *Black, Gay and Under-Age* (detailed in the section 2019).

But regarding Literary Cities: Venice, the convenor introduced himself as the Geriatric Gondolier – literally 'leaning on the pole directing his craft along the canals' – our guide to the city on the water.

This 'tour' involved a reading of 'Charles Harold's Pilgrimage', Lord Byron's 'love letter' to that metropolis. There were then outlined two decisive events in the lives of the peoples of the Lagoon, followed by Edward Gibbon's and Charles Dickens's impressions of Venice.

We then catch celebrated chef Elizabeth David at the Venice markets in early morning. There is a reflection on the singing of the gondoliers by Goethe, and a scene where Hugh Walpole witnesses an execution.

In this City looks at Venice's preoccupations under the skin of the discipline of the Reformation. And scenes from the time of Carnevale.

That was a suitable segue to Bee and Alan coming up to perform their Songs of Italia. In the first set of this sequence the dynamic duo in their impeccable costumes – Alan, with his 'plague mask' above a suit of frills, particularly outstanding – had a largely jolly air with 'Quando Quando', 'Mia Cara Venezia', 'La Postina della Val Gardena' and 'Venezia – la lunette tu'.

After supper, the duo's second set was more traditional, with 'Meglio', and 'Star Sera' and, finally, a forboding tone with 'Come Triste Venezia'.

This was the perfect prelude to the passages from the Geriatric Gondolier's next set, 'Love and Death in Venice'. First, we are in the boat as Henry James urges his 'helper' to push down the clothes of his mistress under the water (reflecting on James's ilicit involvement with Constance Fenimore Woolson in Colm Toibin's *The Master*). Then there is a reflective passage from Thomas Mann's *Death in Venice*, something of an archetype of its time.

We then look at American art collector Peggy Guggenheim's time in Venice, starting with her daily tours with visitors on the canal. She was made an honorary citizen of Venice in 1962 and later a *commendatore*. But her palazzo, despite all the parties she hosted, and the paintings she collected and hung on the walls there, was still badly neglected when she died. There was mould everywhere. The premises were not secured properly and there had been several thefts. The smell of her many cats pervaded as the only perfume then. There is an amusing reference to the Australian PM at one of her parties – a certain Mr Gough Whitlam. There is a summation of how the collection was finally incorporated and left as a legacy to the sinking city – not to be split up by the many cultural hyenas that sought to intervene and secure masterpieces for reduced prices.

There was then a holding of the Masked Bard Ball Game. Two people, a man and a woman wearing masks, get up to dance to music on the beatbox – Andrea Rieu's *Venetian Symphony*, as it happens. As they swirl strategically they converse – asking their 'partner of the moment' a series of questions, bearing in mind at the same time the local rules of thumb: be careful what you divulge! The Gondolier tells each person in the couple who they are in real life. No one else – not even their partner – will know until the questions are answered (though the audience may guess ahead of time!).

The questions (there is a coin toss to see who will ask the first question) are, Are you a resident here, or are you on a visit? What is the essential appeal of Venice to you? Are you an artist, or a musician, or a writer? What are your most famous works?

Famous people played by the players and those people's famous works were, respectively, Charles Dickens (*Great Expectations*), Igor Stravinsky (*Rite of Spring*), Torquado Tasso, a famous singer of Venice (*Jerusalem Delivered*), J.M. Turner (*Wreck of the Temeraire*), Donna Leon (Death of La Fenice), Peggy Guggenheim (the Guggenheim Gallery), Louise Colet (*L'Italie des Italiens*), George Sand (*She and He*).

People from the crowd who played this game included Mark and Stephanie, Bee and Alan – who else? Perhaps you, reader, could play it some time?

After some people read in a truncated Open Section, the Geriatric Gondolier came back for his last set, Albert Morand's apocalyptic vision of Venice's fate.

And the convenor, as a young man in 1977, then told of his first experience of the famous city – beginning with almost going back to sleep on the train and dimly seeing the oil dumps and garbage before the platform at Mestre.

And his subsequent walk – quite happily lost – through the grimy streets of the ghetto… The glamour of the canal nowhere to be seen…

November 2019: Fifties-sixties Sing-sing In the Courtyard

This was the list of tunes and their singers in our nostalgia during and after supper with all songs sung a cappella, singly or in twosomes, or other groups, and 'coordinated' by the convenor!

In fact, he started most of the songs…

'Oh Carol' (Neil Sedaka), 'Who Put the Bump?' (Barry Mann), 'Seven Little Girls Sittin' in the Back Seat' (Paul Evans), 'Walk Right Back' (Everly Brothers), 'Please Stay' (the Drifters), 'A Guy is a Guy' (Doris Day) – a cool performance this from Megan Corrigan, 'Blueberry Hill' (Fats Domino), 'Fever' (Peggy Lee), 'Take Good Care of My Baby' (Bobby Vee), 'Come Back Liza' (Harry Belafonte). There may have been others.

There was also an impromptu duet between the convenor and Willem Tibben of 'Old Friends' by Simon and Garfunkel.

Meantime, the wine flowed and the songs got louder and the evidence got 'clicked'. We were kicking out the year like a mad thing.

Those who had hair still, 'let it down, baby!'

2017

The year was off to a cracking start in a packed house in February with special guests Melinda Smith and Mark Roberts and a special Walk Through Gaza feature where regulars read poems from a modern Palestinian anthology of verse. This event, held over from August last year, actually kicked off the evening, preceding the special guests.

The anthology was kindly provided by Live Poets supporter Shawki Moslemani and provided a vivid window into the lives of poets and people living under occupation. John Egan got us started with two short poems about children's corpses by Dalia Taha. Geoff read 'Sleeping in Gaza' by Najwan Darwish. Charles had us addressing a 'Death Squad' by Muheeb Barghuty. Megan read 'One man Gathering' by Tarek al-Karmy. Helen read the haunting 'A Case of Love' from Aliaa Saqqa. Phil read Isra'a Kalash's 'Fifty years after the Nakba', while Andrew argued Marwan Makhoul's 'Dismissal of Identity'. Marie Mcmillan read Haneen Naamneh's 'Panadol' (thinking it would help) while Willem presented Yousef el-Quedra's 'The world was nothingness'. Graham asked Asma'a Azaizeh's question, 'What shall we do with the addresses of our friends who've passed away?', in 'Mail'.

Melinda Louise Smith is poetry editor for the *Canberra Times* and runs a venue in the ACT, That Poetry Thing, of a Monday evening. Her book *Drag Down to Unlock* was the poetry pick in 2014's Prime Minister Literary Awards (a gong initiated by Kevin Rudd). It is suffused with material both ironic and telling, springing from the 'ordinary' experience. She started by saying, 'I was so moved by what we've just heard (re

Walk). They seemed real poetry. I was afraid my pieces would be caught short in comparison.' She needn't have worried. She started with the title piece from her new book, 'Goodbye Cruel...' then 'What was written in the Sky'. (One wondered, was the graffiti apposite or contrasting?) There was then a middle section principally about suicide with its particular highlight, 'The Gap.' I mentioned I'd first 'met' that poem at the Waverley Poetry Picnic last year. It demonstrated graphically how Melinda knew exactly when to finish a poem – keep a person (the reader too!) 'hanging' – despite the salesman's pun! (Spoiler alert: you have to check the actual poem to find what that observation signifies!)

After supper, it was time for Mark Roberts. Longtime editor of the Rochford Street Press – purveyor of innumerable chapbooks and poetry pamphlets dating back to the 1980s – now an online journal of enduring influence. In interview, Mark was asked about the press's start. It was named after the street he was living on in Erskineville: 'If Virginia Woolf and Leonard could name their press the Hogarth after their address in Bloomsbury, I felt that was OK for us!' The name of the press's first production, *P76*, is a bit better known – after an infamous BMC family car for Australia that frankly bombed in our marketplace. What sort of 'vehicle' was that, one wondered, for the mag Mark started with Adam Aitken? 'The quarterly magazine had owned who could appear in print for ages previous and had great power in that. But in the 80s you produced pamphlets, mags, on Gestetner printers and stapled covers on, and you could get your poems out there.' Get round more corners than a P76?

Mark was asked, what's the biggest change on the poetry

scene you've seen since the 1980s? 'I guess, distribution driven by the internet. You can access so many collections online whereas once you had to go to the library or a bookshop if you could afford that. With the internet, that all changed. It's also meant ultimately that poems are put out to the public so much more quickly and maybe lack the rigour of that final rewrite!'

Mark reflected that we were coming up to Ern Malley's ninety-ninth birthday and spoke of what that famous hoax meant. 'Misappropriation – failed attribution of poems written before – is certainly a factor too today. The net leaves the unknowing public open to that – but it also means you can get caught out.' He cited a few people whose plagiarism has been outed recently. Again, true quality can surely only be earnt. Who could get satisfaction, one thought, out of copying or stealing the work of others?

Mark was asked what drives his poetry. 'I guess describing something in a certain form, capturing it to pass on and, hopefully, uncovering a nuance that connects, that people want to hear more of.'

He then read some poems from *Lacuna* and *Concrete Flamingos*, including a lady's journey into blindness. There was a poem set in St Leonards. And a sequence about his father's final peregrinations – 'his last lap of Bathurst [racetrack]'. The (two) end up at Blackheath for what would be their last pub drink outside the home.

Re the Gazan poems, lots of people came up to offer congratulations for the sequence. Charles Freyberg: 'I really began to understand the situation much more – thank you!' There was the timing, someone said, with Israeli PM Benjamin Netanyahu's visit to Australia that week. That was pure happenstance as we originally planned to run the event in August last year. A longtime Live Poets supporter said, 'Even the poem set in London in that short story where the Palestinian writer has no state, no country, only time before, and she won't change her clock because she doesn't want to "lose" that "connection"'. That is so telling of a people robbed. All she can do is stay in Palestinian time.'

In the Open Section, the standouts were Phillip Radmall's father forensically apportioning every meal each member of the family received, Megan's reflection on Chanel, and Charles's 'Diana – a character of Kings Cross' from a collection he has forthcoming.

Times were quieter in March when Philip Hammial and Rebecca Kylie Law and Andrew Vial featured. Phil (for several decades now from the Blue Mountains but originally from Detroit) was reading from his latest collection, *Testicle to Tomb*. He has produced a staggering twenty-nine books of poetry. He is not shy about tackling controversial issues. In fact, he warned the audience several times this night that if they were sensitive about particular subject areas they were welcome to 'take a walk' during 'this next bit'. Phil has an originality of style too which is not to everyone's fancy – he has few imitators. He says he's been influenced by East European poets. 'Those guys seemed to look at their surroundings (admittedly bleak under a totalitarian yoke) and see through to another reality on the other side. Their work got me to thinking about and incorporating other realities.' Their poetry in fact affected Philip far more than contemporary poets in the USA and the UK. The result is often a story/portrait of a society stratum in ten or twelve lines. There are often strange points of view 'persuading' the reader to indulge his/her curiosity. One poem this night called 'Elephant' starts off with sex – 'it had never been so good' – and ends up with some sort of sculpture being created by the 'couple' concerned – elephant and human, who knows? Maybe! It had listeners chuckling. Others talked about horse whisperers: 'if it was cow-whispering, I'd have to yell out loud!' Or swapping clothes continually with an old woman – or joining women in ECT chambers – your mother or your sister? The dilemmas internally created by conflicting nerve banks. There was a poem called 'Dance Trump' with the immortal command, 'Try charming harder!' There was 'The Authorities' which states, 'you know the penalty for disobedience!' – and the subjects deciding they will comply: 'we always do, always hoping we haven't lost the ability to grow new eyes'. A poem called 'Bytes' defies description outside itself. 'Soft Targets' starts with a drug habit. There is certainly no substitute to hearing Phil 'live' – and it was a pleasure to welcome him back to Don Bank after twelve years away.

Rebecca Kylie Law says that her Catholic faith has an indelible influence on her work. In interview, she explained this by pointing out the references in her poems to candles, prayers, worship, masses, churches – 'a general reverence of the sacred'. This combined in several cases with the physical properties of her life on the peninsula (Avalon) – an existence framed by the activities of the ocean and its weather. There is definitely a sense of someone looking over her shoulder or observing her in ritual activity. Also I find a feeling of 'inhabiting old paintings' in her work. I made her laugh when I said her poems' frequently ordered interiors made me think of the painters Vermeer or Rembrandt. What makes Rebecca's readings special is the way she involves the listener in a shared intimacy – either with loved ones or modes of being or states of mind – or just being conscious of the intercession of higher powers. This was often signalled by gasps of recognition from the audience this night. In her two publications, *In My Days and In My Sleep* (Interactive Press) and *Earthly Darling Came* (Picaro Poets), which she was debuting publically this night, there were painful but accepting poems about her father's failing health ('Waltzing into the Bedroom' was one example). There were ironic poems like the one about a man directing his wife in swimming lessons from the shore ('A Picture') – a process Rebecca apprehended behind her as she was taking her daily dip one morning. There was contemplation of a death in nature ('To a Sparrow') or among the congregation ('Nature of Prayer'). There were more mysterious, eery pieces (re the fish in 'Today's Mail') and spending a night alone with childrens' toys ('Nocturne'). The emblematic role of the ibis in 'Born of the Sacred'. The language was clear but often beckoning into an accepted abstract – a line seemingly first felt and declared uncertainly but nevertheless complete.

Andrew Vial (the third feature this night) an inveterate local film-maker and actor and LP regular, arrived before doors open to set up his laptop and a screen for the short films he was presenting. He was assisted in this by Willem Tibben, but several gremlins were met with the equipment and 'the mode' not talking to each other. After supper, we did see 'Pineapple', which Andrew entered into Tropfest. In this film, a man's serenity in the garden under a flight path is shattered by a series of low-flying passenger jets having him misapprehending – on his mobile – test results from a doctor on his physical condition, with concomitant social consequences. The audience fell about in a guffawing uproar. There was an amusing anecdote behind a film Andrew couldn't get to cast on this night – notice of the content of which had prompted a (threatening) letter from singer Harry Belafonte's legal team saying, in effect, 'you are not permitted to exhibit this without our client's permission. Dispose of all copies or else.' Were gremlins at work this night via some Caribbean voodoo?

In the Open Section, newcomer Clare read a canny shorthand of what can preoccupy one's mind at work. Olga read a snip about lying on (Salvador) Dali's lips – the same forming a sculptural piece of furniture! Audrey Molloy read a piece about how knowledge at successive ages of experience directed the motivations behind naming a child. The convenor read 'Killing Time', in which an answer machine confirmed a chance acquaintance's self-inflicted demise.

Marie Mcmillan was the special guest for April, to be preceded by Beck Fielding with her guitar. The bookings from far and wide in the days beforehand were a clue. This night was another sell-out with forty of Marie's supporters arriving – some of them having to crane in from the porch outside to listen, though we had brought extra chairs from home.

Beck, a young lady originally from Tocumwal on the Murray River, with her booming vocal, astute picking and catchy but not cliché melodies, was over the moon to have such a large audience (and thinking it was the norm for the venue!). She specialised in her own material rather than taking the famous covers route to get attention. With a big voice and a deft guitar style with soulful echo, Beck was asked her opinion of all the singing contests that have multiplied on our TV screens over the last five years or so. Was she ever tempted to have a go at them? 'Bit too mainstream, I think,' was her measured response. Beck had agreed to both open and close the Live Poets sessions before supper. Her first bracket won people over with songs like 'Turning Back', 'Other Side', 'Colour Blind' and 'Whisper in the Heart'. The applause went straight up to the roof as the final flourish faded.

It was now time to welcome Marie Mcmillan. She built up her reading slowly with her more serious pieces like 'Behold the Deer' (inside Saddam Hussein's prison) and 'A Great Hunger', about the effects of famine, with its bitter 'remedy'. 'Letter to Mrs Foley' was elegiac, but on a grim subject – a man beheaded by ISIS. And then the fun started with 'Here Puss Puss!', 'Sniping in Two Halves' and 'Amber's Strip' (a botanical tale). By the time we got to 'Illegal Immigrant' (suffering through a weevil plague), the double entendres were flowing shamelessly. They reached their 'fall-down chuckling' peak with 'Assimilation' and that most famous reference to our most (sexually) infamous cricketer, on the phone at least! Then we had 'Sub Class Visa: 457' ('because I can't say thirty-three you see! But Gina (Rhinehart) is determined that I should hibernasize you!'). These are pieces Marie has slayed us with over the last couple of years and earned her an Open Section poem of the year. Still, you felt, 'She's reached new heights tonight!' She says she accepted my request for her to feature 'as a favour' and 'this has always been your fault for encouraging me originally!' Marie's talent to entertain has gone far beyond any ambition I had for her!

In the Open Section, the convenor read a poem about meeting Yevtushenko, another poetry 'great' who's recently left us.

But here now as we verge on overtime for supper is Beck

Fielding and her finale, 'Make No Time for Love', 'Superman' and the emblematic 'This Girl' – her audience perspiration number – the final refrain going around my head all the next day. Like many I suspect, I was mystified she didn't have a record out yet. Beck assured me the feelers were definitely out there.

The album *Humans* was back on the beatbox as we cleaned up… But who was that guy in the blue shirt in the crowd (a friend of Marie's) who filled in the gaps of our presentation, while we set up this and that, with charming bits of blarney? Someone should sign him up!

It was the occasion of American legend Patti Smith's latest visit to Sydney and the chief chore for the Open Section this night was to channel her work in whatever form they saw fit. The actual Patti Smith piece each poet performed was picked out of a hat. The most interesting examples, I thought, would be those people who could resist the urge to sing, however adroitly. The idea for this segment was an admitted sleeper on the surface but after supper it carried a momentum in a way I certainly didn't foresee. John Egan was up first with a 'reading' of the song 'Citizen Ship'. Barbara almost got to singing 'Rock n Roll Nigger.' Helen Wren lent some special moments – and then kicked out the jams to 'Dancing Barefoot.' Cathy Jones had a real dilemma – how can someone just 'read' the lyrics to 'Because the Night'? Letitia lit up 'Money for Free' – throwing out the lyrics like a hip-hop post. Barvara picked out a poem – the creepy 'Blue Mask' from Patti's book of verse *Auguries of Innocence*. Jill Carter-Hansen's born a cappellist's mind hovered poignantly, glassily, over the poem 'She Lay in the Stream – Dreaming of August Sander'. Last person to take up the mantle was Geoff Yule Smith and 'Easter'. 'Is it a man or a woman speaking?' he wondered aloud, prophetically, beforehand. He 'read' the first page and stopped, telling us 'all' but the chorus. As he came back to his seat, the rest of the audience broke into a raging 'G – L – O – R – I A!' It was simply mad! And a perfect way to celebrate another birthday for Live Poets.

In May, Garry Macdougall was the guest. There was a special called the Travel Rune: Eyewitness Snippets from Famous Journeys and the annual Monologue Challenge. Bee and Alan were also on hand to give us some music.

In the Travel Rune, the convenor read the preface from the I-Ching and a passage from Homer's *Odyssey*. Wil Roach read a haiku from Basho. Helen Wren did a piece from Dante and Cathy Jones ditto from Rimbaud in Abyssinia. Graham Cameron brought it back home with the last words to 'another' from doomed Australian explorer Robert Burke. Willem Tibben gave an offering from Oscar Wilde, Fayroze quoted Jack Kerouac and Danny Lockhart produced a 'road ode' fingerling from Woody Guthrie. Andrew Vial channelled Robinson Crusoe and the convenor came back with a piece from space via Neil Armstrong. His rendition of Amory Hill's 'Bus from Bihaj' (ref the Balkan conflict) completed the set.

We then heard a vague troubadour ode on the air before Garry Macdougall came in from the back of the room – camp mug dangling from his rucksack – obviously being 'patched in' from the road to El Camino! Garry of course is an established guide for travellers through large parts of Spain, France and Italy and divides his time between South Coast, NSW, and those places. The patois and mantra of troubadours in poetry and song is his metier, which has now resulted in several books on the practical realities and the random delights in his profession. He started honing this craft with the plotting and blazing of the Great Northern Walk between Sydney and Newcastle around Bicentennial time. He has gone on since to fashion novels around the time of the troubadours in situ and the echoes in history they have trodden. Here, at Don Bank, he was at pains to tell us a tapestry of tales in twenty minutes or so in pieces like 'The Town that Shaped the People', 'The Town that Cried' and so on. There is an irrepressible originality and wanton eccentricity in how he presents his material – half verse, half song ode, cries and curses – even animal noises that he presses in to service his portraits. It's vine-riding without a safety net at times – but not forgotten easily. Character is uppermost. Like the personality of the 'other' human species you meet on life's road whose vision you would be foolish to discount.

We went to supper puzzling as much as celebrating what we had just witnessed. Thinking, nonetheless, 'It's nowt that a night in the (barnyard) straw can't fix!'

The annual Monologue Challenge featured seventeen contestants (probably a record!) competing for the audience vote. It's the most consistently successful competition we run and never fails to surprise and inform. Players get passed a speech from a play – famous or random, they may recognise it, they may not. In fact, they don't know what sex they will be, what time they will be living in, what comedy or tragedy they are immersed in. Those who can convince the onlooker of their purpose will have the best chance to win the gong. The most eccentric performance can often be the one that lingers longest in the audience's hive-mind. In tonight's edition, Alan Gannaway read an excerpt from *Patty Red Pants* from a twenty-six-year-old woman, Jack is a character from the American Civil War in *Voices Underwater*, Bee is a child-nervous assistant at Macy's department store in *Tumor*, Julie is a policeman explaining his role to a suspect from *Untold Crimes of Insomniacs*, Cathy is a father-to-be who faints as his wife is giving birth in *Little Vines*, Graham plays Nico at an eternal Warhol party in *Valerie Shoots Andy*, Megan is telling herself what to do while an advertisement about battery hens is being made in *Hold This*, Andrew's script is from an eighteen-year-old Korean sex slave at a Japanese comfort station, afraid she's fallen pregnant, in *Falling Flowers*. That will give you some idea of this comp's drift! And the winner was…Alan!

In a vivid Open Section, Bee and Alan performed 'Invasion Day', 'Not Talking to You' and 'Kerking'. Fayroze told of 'Living in a Cotton Candy Mood' and Cathy offered the zany 'Wig Day Out' (a nursing home hymn). Andrew Vial was acting in 'The Stock Market', Ben Hession presented 'Summer Elipsis' and 'Will You Find Your Way?' Wil Roach read some poems from his mentor, Derek Walcott.

In June, we celebrated the fiftieth anniversary of the launch of the Beatles magnum opus *Sergeant Pepper's Lonely Hearts Club Band* and people were invited to interpret or rendition tracks from that album (see Live Poets Players chapter).

Willem Tibben was presenting his recently launched *Surburban Veneer* and there was a special – With Andy Upstairs at Max's – a live memoir in photographs and witness statements of the famous New York rock club Max's Kansas City and the life of Andy Warhol (see Other Major Shows chapter). It was another sell-out night with thirty-one attendees.

Willem, needing no introduction as a stalwart of Live Poets

and the curator's right-hand man, was on before Pepper and did a selection from his new book. This included 'Hard Day's Night' (happenstance on this Beatles remembrance night?). But Bill's piece was nothing to do with the Fab Four! There was a rollicking revisit of 'San Francisco' ('you better get a flower in your hair!'). There was 'Back Up Hermannsburg' and another telling take on Aboriginal museumology outback, 'Albert Namitjira's Ute'. There was the drama of Bill's father's milk truck breaking down on the biggest hill on the farm (in the 50s). Lastly, still in the rural 'out there', 'Agatha in the Dry Run', which Geoff Yule Smith later called a 'perfect bovine imitation'. Bill, as usual, had struck many chords in how we view our place in this space here.

In the Open Section, Geoff Yule Smith did some songs: 'Let's Make the Most of Things' and 'Love's Place'. Kari did three Shanghai poems (and keenly regarded the 'Max' scenes!). Maggie Mason did a lively, sassy 'Bit on the Side'. Olga K performed 'Oh God' and Jim Quealey did a poem re the 150th anniversary of Henry Lawson's birth. There were lots of performers in the audience in the first part keeping their powder dry until we got to the Pepper special.

July had a Latin-American basis. Mario Licon Cabrera was launching his translation of three contemporary Mexican poets in the Vagabond Press American Poets Series. His 'partner in crime' in the past, Gilmar Munoz of Ecuador, was here with Brian on trumpet in a sequence, 'Bossa to Bolero – from Shadow to Sun'. There was also a special: 'Reading from the Book of Lists', another Shaun Usher production. Once again, we had thirty people through the gates in this bumper year for attendances. Obviously, we were doing something right!

The three Mexican poets in Mario's book were Mijal Lamas, Mario Bojorquez and Ali Calderon. Mario read with passion and gravitas a selection of the poems in English and then Spanish, though some times this was reversed. He also spoke with the convenor about particular qualities he saw expressed and the process and approach of translation more generally. They then combined, the convenor reading the English and Mario the Spanish of some poems the convenor had chosen, including Calderon's 'Mexican Democracy', Lamas's poem to his father and Borjorquez's 'The Eye of Time'.

Gilmar and Brian were a hoot of contrasting tones. The brooding Spanish guitar offset with the trumpet's irrepressible flamboyance continually enlivening; the byplay in modes and gestures between the two players circling back to reiterations and fresh interpretations, the next round in the circle. This enabled collusion and separation both, from the more on-the-surface Bossa and the introspective and ritualistic Bolero styles. The audience was plainly entranced, soaking up the ambience, heads and torsos dipping and rocking. We were right in the club, at the feet of the maestros in the moment. We didn't want to come to the end. We went to supper, heads buzzing as the lights were doused and the house music came up.

The reading from the *Book of Lists* posited numerous scenarios, preoccupations in a life, portraits of certain times – private moments of the famous that the public might not otherwise ever come to know, never more effective than being read aloud now – to people's memories of heroes and villains in the main. Thus, after the convenor got things started with 'Our Reliance on Lists', George Clark read 'How to be a Cowboy'. Kerry J read 'Rules of Good Parenting' (from Susan Sontag). Graham presented 'Ten Commandments for Con-Men', Olga read 'Wartime Golf Rules', Cathy offered up 'What I Must do Better' (by Marilyn Monroe). Caroline announced 'Advice to Young Ladies'. Megan outlined the fundamentals of 'The Anti-Flirt Club' and Jayne detailed the 'To Do List' of Leonardo Da Vinci.

In the Open Section, Raghid presented his poem 'Land' in English and Arabic. Olga had us appalled with her 'Experience at Centrelink – in an Online Application' (poor girl!). Jim Quealey meantime read 'Capture or Captive' and Cathy tickled ribs with a 'Day-trip to Dee Why'.

August saw the visit of David Hallett and the running of the annual Short Fiction Cup. There was also the special A Letter to People in Power. Just how would you couch your case against the system in correspondence form?

At the start, there was a minute's silence for the passing of (Doctor) Gurrumul Yawapingu in the NT the day before.

Hallett, who (so long ago it seems, now) famously contested with Live Poets Society's co-founder Sue Hicks whether his Live Poets venue in Lismore had operated longer, has built a formidable reputation over the years in spoken word performance. On this night, he was a man wanting only to strut his work – a man determined not to be 'interviewed'. I felt the dead air in our exchanges having assumed he'd okayed a certain Q and A as part of the plan. But our frailties are forever pursued by detail.

I like David's often dazzling wordplay and his ability to persuade the onlooker of his viewpoint. But much of it, looked on baldly, presents still a first world bleating about the problems of those outside its experience. He reverted finally to fundamental 'goods' – the Bridge is Love et cetera and vice versa – to consume and be consumed, no miracles here, to 'live and be loved – that is all'.

It was interesting to compare his style with another performance poet who was on hand this night – Tug Dumbly. TD knows the only way to learn to swim is to get into the water, even when fighting through it, and enjoy the journey of rising up from it, no matter the absurdity. Encourage your audience to take on your 'struggle' themselves!

David made telling points in such pieces as 'Nimbin bubble, God-Forsaken?'; for example, on 'just this solitary sphere / a breath of life / this tiny, troubled tired and wasting / bubble'. He regaled us with the rumbling, tumbling 'This poem was not made in China – yet'. 'Last Drinks at Byron Bay' hit at our inner hypocrisy with its ducking and diving over world issues (there are so many pressing) but 'we don't talk about them – its Mother's Day'. It's what happens – the reaffirming of the status quo in these fortunate climes. It was a dagger to our 'all lotuses, here' outlook but, like a history of failures, that fallacy, too, gets repeated, almost as a default.

The Short Fiction Cup this year had only four competitors, all so different in tone. Bob Howe's 'Fiction Cup Entry' was a comedy. Slowly, a hero is unravelled, with political overtures woven in what's more, until he confronts a foe unsurpassable. In 'Recall', Jill provides a view of birth from within, although crucially we don't get to realise that till about two-thirds through. Before that, we rely on sounds from emotions as we deduce feelings not language. Olga Kulanowska's pacing and gravitas in 'Broken Promise' are A1 and hinge on angles to apprehend insights with luck. 'Dinner at Lachlan's' was Graham

Cameron's entry. His preamble and the first half, in fact, is nothing less than known and dried. We've all seen those movies, we've been on those dates and felt those 'moments' arriving to envelop our better judgement – but then…

The last vote called was decisive. Graham – so many times close, the bridesmaid – finally nailed the prize! I've scarcely seen a happier man!

There were only two entrants for our third feature, A Letter to People in Power, which was surprising, as there are so many grievances that could have been touched on. Tug Dumbly's address to the poetic zeitgeist of Australia (specifically, Dorothea Mackellar, favourite of classrooms and librarians) in 'I Love a Stunted Country', and Mr Cameron's dispute of a toll charge and trying to reclaim the money, which had a long list of unsuccessful instalments!

Earlier in the Open Section, Tug Dumbly magicked up 'I Might be Wrong, Day'. Richard Coady, doing his annual appearance promoting the Timestream Picnic in Sydney Park, read 'Invasion Day, 1992' and a poem by Emily Sender. Jemma wanted to read something so I picked a page number from *Light on Don Bank*, our fifteenth anniversary collection, now passed on to all newcomers to the venue. It was Jill Jones's 'While All This was Going On'. Jemma then returned the favour to me and the choice was Yvette Christianse's 'Look, how I feel I am Moving Away'. Olga K came up with her sassy 'Tid – bit – Bitty?' and Willem Tibben read two from *Veneer*: 'Fish Tank' (Fuge) and 'Puffer Fish' (Your Last Kiss).

The Live Poets Players took the stage in September for In Arles, Provence – the Trial of Van Gogh in poems written where he painted his famous pictures (see Live Poets Players chapter).

The special guest was Katherine Gallagher on another trip to her home country from the UK with her latest book, *Acres of Light*, from Arc Publications, with its bright cover based on a Pierre Vella painting.

The interview with KG was delightful – reminiscing doing/sharing shows in the UK. (She is one the most hard-working poets I've ever met and knows so well your progress only starts with writing a poem!) There was wonderment at her range of subject matter which she answered with a beautiful quote: 'I love how you can get poems from anywhere!' In this book's case, all the way from Palestinian poet Mahmood Darwish – 'We Live Life When we Can' – to discovery of London 'snow' while writing about the Australian bush our painters 'wrote' in 'Presence of the Trees'. There is caring for the environment – 'Tree on the Underground' – and the form borne out by love's fire in an Iranian love ghazal. There was music too, inevitably – chamber chords echoing moods – and John Lennon (and the other Beatles) when 'no one could shoot down the song' (re Lennon) and 'no one was too young or too old (anymore) to enjoy' (the Fab Four's oeuvre). Not to forget poetry in education if only in Ireland: 'from where PhDs are written in verse'. Long may Katherine continue her Oz visits before returns to her French husband and now teenage son in Golders Green, London!

The night's third feature, Building a Limerick, which invited two teams to compete in the process, seemed a quirky enough concept in theory. In practice, it meant poets unwilling to compromise and nail the form. Ideally, there would be the classic aabb rhyming scheme, with the final line in mirror-metre to finish. Neither team could settle on the second a – the first was so stand alone: 'Christ! What rhymes with orange?' If we did it again I would have some players on the bench that could be substituted with another approach after, say, two failures from the originals, but the idea just bombed this night!

In the Open Section, Willem Tibben read 'Albert and Vincent' in sympathy to the main show. And Marie Mcmillan revealed her entry in the Australian Poetry Slam Final: the rather porcelain-on-leather-leaning 'Robot Love'.

For October, we had a poetry and a music guest. Jim Low with his latest production from the Roweth (Folk) Studios, *Journey's End*, and Mark Mahemoff's latest book of poetry, *Urban Gleanings*.

Jim's evocation of the past and present in the Blue Mountains and environs continued to reveal human endeavour in our wide brown land. 'Just Fair Game' and 'Turon Valley of Gold' recalled Chinese miners' experiences. Then there was the story of 'collaborator' Jim Hooper in the 1940s. Polly Flood, a proud tribal woman, played accordion for music-lovers in Walgett. There was an enduring line re the lore of the tracks: 'I judge a town by its railways and churches'. There were 'Pieces of Childhood' (Jim used to live locally) in references to the Orpheum, Cremorne and the MLC building, North Sydney and the title track paean to the Dividing Range: 'you're my journey's end, my lifetime friend'. In 'Oh so Blue', 'wild birds fly in the cerulean sky.' Jim's accessible, easy tone made discovery a natural pursuit through a backyard where few, truly, dwell.

Mark Mahemoff has produced four or five books now but has had an understated poetic career. His economy of form is a key weapon in his urban investigations – whole situations unveiled in a line or two – and he is deadly on finishing off with last lines unerring in their aim. There were many things to like here: 'Goodge Street in Glebe' recalled Donovan under a foreign sun. There's land-release irony and comment in 'Kellyville Holiday Farm'. '80 Candles' is about his grandmother. 'Grid Fault' remembers a shocking anniversary, while 'Trope and Africanstance' overburdens the glue holding everything in place in its vigilance. Yet 'Still-Life' sheds frangipani perfume on some city streets. 'Monumental Case' is a signal for all the other utilities we take for granted. In 'Double Rainbow', pools of hope are left in every street. 'New Premises' reflects on his father's clearing out his business and the writer realising another part of 'being a son'. 'Rainy Twilight, Victoria Park' relativises the packed-together-many in rush-hour reflections; similarly, 'Beside the Sleepers'. 'Speaking with Tears' is comprised of lines from letters from refugees in detention centres to the authorities.

We should hear much more of Mark's work.

In the Other Archibald comp, there were just two entrants. 'Ode to Wendy Wu (tours to China)' by Cathy Jones and 'Vibrant Covers' by Janet Eade. They both attracted ten votes each from the crowd.

In the Open Section, Clark Gormley did a persuasive 'Something to Tell You'. Des Maddalena was cautionary in 'I'm Just a Scientist'. Andrew Vial did a Michael J. Fox piece, 'The Actor's Audition', and Mark Marusic, recently back from the UK, recalled the Grenfell Tower housing disaster and tickled memories with the railway mantra 'Mind the Gap'.

So we got to November again and special guest Wil Roach and his West Indian family's opus, *Year at Sea*, and George Clark presenting his book *Crossing the Divide*, while there were literary references to the Art Gallery's latest exhibition in 'Voices From the Dutch Golden Age'.

It was yet another sell-out in a bumper year – forty-one patrons crowding the Don Bank sitting room and hanging from around corners.

Clifford and Shirley, the parents of Wil, are the stars of *Year*. While his wife awaits the birth of their first child (Wil) in Barbados, father has taken a boat to the UK to lay the ground for his brood's translocation to the mother of the Commonwealth. What we hear are two voices reading the couple's letters to each other. We hear Shirley, voiced by the other actor, Jason Philips, and see Wil 'saying' Clifford from the spotlit lectern specially brought in for the occasion. The interaction, reflecting their respective characters, is frequently startling. For instance, Clifford upbraids Shirley for her delays in putting pen to paper: 'you must write today, every day!' But of course Shirley, preoccupied otherwise with confinement and friends' fortunes, responds when she does, 'everyone in the town asks about you!' She rebuts his criticism: 'That is the way it is – mind your tone, Clifford!' He's always complaining about the fog in London (rare as snow to Bajuns!). She feels the weight of baby Wil: 'how he hangs down so low today – like he wants to come out!' and the tiredness remorselessly sapping her strength. In his fondest moments, Clifford announces, 'three million kisses coming just for you! You know you're the only one! Hope you enjoy them!'

This presentation captured the imagination. We felt privileged, humbled by the tale. Wil was afterwards interviewed by Veronica Hannon, during which he said it was a plan he long harboured – to read their letters back to his mother and father in some sort of family ceremony. It was no longer possible now – and that's what drove him to assemble *Year at Sea*.

George Clark's set from *Crossing the Divide* was measured

and indulging – we were guided step by step through his visions from his farm in Oberon under starlight ('4 a.m. on the family farm') to the heavens' reach from foreign clime to the cosmos ('The Greeks' and 'Those Wandering Stars') and how humanity has seen itself through the ages ('Culture Lag' and 'Divine Madness'). The failings of war ('Poetry Cannot Breathe Life') to simple irony and humour ('Vanessa's School Poetry book' and 'The Farmer's Hat'). This is earthy but big picture stuff. Time-honoured individual strength born out of vulnerability and history's frailty – in concise, unhurried phrases. Nerves held tense before judgement. Released in simple occurrences that linger and instruct.

The third feature took us from Rembrandt's self-portraits to Vermeer's sense of order before the shattering on a day a munitions store nearby blew up (he struggles afterwards to reassume his daily 'pattern'): 'I am alone – the wife once more with child. Is this – finally – ruin?'

That's a long way from the 1629 voyage of the *Batavia*, later wrecked off the WA coast. And marooned mutineer, the cabin-boy Jan Pelgrom de Bye, recalling the frosted streets of impossible home scarred by skaters' scythes – Jan, knocking on the door finally and his father, adrift in his treasures, will not answer.

The Open Section to end the year was subscribed to the brim. Bee and Alan did three songs: 'My Guy', 'Baby Please Don't Go!' and 'I'll Make You Happy'. Jill rendered 'Fly Like a Cockatoo' and 'Unchained Melody'. Helen Wren read John Dryden's 'St Cecilia's Day' – on the saint's day! Amory Hill, long time away, came with his son and a friend. Phil Radmall's 'Kangaroo' simply glowed – an incandescent surprise.

There were the Un-Darwin Awards announcements and a reiteration of comp results through the year. Monologue Challenge, Alan Gannaway; Short Fiction Cup, Graham Cameron; Other Archibald, (deadheat) Janet Eades and Catherine Jones; Orange Wig Award, Geoff Yule Smith's 'Mr Kite' (and 'Gloria!' ref Patti Smith), Olga and Megan for being the Strawbs on 'Pepper' night; Open Section Poem of the Year, Olga's 'experience' at Centrelink – more a vivid experience 'live' than a poem per se.

And sincere thanks to the increasing supporter base in this quite remarkable year.

letter to frank

dear frank
they are opening up urban consolidation corridors
that means big apartments knock down grandmother's
house & build a skyscraper!
like you i want to be a construction worker/
                                            poet
tho my silver hat would have a union logo
                                       on it
no charms in my pocket but I am
charming
& i have a copy of the planning regulations
which i am rewriting in the style of the new york
                                       school
when i'm finished i might go and see les
to see what the poets in ukraine are doing
do they write poems while riding on girders

i catch the train to st leonards & lose internet connection
bloody vodafone
                                       but no matter it reconnects after
a second and all i've lost is some punctuation
which i'm not using in this poem
st leonards has already been consolidated
& all the construction workers have gone home
maybe to write poems

Mark Roberts

Grand Theft Auto

Want to know how it happened?
I'll tell you how: a 3rd rail stoush
with a six-mule handicap, Hunky & Dory
sorting out their differences – who
nods when & if it's a sin to grin
at the great man's funeral. As expected
I say 'Why not?' I say 'It's time (while we're at it)
to sort the grannies, which die today & which
on Thursday next.' Are you motivated
to conjure up a regret? I'm only asking because
the riding in these parts has been a bit too roughshod
for my liking lately (No, I don't share Teddy Roosevelt's
enthusiasm for). When we got to that beach we saw
that he'd made a right royal spill & wasn't prepared
to clean it up. Kinfolk curlicues & a making whoopie
scam – he left us no choice, we brought them to bear
& boy did he clean; you could have whistled
a dozen dogs home: sheer delight, let's sit tight
& watch the clouds roll in; forty days
& forty nights & they're still coming; maybe
we should finish carving that canoe; maybe
you could toss a few of those asylum pennies
our way; we're about to get all gussied up
& make our way to Golgotha; me & Garibaldi
if we get there whole the plan is to play
the local hoi-polloi fast & loose, vamp
their plugs, spill their beans, with any luck
might even flog a few copies of my latest
The Petrochemical Songbook. 'OK
everyone it's time to sing along; – Gall
upon gall, 50 miles of RCA!

Philip Hammial

Heidelbergian Psyche

'Only those things are beautiful which are inspired by madness and written by reason.' André Gide

A family of kangaroos lounge in a grass clearing
between the river and walking track. To their left,

large, sprawling manna gums whose long bark drips
toward the water and sways in the breeze; to their right,

a line of neatly segregated maple trees, mature
and blazing in their hot red flashes of autumn.

On their sides, large and small, propped up at times
by a lazy elbow, the animals formation is elongated

as a landscape painting. A seasonal sun hangs near the
ceiling, casting its mild light across the group at a

dusk bound diagonal. The air sparking with the sharp notes
of bush oils. In their stare, the task of a wide Yarra crossing.

Rebecca Kylie Law

My Prometheus

You mightn't care a jot
but I'm hot, yes, hotissimo
for Roger
and he's a robot…

Found and researched
in a lab
he's absolutely fab.
There was no Baron Frankenstein
but he's different…like
a creature in a pantomime

He's my chess mate, my checkmate,
never rude,
always nude,
never visibly priapic
private parts kept in the attic

He's my Titan in titanium,
my Knight in
shining armour
not a farmer but a charmer
whom you might think exotic
but I find
robotically erotic

Desires?
They will be tabulated,
algorithmically calculated,
algebraically validated,
programmed
and
in an affidavi…circulated

I'll never need a maid,
but the problem is
how to get laid?
It's metallic virgin territory…
I think that's how it's labelled
for doin' 'you know whatsy'
with the differently abled

So, I ask you to imagine
when he brings his potent power
to my pristine virgin bower
where I know he'll me deflower

Gives me a screw…
driver,
a tin opene…
'C'mon babe,' he says
'My nuts and bolts unlock
for voltage that'll shock
an' make you
R O C K.'

Marie Mcmillan

The poem is entirely fictional and is neither based on nor has its genesis in any human experience. The ideas in it were conceived and brought to fruition before any discussion in the media about robots and sex toys.

Crave Love

(Pezanas, southern France)

Bumping into you, Pezenas
green-framed on Michelin map
knowing you and your charming Molière
giant of French theatre, seasons you
with hilarity and storm, imaginations fired.

Your Rue Jean Jaures is wide and bent
like a beggar, Champs Elysée with a limp
in memory of his assassination, regrets endure
shops closed, architecture scuttled…

Pezenas, prosperous and love-crazed
keeper of Langue d'Oc, lonesome for Molière,
you gather craftspeople to your galleries
decorate your good self with statues of bronze
musée and oiseau, cats and dogs unleashed.

Your people sweep, serve and converse the good air
sell knick-knacks and handbags of leather
your visitors see shadows for nothing
courtyard studio with a ceramic giraffe
cane flamingo and gorillas with erections
hidden behind frightened palms.

Expectant tourists borne on carefree wings
Meet thunder storms before
retreating to cafés of innocence
'*Bon Jour*' and '*L'addition, s'il vous plaît.*'
Pezenas serves lashings of poetry
with almond panache
cream of onion soup
all your ways lent to welcome…

Your halles turn heads
visitors drawn to one-euro musee
There! See impatient Molière in the backroom
breathes sweet lavender and musk
launders his clothes in hot water
shatters crockery, offends the mistress
and bites his tongue.

Molière strips their pretence
mingles with diplomacy, the women
under high hair, heels, doublets and cuplets
powder and lace (a fainting spell so easy to waist)
the men without baldric and sword
itch in tights that harden the nipples.

Jean-Baptiste sits with ink and quill
milk and dill, all genius for the noble nothings
gifts wit and mirth to a master's babble
servants gathering by the pink-striped pantry
plucking ducks with duplicity

Scullion of rumble and gambol
piping-hot denial, cramp and scornful brogue
giggles in the kitchen, potent broth and cough
and Madame wiggling her toes
glances sideway to a fellow enrapt in rags.

Garry McDougall

Caribbean Jewel

Dedicated to Derek Walcott and Dr Arthur Drayton

As the sun sank into the hush of the night sky
nature's angel whispered a message…effortlessly carried,
through the fragrant warm air of sleepless St Lucia,
foretelling that a soul man's bright journey was
destined for a starry graveyard – and immortality.
Those who were watchful that night
caught the whisper and heard tell
how his soul would fly, high, high, high
past the darkened Piton Peaks, as if in mourning,
for an Island son – his face no more reflected,
on the deep, azure sea
from which offerings of a profound knowing
and unfathomable intelligence, sprang.
It has been shared with us without equal.
The timbre of his voice silenced for now,
a rich depth as if holding another time,
his destiny fulfilled. It was time to rest.
His literary gifts all spent in honour
of his calling. Yet the bitter-sweet irony
of human rejection lingered,
would give him pause to reflect
from a distant place, unknown to human sight.

Wilfred Roach

hume and hovell monument

the photo
among the eager mt hunter schoolchildren
crowded into place around that appin monument
eric is near the front one of the littlies posing
allen eldest at the back taking it all in
surveys the moment approves the arrangement
smiles out to the milk blue air and razorback

and i remember in the days after allen's death
eric in tears and me leaving not because i was going
not to hold me just revealing himself as brother
man boy alone i was already much too late
but i should have stayed

now it will forever be too soon too late
the gulf i did not cross that night
because of what was left unsaid
everything shrinks but nothing closes

I'm standing by the monument
there are cars passing on appin road
the barbed wire strands still here

keeping out cows i climb through
to stand with them

as if i am a kid

Willem Tibben

Day Trips to Dee Why

What a special person I am,
lots of friends wishing me well,
they often go globetrotting and leave me behind,
do not fret we'll be back they tell,
'Here's a tissue, do not cry.
When we return, we'll go on a day trip to Dee Why!'

My friends are so very good to me,
I receive lots of postcards from exotic places,
beautiful beaches with golden sands,
leisurely lazing contented faces,
their words are few, 'Wish you were here!'
'Never mind we'll still have our day trip to Dee Why!'

Cascading chasms weeping waterfalls,
tranquil turquoise waters drifting by,
glorious gardens delightfully displayed,
rolling rivers meandering mindlessly,
I dream and sigh.
All I have are day trips to Dee Why!

I once travelled on long forgotten tracks,
through towns with cobblestone streets,
surrounded by snow-capped mountains,
fabulous fortresses firmly on guard,
but now I wonder why
its day trips for me to Dee Why!

You can have the rolling green hills,
blistering, bubbling volcanoes ready to burst,
enjoy the Seven Wonders of the World,
give me the sun, the sand and the surf,
oh joy! Beauty before my eyes!
All day, every day are day trips to Dee Why!

Cathy Jones

Tiger behind those rubber trees

1950s British Malaya

Our young family was left to the elements with just my blind great-grandmother, grandmother and grandfather to visit us out of the blue.

Our house was a big old English stone mansion in the midst of a jungle and a dark rubber plantation. Father owned an old Japanese motorbike that he would get to work and back. The house was sturdy enough to withstand the heavy thunderstorms, flooding and the elements of the tropics. The marble floor I remember as a child was cold, the kitchen was immense, dark and ominous. We children roamed like wild animals!

There were loads of places to explore. Giant fig trees that we named 'tarzan tree' as the roots of the fig tree were long, tangled, gnarled and sturdy to climb. It was our saving grace when it came to a wild goat that did not like children – as soon as we were in its sight, he would charge like a bull, at full speed.

We would run screaming, laughing and climb on top of that fig tree, like wild monkeys, to get away from that crazed goat with big horns! For a girl, I was very adept at climbing the trees in this neighbourhood with my brothers. At midday it was a different story. Father had warned us about the wild animals that lived in this remote rubber plantation.

We were banned from venturing too far out from our home, or anywhere near the well, that held our water storage. No close neighbours or a telephone. When it flooded, we were isolated from the rest of the world.

The farmers and villagers discovered a little path that led to their homes, via our house. Wild boar and their piglets, wild hen, monkeys, wild buffalo and snakes – and most of all a tiger! – would venture close to the house to forage for food. The striped creature was spotted several times over the period of my childhood.

Our house was surrounded by dense jungle and rubber trees. We younger children were terrified of those monkeys and the dark house. Monkeys would venture, bold and brass into our huge kitchen, grab our breakfast along with the utensils. They would climb over the wooden beams into the house, and threaten us with their very sharp teeth.

Grandmother hearing the children's screams, would curse in Tamil and Malay at the monkeys with a broom! Great-grandmother would laugh and giggle banging her stick, hearing her daughter curse or the children playing up, or the 'resident ghost' terrorising the household. Being blind, her senses were very acute. She could hear us creeping under her bed, and she would swish that walking stick of hers like a weapon.

At midday a Malay farmer had decided to rest, with his goat and cows under the shade of a rubber tree. While he sat eating and performing his daily prayers, he was unaware a tiger had sat – watching its prey. Swiftly she crept closer and grabbed the goat and disappeared into the sinister dark of the rubber plantation. There were heaps of stories about farmers and livestock being attacked by a tiger or terrorised by rampant wild elephants all throughout my childhood.

Years later, a local hunter from our hometown, killed the tiger. The British have hunted out our forests of the wild animals that roamed free. Wild boar, sun bears, Asian armadillo, breeds of monkeys, elephants, rare leopards and most of all our tigers. Anything for a trophy.

This magnificent animal in its prime –a female – was just hunting for food, to feed its young cubs in the forests that were disappearing for planting oil palms and rubber trees. The tiger was laid out for people to poke and prod its beautiful fur in the main town area. We children were fascinated like all the other locals.

We ran all the way, from home with my brothers, to see this tiger whose capture spread like a bushfire to the neighbouring towns and villages.

The local police were unable to control all these hoards of people who trampled through, like a bunch of herding wild buffalo. It was chaos. I did get close, touched her gently – and shed a tear for her cubs that would be missing their mother. This moment in my life had a profound effect on my young life. My disgust at the zoo, the circus that came into town. I just did not condone the disgusting treatment of our wild animals in a cage.

Dona Samson Zappone

The empty stage

dust settles
on microphone, trapeze, on grand piano,
the words of the song, words of a poem forgotten,
spiders are spinning their world all around the stage
the lacing of webs is the only dance,
a rat
stars centre stage every night
for no one,
outside, the stage door scarred by plague
the theatre sleeps through winter
sleeps into spring –
now
the law is 'no singing, no dancing, no mingling'
now
the stage is a tiny handheld screen
the wall of sound a pair of headphones
now
the show is virtual
an instagram, a tweet,
the movies repeat, the old songs repeat,
now
music is machine
the beat is algorhythmic, the lyric is predictive text;
the hours creep past
the weeks fly away
warm wild August winds blow the mad trees
dazzling fireworks of parrots rise to meet the wind,
words fall across the page
taken by the wind,
the year's doors are closing
the borders closing in around us,
the masks of theatre – comedy, tragedy –

David Hallett

The Year of the Tree

I carried a tree
through the Underground.

It was hard. At first,
people scarcely noticed me

and the oak I was lugging
along the platforms –

heavier than a suitcase
and difficult to balance.

We threaded through corridors,
changing lines: up and down stairs,

escalators, and for a moment
I imagined everyone on the planet

taking turns
to carry a tree as daily rite.

A few people asked
Why a tree?

I said it was for my own
edification –

a tree always
has something to teach.

*

Sharp gusts
whirred through the corridors

rustling the branches
as I hurried on

past the sweepers
picking up rubbish, scraps of paper.

*Be sure to take the tree
with you,* they said.

*Don't worry, I'm taking it
to my garden,*

the start of a forest.
When people stared,

Relax, I said,
it's a tree, not a gun.

Katherine Gallagher

Time Is Memory

We put the clocks back to see the sunrise, look
but be careful not to make a black spot in your vision,
black turns to silver as ducks swoop on the dam
Akhenaton's ghost bows down to the east, thanking
the stars for dimming their vanity. A single currawong
on a dead branch looks at the empty autumn vineyard.

Last night the rain fell out of the night sky as though
it had been suspended against its will and looking to
regain contact with the earth after late hot spell. Then
this morning on the wireless, each note had meaning
like a conversation between man and his maker. We
don't need rock star treatment to find truth and beauty.

I comb the beaches of memory in those days when I
was hurrying north to the next encounter in another
country. Further back, red and green sugar drinks,
cricket, and the ball lost in the choko vine on the shed.
The cicadas and their seven year miracle. Living close
to the sandstone nature and angophora forests,
invaded by privet and morning glory from Europe.

Friendships taken for granted, but mountains and rivers
explored while our minds were left fallow by sun and sea
testing ourselves against nature. I find things in poems, lines
I wish I had written. But who we are, I do not know.

George Clark

Monumental Care

We are pleased to announce,
in addition to general maintenance,
a monument care service.

For a small annual fee,
if you cannot attend
to your loved one's grave,
we will remove leaves, debris,
bird droppings and weeds,
wash it down fortnightly,
and report any damage or decay.

As for your grief
which waxes and wanes;
the guilt and regret
that claws at your dreams;
all the love and hate
that went unexpressed;
that's none of our business:
we wish you all the best.

Mark Mahemoff

the other thing
to Brett Whiteley

Here, you can live outside yourself
and not be crushed by the forces that tell you
get back in.
With the other thing, it's not all decay
or adjusted curves, and non-sexual nudity
it's what it removes, what it adds
and it's where I don't have to be
neither knowing or unconscious
of what is real or abstract
it is all sensation bound.
It's all for you to view this triptych in terror
screaming baboon, attenuated arm, and wild child
and if you listen carefully, you can hear
the syringe sing its big H licks.
Outside yourself, where it takes you, there
is pure style, forms undreamed, designs unbound
and days of freedom I can't find anywhere else.
Outside, you never want to go back in
you find the ecstasy in squares
delight in silence
and a mind space, like no place
you've even been.
Until I'm dry, and crushed back in.

Rob Kennedy

LIVE POETS' SOCIETY

Poetry on the Northside, Wednesday April 4,
Cafe L'Orangerie, Young St, Neutral Bay.
SPECIAL GUESTS:
Vera Newsome, Danny Gardner
and singer-songwriter Paul Cook.

Poetry, music, pasta and unlimited coffee,
$10 from 6.30pm.
BYOG.
Open section — all welcome to read.

*Performance and coffee only 19, 8pm.
Inquiries to Var Hicks. 908 4527 after 6pm.*

Poster of first Live Poets meeting.

Live Poets' Society regulars in Litmus Suite, the group's first anthology, 1991.

Time of Magic poster of Uri the Russian storyteller, a Live Poets regular.

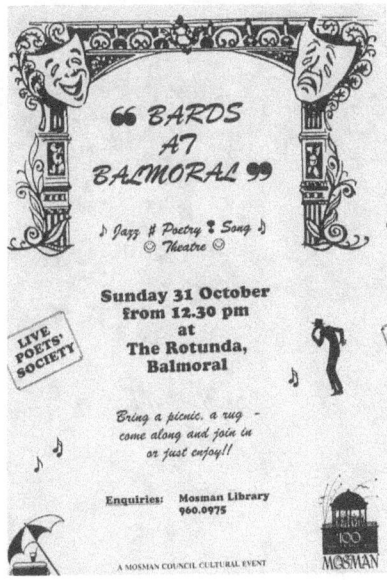

Bards at Balmoral PR leaflet, 1992.

Sketches of Live Poets regulars by Robin Norling, 1998.

LIVE POETS @ DON BANK 20th Birthday Celebrations
At Don Bank Cottage 6 Napier St North Sydney
28th of April 2010
Convenor: Danny Gardner
Performers in order of appearance:
Buck N Deanne (Folk and Blues) Dulcie Meddows, David Tribe,
Chafic Ataya, David Wansbrough, Brian Bell, Hilarie Lindsay
Pip Griffin, Molly Kennealy, Les Wicks, Carolyn Lowry,
David Falcon, Paul Knoebel, Andrew Viall, Michael Buhagiar,
David Chung, Moira Boland, Danny Lockhart, Peter Wagner,
Bob Howe, Ed Wilson, Sri Bhagavadas, Nashaa Hamody Abdul-
Hassan, Ava Banergee, John Powrie, Ann Jarjoura, Sheryl Persson,
Melissa Paris, Lee Cass, Frank Ezbury.
Camera: Bill Tibben.

Special Thanks to North Sydney Council and Stanton Library
Martin Ellis and Sue Shaw.

LIVE POETS AT DON BANK IS 20

Live Poets is 20! DVD cover and program, 2010.

'The 1890s poets and music come to the Farm' – Live Poets @ Don Bank, July 22nd 2015.

the Ceilidh Collective.

narks by the owner of Don Bank (Captain) Benjamin Jenkins - reflections on North Sydney
onial poets – a reading of Barcroft Boake's : 'Where the Dead Men Lie'.

an: 'Australian Bards and Bush Reviewers' and 'The Uncultured Reviewer to his Cultured

atterson: 'Saltbush Bill'.

: 'When London Calls', 'In Arcady' and 'the Old Bohemian'.

Brennan: 'the pangs that guard the gates of joy', 'my heart was wandering in the sands',
battles I would win?'

e: 'the Truest Mate and 'Child Newsvendors'

the Ceilidh Collective.

ins - Ref The Country vs City Debate.

n: 'Up the Country'

atterson: 'In Defence of the Bush'

Reflection on John Shaw Nielson – presented by Bill Tibben – 3 or 4 poems.

Mary Gilmore: 'Men of Eureka'

A B (Banjo) Patterson – 'Man from Snowy River'.

Louisa Lawson: 'Lonely Crossing' 'the Hour is Come' and 'the Reformers'.

Music from the Ceildh Collective to finish.

Presented by the Live Poets Players:

Ed Wilson

Marie Mcmillan

George Clarke

Mike Richter

Bob Howe

Willem Tibben

Barvara Hush

Danny Gardner

And the Ceilidh Collective: John Coombs, Jill Rowston, Di Churchill and Penelope Grace.

Many thanks to North Sydney Council and Justin Sheining in particular.

*Program for 1890s poets and music come to the farm,
part of North Sydney Council's 125th anniversary, 2015.*

NEWS

No longer naked, this poet is ready to report

ENTERTAINER Pat Drummond was a legend on the lower North Shore for his Friday night appearances at the Wrest Hotel at Milsons Point for nearly a decade during the late 70s and early 80s.

The singer, songwriter and bush poet is also a member of the highly successful Naked Poets group.

Next week, however, Drummond will move from naked to live poets when he is a special guest at the Live Poets' meeting at North Sydney.

Drummond will leave his Naked Poets persona behind and appear as one of his favourite characters – a 1940s newspaper reporter who travels the country interviewing ordinary people.

He will perform a number of songs based on his interviews.

Another guest will be Sydney poet Stephen Edgar who has published six collections of poetry and was awarded the Philip Hodgins Memorial Medal for Literature in 2006.

The meeting will be held on Wednesday at the Don Bank Museum, 6 Napier St, North Sydney at 7.30pm. Tickets are $7, including supper. Phone 9895 6956.

Poet Pat Drummond as a 1940s newspaper reporter.

Artwork for Weimar Cabaret poster-board, 2015.

for sausage ice cream

KATE CRAWFORD

THE Live Poets' Society of North Sydney had its eggs served sunny side up when an Irish poet was a special guest last week.

The poet's name is Dan Eggs and he's well known in Ireland for his humorous rhymes.

During an Australian tour, he met Live Poets' Society stalwart Danny Gardiner (pictured) to make a guest appearance at the society's regular meeting last Wednesday night at the Don Bank Museum at North Sydney.

With a brogue as thick as Irish mud, Eggs talked about his poetry and read several of his favourite poems, including *Me and My Mate Martin* and *Coffee Shop Song*.

"People were laughing so much they were rolling around literally with tears in their eyes," Gardiner said.

Eggs also talked about his latest exploits, including winning an Irish ice cream eating championship by downing 40 cones in record time.

"My favourite ice cream flavour is sausage."

Eggs says he is aged somewhere between 21 and 82, and has been writing poetry even before he was born, claiming to have scratched out a few lines on his mother's womb.

He's been known to refer to his poetry as "a stupid old pile of s**t" but he's a popular guest on Irish radio and is often referred to as "the Blagger from Belfast."

No Longer Naked Pat Drummond and 'Eggs' Dan.

Artwork by Keith Hansen.

POETRY

VERY HAPPY VERSE-DAY

POETS MARK CLUB BIRTHDAY

Kate Crawford

THE Live Poets group at North Sydney have remained alive and well for 25 years.

The group is celebrating its 25th birthday this month and holding a birthday party next Wednesday.

"There will be a massive open section for poets, storytellers and musicians on the night and everyone will be invited to present their fondest (or weirdest) memories of Live Poets," said convener Danny Gardner.

Playing on the movie title *Dead Poets Society*, the Live Poets Society was formed in 1990 by Gardner and former *Mosman Daily* journalist Sue Hicks, who now lives in the UK.

The first meeting was held at the Cafe L'Orangerie on a rainy night and featured the late poet Vera Newsom.

Meetings were held at the cafe for about a year before the society moved to a new venue, holding monthly meetings at the Don Bank Museum at North Sydney.

Beth Hicks and Gardner were presented with Centenary Medals by North Sydney Council in 2003 for their contribution to the cultural life of North Sydney.

In 2007, the group changed its name to Live Poets @ Don Bank.

"We give people the opportunity to enjoy poets live rather than reading books or looking online," says Gardner.

"We also give them a chance to express themselves and dip a toe in literature's ocean."

The birthday party will be held at Don Bank museum next Wednesday, April 22, at 7.30pm.

Entry is $7 including supper.

For more information about the party phone 9896 6956 or email dannylivepoets@yahoo.com.au.

Sue Hicks and Danny Gardner receiving their Centenary Medals in 2003. Picture: VIRGINIA YOUNG

Mosman Daily article on Live Poets' 25th anniversary, 2015.

Kate McClurcan at the Monster Music Mash, 2015.

The Harmony Trio at rehearsal, 2015.

Poster for Sydney, My Muse (with Diverse Poets), 2016.

The 'Strawbs' (Olga and Megan) at the Sgt Pepper anniversary, 2017.

Upstairs at Max's and Pepper poster-boards, 2017.

The psychedelia of guitarist Dirk Kruithof, 2017.

NORTH SYDNEY

Warnie in her sights — but mozzies first

Wordsmiths to ply their trade at Live Poets at Don Bank meeting

Kate Crawford

Irish poet Marie McMillan. Picture: Gunther Hang

IRISH-BORN poet Marie McMillan has the gift of the gab.

Her poems are a merry jig around every subject from shagging Warnie to rebutting her butt.

The retiree will be special guest at Live Poets at Don Bank on April 26 and she will be lining up her larrikin poems likes pints of Guinness.

"Why do I like poetry?" she said.

"Because I am Irish and the Irish love words."

McMillan is known for her funny and self deprecating poetry – sometimes skirting the politically correct.

"Better to laugh at yourself," she said.

Mosman Daily article on Marie Mcmillan, 2017.

Three Live poets: John Egan, Ed Wilson, George Clark.

Beck Fielding and Paula Harris (inset), 2018.

The art of Sue Bacsi and Fixin' to Die background, 2018.

Amy Bodassian.

The Faraway Eyes, Vashti Hughes as Mum Devine in Homage to Darlo, and the Convenor, 2018.

The Short Fiction Cup chapbook.

Live Poets @ Don Bank

Bee Perusco in Homeless, with Lou Steer in Ballad of Frida and Diego, and with Alan Gannaway in Songs of Old Italia.

Three Faces of Blue with the Convenor (foreground), Andrew Vial, Graham Cameron and Wil Roach, 2018.

Geoff and Jade promo.

Ali Whitelock's and my heart crumples, and Willem Tibben.

James Griffin at play.

The Heide flashmob at Art of Modern Love, 2019.

50s Swing Sing in the Courtyard, 2019.

Ed Wilson and the Hard Quiz brass mug he won.

The Words Behind the Poems

There was a time before there were any major interviews with poets conducted at Live Poets – that is, distinct from their actual readings/performances being recorded.

But then one night in 2006 Martin Langford was due to be the guest to present his latest book, *Microtexts*. That last Wednesday in June, there was an electrical fault at the door where people paid to come in and I had to relocate inside the sitting room. And Martin had a confession to make when he arrived. He said, '*Microtexts* is not really a book I can read from. It's much better if I talk to someone, say, about its content and what it hopes to do for the reader/writer.' So talk is what Martin and I did. The interview/discussion was recorded on tape – and the author interview at Don Bank was born.

What was the essential importance of this breakthrough? The audience got something extra out of a featured appearance – background and insight into the poet's motivations and methods and the concept behind the book or project presented. The poet/musician obviously got a more comprehensive chance to tell the audience about his craft and how it was fashioned. From then on, every 'special guest' had the opportunity, if they wanted it, to have a discussion/interview with the convenor about their work in poetry and the latest book or CD they were promoting. And, if there was time, there could be a quick Q and A with the audience before they read their poems or sang their songs and played their music.

There have been some memorial outings in this genre. Not long after Martin, we had interviews with poet and publisher David Musgrave and performance poet Skye Loneragan.

Musgrave's interview was notable for two answers he gave. One, on his experience of the 'black dog' of depression: 'It was [basically] not having one iota of motivation – a total inability to write, what keeps you going. When all that happens, you're left with nothing. It's nothing to do with reason. If you could analyse it, you could reason a way out.' And the visibility winning the Newcastle Poetry Prize affords: 'The results of those prizes are the subjective thoughts and feelings of a couple of individuals – the judges.'

Skye Loneragan on 'selling' the possibility of entertaining people in queues while they are waiting to do something they have to do rather than want to do. 'The sense of having to be somewhere else in our head from the pain of this space we don't want to BE in! For the most part. WE LOSE THE WILL TO LIVE YOU KNOW!' she said, to the audience more than to me. 'What would happen if we could dismantle the anonymity to each other in that queue? By interjecting another experience – some stranger, PERFORMING, to and for you. Huh?'

There was a major conversation with John Tranter, reliving the 'revolutions' of Australian poetry in 1968, forty years later. There was singer and musician Pat Drummond one moment being, officially, a naked poet – and the next presenting a cast of characters as a reporter: 'travelling Australia interviewing people' in 'Tales From a Local Rag'. There was Queanbeyan performance poet Omar Musa remembering 'having to' do Shakespeare in high school. Ouyang Yu (ex China) justifying his claim to be 'the ungrateful immigrant' and seeking Oz publishing grants. There was Tara June Winch learning how to negotiate being 'this apparently amazing indigenous talent' according to her publisher, trying to write a second book and take care of her new baby.

Ketut Yuliarsi trying to keep Bali languages alive and advising the young of his people not to turn into whores for tourists: 'always with that [he pointed to the mask he encouraged others to put on before performing] as well as the dollar in mind'. Dorothy Makasa decrying the local paper mystifying her as a poet when she was presenting 'incantations' in the local-to-Zambia style – and 'why do you think I know so much about griots?'

And so many others. There were also those poets that were almost impossible to formally interview – Mario Cabrera comes to mind, and Steve Smart, say. Those who were difficult, like Dave Hallett. Those who were impossible to stop once they got started – like Tug Dumbly, and Robert Adamson (when he was a guest on a night with Kate Lilley – discussing her mother Dorothy Hewett and Kate's identity in the book *Ladylike* – there were almost two hours of interview recorded). There were poets who made any attempt at an interview redundant – Billy Marshall Stoneking and his partner Christina Conrads, and Craig Powell feature there.

There are no interviews in full in this book – the main points of many are accessible in the Year chapters. But I can't finish this piece without including a conversation with the late, lamented Les Murray which I think poets and audience would appreciate. It was on the occasion of the launch of his latest *Selected Poems* in 2014.

Danny Gardner (DG): I notice you did the regulation fifteen minutes.
Les: What?
DG: After about that time, I've noticed, a get out seems to kick in.

Les: No one had got to the point where they were shuffling too much – so I thought, that's enough.

DG: Forty years of poems – it's a hard canon to imagine. Was there a temptation to change things, the poems, in any way?

Les: The good poems won't let you do that. They stand on their own. What you put down then still stands – you just know it.

DG: Do you remember every one intimately?

Les: I could probably write some out from memory at a pinch, with a bit of cribbing.

DG: You mentioned depression twice – once when in late teens and then again at fifty. Were those occasions, let's say, touch and go?

Les: The Black Dog, yes. I was never going to suicide. The trick about it is it never drives you to that point, but you never really defeat it. With luck, you write yourself out of it…you can write yourself out of most things. And in that mode you're allowed to be lazy. You don't really get rid of it [Black Dog] but you can maim it seriously now and then.

(A woman came up for an autograph and leaned over to say, 'Some of these bushpigs [poems] keep us going in the country!')

I later thought, that may be what it is about Les. He's a link with the country – attitudes, point of view, perspective – we can't, don't want to let go of. It still remains essential to the idea of Australia, wherever we're living. But we're still a little embarrassed by it as well.

Les: It's the home of irony.

No one could argue with that.

2018

We wanted (as always) to start the year with a bang. We had three ladies ready to give us something special in their indubitably different ways, in the order Barvara Hush, Ember Flame and (from Melbourne) Amy Bodassian. We had a lot of Facebook interest and *thirty-three* people came through the doors. Yes, another sell-out, folks.

Tyler Mitchell sent out his jazz rhythms from the Smalls Club in Greenwich Village as people were entering the cottage.

With a short first Open Section done, Barvara was introduced by a poem 'Village' by Bob Holman, read by the convenor, which starts, 'I live in the Village / Not just any village / Not just every village / Where the City / Becomes a Village / That's my Village / Where the Intercontinental / Becomes the neighbourly experiential / That's my Village / Uptown Downtown Lodown Notown / That's the place that's Home Sweet Home Town. / The Village is where I live.'

Barvara, using an audiovisual presentation, took us through her time as an artistic free spirit nursing in the 'Hattan. Her story ran from daunting initial scenes in Washington Square and Central Park to fighting eviction and helping to save her apartment, and that of many others, in the tenement building that became her home. The joys of art and a major relationship strengthened and pursued her nevertheless. She ultimately had to decide what would give her newborn son his best chance. She came back to Australia with Jay.

But NY, once it's lodged, never really leaves you. I am reminded of the writing about Manhattan by feminist American critic, journalist and memoirist Vivian Gornick (author of *Odd*

Woman & the City) – what she thought gave the individual their place among millions in that sceptred isle.

Ember was up next to talk about what she's been doing in Manhattan, where she divides her time year on year, amidst the famous and obscure venues as, like Barvara did, she pursues her dream. She told how the 'I've got a Crazy Idea' series anchored her to the club of choice and her compatriots there, rich in comedy and wonder. Ember's poem 'Living in the Dream' put a lot of illusions straight as a set opener. You-can't-do-that Hilarious was 'I've Got a Crazy Idea – to Descend into the Sewers'. ('Still with me?' she then purred.) 'Ginger Pubes – the great wars' followed. A scary sensation came from 'The Drop' and intrigue/malice in the 'Corporate Jungle' before Em brought it all back home again with her sketch 'Alexis from Dynasty takes on Donald Trump'. As it's been said many times before of this mistress of the burlesque, 'Ember, you've done it again.'

We came back from supper for Amy Bodassian. She and the convenor chatted about her appearance at the Woollahra Poets' Picnic the night before. 'It was certainly a bit less hangloose than a more intimate gathering!' she laughed. But the smaller spaces such as Don Bank provided enabled Amy to invite us to her OCHD world – to lure us on a trip where nothing seemed ordinary and strange obsessions disordered logicality. We were with her through the sanity attacks – this beautiful stranger we could not safeguard in the final analysis. It was raw stuff! You left your faint heart at the door. The details of Amy's set did not arrange themselves into discrete focus separate from each other. What we and she went through we could not soon forget.

In the Open Section, Kate Mac got us going with a rousing

Eric Bogle song about the gun lobby. David Wansbrough did a magnificent Yevtushenko piece and Raghid made us 'feel' Damascus calling.

For March there was a Japanese feel for David Gilbey's guest spot and Pip Smith had a disturbing tale, with interview to purvey, around her debut novel *Half-Wild*.

It was a great pleasure of the convenor to welcome at long last Mr Gilbey, who would read from his book *Pachinko Sunset*.

In the Open Section, to start proceedings people read pieces from a book of Zen poetry. As patrons came in, they were presented with pieces of bark with messages written on them. This echoed one of the traditions of the celebrated Cherry Blossom Festival, whereupon young lovers, who were not permitted to meet individually by their parents, communicated with each other by 'coded' messages 'tied' to the cherry trees.

The convenor reflected on 'ukiyo – the floating world' in Japanese art before beginning the evening with his Zen poem 'Not For Me'. Sergei Yalichev, a long-time friend of David Gilbey, then read in Japanese and English a Matsu Basho poem from the seventeenth century. Cathy Jones offered up the poem 'Thoughts at Sea' and John Carey, an LP regular of long standing, got us in a comic mood with his 'Our Emails', which wickedly spanned the gamut of online interactions and the respective sources of all those spams and scams we know and hate.

David Gilbey, in a resplendent red suit, was then interviewed, citing his years teaching English in Japan, his past at Charles Sturt Uni and his role as the convenor of Wagga Wagga Writers Writers. Gilbey's verve and enthusiasm in performance of his *Pachinko* pieces enabled us to eavesdrop retrospectively on his experiences with his Japanese students, which he frequently referred to as 'a confirmation only of his ignorance'. A poem called 'Sendai Lasagne' is principally about the difficulties of cooking the dish for a multitude in an apartment with only one hotplate, a frying pan and a combined toaster/oven/microwave (?). 'Oku Matsushima' is set on cliffs that sit like 'wire-dredged slabs of creamy tofu'. 'Writing Class Sonnet' results in fifteen lines of a potential tourist's fractured suppositions about life in Australia. David Helfgott's actions in concert were rendered as 'wrestling with Liszt's B minor sonata, like a monkey chained to a roof...his impossible intention to grasp the whole world / in a fist full of chords.' The Sumo poem 'Yokoyuna' featured 'baby giants, the Mongols...birthed from their stables (facing) each other across the pounded clay of the dohyo' to become 'leaning together, breathing heavily / wandering islands momently stalled / in an ebbing Sargasso' before the ultimate confrontation. Several pieces were haibuns – a mix of poetry and prose. Meantime, there was an anecdote about Aya, a visiting Japanese student, who learnt a new Australian phrase from David's children while staying chez Gilbey, Wagga. It was 'shasha' (show us), as in the expression 'shasha tits!' David made unwitting use of a malapropism in his poem 'Intercultural Communication' when taken out to a year's end dinner by some of his students – alumni of Miyagi Gakun Women's University in Sendai, Japan. David tried to explain his full stomach at meal's end by the phrase 'onaka ippai desu – I could not manage another mouthful'. But David in fact had said, 'inaka oppai desu' and was troubled by the merriment that followed. The translation in Japanese was 'I have the breasts of a countrywoman!'

This was a most delightful session and the convenor decided

to bridge us to the next mood gently with the poem 'On His Baldness' by Bai Jayi, before he introduced Pip Smith.

Pip used to run the monthly writing event Penguin Plays Rough and was the adjudicator of Live Poets' very first edition of our Short Fiction Cup competition. But tonight she would be interviewed about her hit fiction debut, *Half-Wild*. This book was inspired by the life story of Eugenia Falleni – a woman from Italy who became a man (Harry Leo Crawford) and was also known as one Jean Ford and had two marriages with members of the fairer sex and ending up murdering one of them in 1920, to protect his/her identity. The book was divided into four parts. The casual observer might think Pip had given herself an insuperable task especially for a fiction debut to write a novel about a story that screams, 'Nothing stranger than truth!'

'Why did I think I could do this?' Pip asked herself. 'Present the thoughts and actions of this man/woman in her various guises.' She knew she had to somehow get inside the mind of Eugenia to depict her bizarre life experience successfully. Her first exposure to Falleni was her photo in the Justice and Police Museum in an exhibition of Sydney's most notorious criminals. Before the camera, the prostitutes of the time put it all out there with their come-ons et cetera; the crims were tough guys acting out their self-image. Falleni, by contrast, was a picture of uncertainty. A woman dressed in a man's suit and tentative under scrutiny, unsure if he/she was 'presenting' successfully. Pip was immediately struck, fascinated by what this person put herself through, what she felt she had to do. Pip said that was her challenge: 'to try and demonstrate how that worked. Put the reader in Falleni's place – if I could.'

Pip admitted she got tremendous support from her publisher and a very good agent, which meant she didn't have to flog this 'wild idea' around on fishing expeditions to various publishers. She was also on a grant while she was writing. But 'I got stuck!' she said when she had to bring the figure of Harry Crawford (Falleni's male alter ego) to life and to have the reader 'cross that bridge successfully with her'. She was frustrated too when the non-fiction book about Falleni by Mark Tedeschi came out and dreaded going back to her task unaffected by it, if she could manage that.

The climax of the book, inevitably, was Falleni's trial. Pip had the clever idea to see this pivotal event through the eyes principally of the 'middle-class women' who flocked to the proceedings. This fascinated cohort were 'of a certain age – and they could not help but wonder, internally, if they could do what Eleni did.'

Pip stressed that her principal aim always in writing the novel was to 'encourage people to feel Falleni's motivation'. This mission was never more tricky than when Falleni as a man had intimate relations with his/her wives. One of the highlights of the trial, salacious though it might have appeared, was the 'unveiling' of the attachment Harry (Eugenia) strapped on in the nuptial bedroom.

The audience at Don Bank was genuinely inspired by Pip's achievement. The fact that she came to see 'what else but fiction could make that double life real?' To portray what it is like to live as a man at one time and a woman at another – in the same body – against all the things others expect of a man and/or a woman in the context their experience lends. 'Who we are construed as being by the people around us.' And the question,

'What would I discover about myself in the writing process and the "inner prisons and protocols" my thinking/motivations as a man and then a woman demand?'

The book has been the making of Pip from being a short story writer of some import to the cusp as a major literary talent.

We went to supper buzzing.

After the interval, Olga read 'On Founding a Retreat' by Xie Lingyun from the Zen poems. Jill in a preview of her guest reading next month did some children's poems. Raghid, fresh from his book launch a couple of weeks before, did a fine piece in English and Arabic about the moon teasing him in all her disguises as a mistress. From Zen poems, Phil Radmall read 'Miscellaneous Lines from My Lair' by Betsugan Enshi. Graham read 'Poem rhyming with the Monk San's Trip to Kanazawa' by Guido Shushin. Caroline Turner weighed in with a haiku or three – the first original poems she had read at Live Poets, she said. Clark Gormley couldn't resist his comic bent with 'Clark's Nerdy Science Show' and 'Test Tube Baby'. Mark Marusic did an engaging ditty about La Perouse, the explorer. David Falcon reminded us of how 'the river holds the drowned'. Geoff Yule Smith rendered '1999' and 'Being a Composer' and then people noticed the piano keys on his tie! Andrew Vial used his message on a dried leaf given him at the door: 'the train leaves at 9', and launched into a child's story about a snake he bought and ate – a sort of 'Pitchfork Disney' remake from what won him the Monologue Challenge last year. Then Marie Mcmillan, who earlier had said she was too exhausted to do a piece, let forth with 'Discrimination' and 'Robot Love'. That prompted David Gilbey to suggest she come down to Wagga Writers for their Raw Roar Comp! Finally (almost), Live Poets first-timer (as a reader) Lynne Fairy hit the bullseye with her quiet, developing saga inspired by listening to talkback radio.

The convenor closed proceedings with Han Shan's 'In the Third Month' from the Zen poems, ending with the couplet 'with all that glitter of outward loveliness / how can the Cold Mountain hope to compete!'

April saw a surprise visit from Randall Stephens up from Melbourne. The special guests were Jill Carter-Hansen and Philip Radmall with his latest from Ginninderra, the collection *Earthworks*. It was a birthday issue, so we had a reading of what happened on the very first night of Live Poets' Society at Neutral Bay (from *Light on Don Bank*) and other readings – 'I Am Jamal Al Hallaq' and 'Carapace' by Dexter Dumphy from *Can I Tell You a Secret?*

And, because it was Anzac Day, 'War is Over if you Want it!' – the famous saying in song by John Lennon and Yoko Ono – and voices of war past and present, for and against.

There was a special announcement about the Short Fiction Cup chapbook where entrants over the comp's first years were asked to tender their best stories.

Jill got her set going with 'Dark Vision: through 30 Hours' then a couple of children's poems and 'War War War', something of an anthem against loss. There was a story of farming life in wartime NZ: 'how is it people in planes kill themselves in places like this?' More prosaic was a campaign against a fox called 'Hercules' – 'his hunters had to wear a sheepskin disguise to hunt the rogue down'. I was thinking there might be another a cappella song but 'that was all she wrote'. The display of photographs and paintings on poster-boards behind her was also a signal of Jill's many other talents.

Phil Radmall started *Earthworks* with an early poem in that volume: 'Seascape'. He added, 'God should remain a mystery sometimes – leaving us access to spirit things by "other" means.' There was then 'Grounding', a series of poems ('Farringdon', 'Bedrock' and 'Cunjarong Point') that, as a suite, snared Phil third place in the prestigious Newcastle Prize. 'That first time (I was third) was when my first wife had just died. My mother and her sister had also died and I went back to the UK to process the "job lot"!' he added sadly. He then also read – not in the book – 'If Poetry Were Soccer', which reflects hilariously on deathless promotional adages about winning and losing, not as a physical athlete but as a poet! He then read his becoming-famous at the bank 'Kangaroo' and another stray, 'The Somme', in deference to the night's theme. All in that sonorous, modulated tone that, as another long-time supporter of Don Bank has said, 'carry their rhythms so eloquently – there are not so many long-liners among us that can do that'. It also struck me that Phil's meditations on landscape are like throwing out belay lines across difficult terrain to his companion – and there is always one, even if it's another part of himself – to ensure everyone gets to the other side safely. Phil later had another tragedy to contend with – that of his artist-brother. The art of painting he pursued that in ways echoed Phil's voyage in words. 'In that, you have this working backwards into the making.' A chapbook later resulted from that joined learning (in 2019).

In our 'War is Over if you Want It' segment, Ann Jarjoura was unrelenting with 'Investigation/Disintegration' and 'We Don't Give Peace a Chance'. Michael Bartok offered up 'At the Graveyard By the Sea'. Cathy Jones read 'A Critic of War'.

In the general Open Section, Randall Stevens was evocative

in his 'Keys to the Kingdom' (of Injustice?). Willem did 'Last Plane Out of Saigon'. Helen Wren came next with 'Finke River, Old Tree'. Charles Freyberg's long '2014' ('What Did My Grandfather Say to Me?') riveted attention as the question pulsed beyond everything the world leaves unsaid. There are glimpses of an answer, the key to forefathers' past (yes, in war): 'why I am like I am – that I can't seem to rest until I recall them. Live through that dream again – and who can demand any experience recurs or comes back in a form we can recognise?'

This sent us back out into the night to plumb those echoes if we could.

In May, it was time to welcome back 'that girl' – Beck Fielding – along with the annual Monologue Challenge and our travel-oriented theme, this time from a Lonely Planet book featuring writers conveying their solo experiences in remote climes and situations – the startling *Voices From the Middle of Nowhere*.

In the Open Section, Shafic Ataya got the ball rolling with a poem from his new book, 'Alive – we shall Go to the Stars'. Cathy Jones took us to the 'Promised Land', in hot, dusty drives in her childhood.

We then had the annual Monologue Challenge where performers inhabit a text they are handed and the audience votes on the result. Michael Cowdred had booked a seat at Don Bank for his first visit and duly arrived with partner Tracey. He immediately said he would like to participate in the Challenge. He picked the number one out of the hat – a passage from the character Anne in a Stephen Berkoff play – and proceeded to enact a powerful representation. Graham, Andrew, Megan, Wil, Helen Wren, Michael Bartok, Marie and Tatiana – all regulars – with some fairly compelling scripts from (UK) people like Kate Tempest, Vinay Patel and Pat Kinevane – and Bertolt Brecht (Galileo) – also took part. Michael took the gong on his debut by one point!

We then came to the Voices from Nowhere. Gareth McCormack's meeting a bear in the wild was 'relived' by Graham Cameron. Andrew Vial inhabited Tom Parkinson's tale in the Sahara. Caroline experienced altitude sickness as written by Caroline McCarthy in the Himalayas. Phil had to get help after busting an artery in a remote part of South America as Karl Bushby described it. Danny had to be creative in a crisis after a malfunction with his bathyscape submersible leaves him exposed in his his deep-water suit, several kilometres below the surface, as related by Craig Scutt.

The significant thing was these people all obviously lived to tell their tale and have it published by Lonely Planet!

The guest of the night Beck Fielding was then introduced. Last time at Don Bank, she had been amazed at the number of people that had turned up – principally to see Marie Mcmillan. This night, she was much more relaxed, with anecdotes about what she'd done recently – setting up an audio studio which had resulted in a CD (which she had for sale this night, natch!). She then gave us a dissertation re the qualities of her Mack guitar which she had acquired recently: 'without being totally techie about it!' Her set then followed: 'Time for Love', 'The Other Side' and 'Moving On' – 'three upbeat songs but now we have a little turn!' A more reflective mood followed with 'Find My Place', 'Every Day', 'Living in the City – no Turning Back' - 'in full roar!' – ending with the question mark of 'Stuck on Blue'. 'That girl' got another rousing hand and people keen to secure some merch! Live Poets has so often been as much about music as words!

In the Open Section to finish after supper, Andrew took us back on stage with the gnomic but fun cricket selection game 'Who's Wicketkeeping? – Watt's at First Slip?' Phil Radmall introduced the 'Repton Warrior'. Mark Marusic offered up a 'Wild Ride'. And then there was Olga. Or rather there was Megan being Olga as she read one of Olga's poems. Then Cathy was Olga saying 'goodbye to Live Poets'.

But where *was* Olga? 'She's back at home – packing!' She's off to South Australia!

In June, the Special Guest was 'old Live Poeter' Tony Scanlon on the back of a new book of his selected verse (edited by another original Live Poet, Sue Wildman) recently published and launched at the Carrington Hotel in the Blue Mountains. There was also a tribute to Dulcie Meddows (see separate story, Icons of Live Poets) and a special, 'Three Faces of Blue' (see chapter on the Live Poets Players).

The convenor read out a tribute to Candy Royalle, who had recently died, and recalled fondly the feisty performer's appearances at Don Bank – particularly her 'fire' at the Manhattan speakeasy remake. There was a brief look at the Biennale, for the program was already crowded.

The Open Section was led off by Geoff Yule Smith with 'Guns Are Bad' (not a poem) which was a reply to Kate Maclurcan's song earlier in the year. Katherine Anderson, here for Dulcie's tribute, did a piece called 'Echoes'. Cathy Jones's contribution this time round was the quirky/mysterious 'How to Dispose of the Body'. Mark offered up a poem about a statue of Henry Lawson at Grenfell. Roberta Lowing presented her poem from *Ruin*, 'By Ourselves, Nothing'. Andrew Vial's piece was 'Disconnection', while Jill presented 'Not a Love Song'.

Catherine's friend Oriel gave us a moving 'Light and its Shade'. Caroline agreed to read David Kelly's 'Better than Saturn' from the Live Poets anthology *Ten Years Live*.

Tony Scanlon, though of ailing health in the last few years, lifted in his guest spot with a performance of erudite light and shade of several of the best poems he has written. There was the elegiac authority of the early years in the Northern Territory with 'Flying to Papunya', 'Python' and 'Forest Kingfisher'. There was an interlude in life-moments of 'Flying Blind'. A return to the single man time, 'Brandavino Days', which glittered in the original Live Poets presentation in the 1990s. He finished with the convoluted tale of the unwilling tourist on his wife's shoe-buying expedition gone bung ('Lost in Venice'), which had the crowd eating out of his hand. Tony – barely capable of anything beyond a whisper by then, the guttural authority long since surrendered by anecdote and verse – then beamed at the convenor at the applause (not skiting but), 'Rarely read better!'

July was dedicated to 'Homage to Darlo' (see chapter on Other Major Shows using Music and Art). But there was some Open Section featured that was outside that compass. Shafic was back with more new poems: 'Photons' and 'Empty Call to God'. Cathy Jones echoed something of Kings Cross with 'Naughty Shed'. Andrew Vial read 'To My Wife'. Graham Cameron did a rehash of 'Stuck in the Middle of Nowhere' by revealing what happened in his bear tale after the preamble he gave us in 'Nowhere' last month (he brought along the book the original fragment was taken from). And there was a poem from the irrepressible Olga – 'Entranced by the calmness of ocean / echoing rays in a soundless way / I let myself follow the rhythm / of gentle ripples teasing the sand / just like a summer's love affair / that whets your appetite – to leave you bare.' 22/23 June 2018, Henley Beach.

In August, there was a book launch (which we don't normally do) – Emeritus Professor Elizabeth Webby unveiling *Glass and Stone* for dear friend Assad Cina Aleem. Assad was the convenor's colleague in Auburn Poets & Writers – several others of which – Maureen Ten, Sri Bhagavadas and Dorothy Makasa – turned up to honour Assad. There was also the music of another compatriot, Fadeel Kayat and his aosante, a harp that produced simple, miraculously delicate echoes 'like footfalls in a cathedral'. Fadeel commented, 'The strokes must be so exact!' He then read a joke about desire being found in a tree in the desert originally. All of which served to set the scene for Assad's reading with friends.

The man himself read two poems in Farsi to Fadeel's music: 'Journey Through the Night' and 'Morning Bird'. Maureen then read 'Perfume'. The convenor presented 'Wild Wind' and Assad's sister read a verse from 'Axes'.

Elizabeth discussed the nine poems in English mainly, reflecting on the devastation and darkness of war, in parts of 'Dark City', 'Doves', 'Wild Wind', 'Morning Bird' and 'Red Desert'. She then read 'Axes' in its entirety. 'It forces you to reflect on the dark pain of suffering of the Afghan in history and compared to now. But in "Axes" there is hope.' Later, at supper, we had recourse to Assad's wife's aromatic sweetmeats as the proud author poured a wine – 'not from the [Kabul] district!' – as a toast.

Our other special guest was Paula Harris from New Zealand, who began by referring to her analyst ('as anybody with self-esteem issues would!'). 'He likes poetry,' she expanded. 'He told me, you should spend a lot of time in bed 'cos that's what you do when you're depressed!' We weren't quite sure whether she was joking or just bitter. But Paula's pieces stood for themselves: 'I Decided to Go to Dorothea's Book Launch in Manhattan' (the story of how she actually didn't go was as inexplicable as it was, finally, logical!). 'Sex as a Solution' (to a situation of connection?), 'To a Man' and finally 'If I was a Queer (but then I am!'). Paula was a past winner of the Whitireia Prize in NZ, has been published in NZ and Australian poetry mags, and, lately, has been getting attention overseas. 'I am extremely fond of dark chocolate, shoes and hoarding fabrics for various undecided projects. I've been writing since the dawn of time and performing over the last twenty years. I bought a house in Wellington in July. I fall into the weird space between performing and page poetry.' Later this year, she would be a writing resident at Vermont Studio Centre. Paula didn't linger long. She had not wanted an interview particularly. But we went out to the break with her images laying their down payment on our cognition.

After supper there were also people quoting aphorisms from the Wicked Words of Wilde, including usual suspects Andrew Vial, Marie Mcmillan, Catherine Jones, Bob Howe and Graham Cameron.

What about the Open Section? Raghid presented 'Fatimah' in English and Arabic and 'Not Coming to Aman' from his late friend, Ghassan. Megan read 'Breaking Brian'. Bob Howe rendered 'No Name' (a man contemplating a gun?). Mark read a poem found on the walls of a shed in his urban meanderings. Cathy Jones offered up 'Stage Telling', while Jill took us out with 'Currawong', 'Powerful Owl' and 'Raven', which were part poems/part songs on the wing.

September took us back to Politics in the USA in 1968 with the special Feel Like I'm Fixing to Die Rag – a forty-five-minute show with songs from the era by Bee and Alan, and commentary and poems by the convenor (see chapter on Live Poets Players).

There was also a Literary Cities Special, Verses from Prague, by several authors – rendered by people from the floor in verse and story. Tatiana read a poem in Russian about Prague. The convenor followed with a passage from 'The Spirit of Prague' by Ivan Klima and another concerning the emblematic Charles St Bridge from John Banville's *Prague Pictures*. Caroline then read another piece, 'Where do you locate the real Prague?', from John Banville. Among the poems were Joseph Hanzlik's 'Mirror Poem'('It's never too late for two people / who read a poem together'), Viteslav Nezval's 'Hundred-Spired Prague' ('with fingers touching the stars / on the abacus of night') and 'Panorama of Prague'. There was also 'The Suburb' and 'The Old Clock in the Jewish Ghetto' – famous with tourists. Hanzlik was back for 'Memorial', and Kamil Bouska reminded us of the atmosphere at the time of the Velvet Revolution in 1989 with its unforgettable refrain: 'again I am running down the school hallway', the boy reborn but now faced with challenges he hadn't foreseen in 'that long shadow…an invisible hand is dragging me from schoolwork to history.' All a reflection hopefully of how the jewel of Eastern Europe has influenced world views.

Dorothy Makasa led off the Open Section with 'African Eagle'. Lynda Lovechild, to the tune of the Rolling Stones 'As Tears Go By', rendered 'As Cars Go By' (as the Westconnex mess poisons those who can only look on!) followed by her emblematic 'Bag Lady' and 'Ads from the Fifties', which almost formed a guest spot! Geoff did a poem and a song, 'Warm and Exciting', dedicated to the Spirit of Progress (a train). Janet performed 'Grinder'. After his parents had finished with 'Last Train to Clarkesville', which should really have been in the Fixin' set, Remy did a poem called 'Being Different'.

October was set to be busy. Edwin Wilson was presenting his comic memoir about his uncle, Oliver Bainbridge, who traced a lineage back to Horatio Nelson. The Short Fiction Cup had been deferred from August when we had Assad's book launch and there would be readings from a classic poetry book of the past, *Rapunzel in Suburbia*, by Dorothy Hewett.

Live Poets has been the site of many of Ed Wilson's book presentations over the years. The Powerpoint this evening was set to relay highlights of a quite remarkable tale. Ed's chief inspiration as a child, his great-great-uncle Frank Nelson. He was born in 1877 in Upper Copmanhurst (northern NSW), the son of a pioneering bush schoolmaster and bandmaster of South Grafton, Andrew St Clare Nelson, who claimed descent from Horatio Nelson and Emma Hamilton. Tiring of life in the slow lane, and perhaps with a sense of Nelson entitlement, young Frank stole money from the South Grafton Post Office where he'd been employed. He spent a year in Grafton Gaol, after which he was thrown out of home for 'disgracing the Nelson name'. He had earlier expressed a desire to procure the head of an old Aboriginal man for 'scientific research' – but now Frank left town under a cloud with five shillings on his person. He changed his name to Oliver Bainbridge and lived by his wits – successively as explorer/anthropologist, apologist for Empire, writer, orator and most probably as some sort of spy (where 'writer' was his cover). In so doing, this unknown colonial made a name for himself in London and America, mixed in the exalted circles of the royalty of old Europe and had three audiences with the English king (Bertie, or Edward VII), and with American presidents Roosevelt and Wilson. He had been ambassador to King Ferninand of Bulgaria after the Balkan Wars, and had escorted his queen to America, and had spent time in India, China and Japan. All the while of course firing our Ed's mind with all sorts of wild imaginings and ambitions in such a glamorous stead!

Yet despite all the excitement and superficial glitz, Bainbridge's life had been also impecunious and often tenuous. He had lived and died by the word countless times in the diplomatic sphere. But he had a sticky end. He was 'taken out' by the IRA, aged just forty-five, in Sydney in 1922 at the beginning of the Irish Civil War. He was buried in a pauper's grave in Rookwood Cemetery.

It had taken almost all Ed's life from childhood to now to track down the truth. He convinced the audience at Don Bank in image and word of his quest, as evidenced by their awe at his exposition before them. The book was a talisman to this calumny made flesh – his uncle's fate. There are so many levels to our Ed! 'I think that was the show of the year' Geoff Yule Smith told me.

The Short Fiction Cup was the other big noise of the evening. Bob Howe presented 'No Name'. Geoff Yule Smith told us of 'Anne's Kingdom'. Mark's story was 'A Big Tree.' Graham Cameron took us through the marathon paces of 'Whatever it Takes'. Jill Carter-Hansen presented the whimsical ditty 'Harry's Questionable Eating Habits', while Tatiana's tale was called 'Parting'. Jill won her second Short Fiction Cup by a clear margin, but there was some conversation around whether a poem can be a story. There is always some intrigue about the SFC. It remains our most popular competition.

In the Significant Poetry Past feature, the inimitable Dorothy Hewett's 'Rapunzel in Suburbia' yielded rich material in sass and protest. Graham read 'Professor Quixote'. Danny offered up 'Living Dangerously', 'Death of My Mad Mother' and 'Memoirs of a Protestant Girlhood'. Jill finished the segment with 'Blue Moon' and 'Underneath the Arches' with Stephanie and Caroline assisting.

In the Open Section, Megan read 'Love Is'. Alison proffered 'Noting the Hunger' and Mark offered up 'Time Frame'. Ed manned the flow at supper with people ready to hear more of his radical relative!

So we came to November, where the bannered Western Sydney attractions were Jennifer Maiden from Penrith and the Duck River Band from Parramatta. A third feature was going to be a reading from the antho *To End All Wars*, but we had to put that aside apart from Jennifer's rendition of 'Into the Bodies of Poor Men'.

The weather on the way in was calamitous rain and raging winds. Jennifer rang me as we were en route to ask if it was still on. I replied, 'As long as it's safe for you and David to make it in the car.' It had not deterred the band in the least as they arrived while we were setting up complete with mike stands and amps and clarinet, Irish drum, mandolin, guitar, harmonica, flute, whistle and finger accordion. I waved hello to Michaela Simoni, who I've worked with at Auburn Poets & Writers for many years. Her fellow players were Simon Ferrugia (her husband), Nancy Nicholls, Eric Eisler and Dot Newland. Michaela and Simon led the intro. The beautiful 'Inch by Inch' was followed by 'Morning is Broken', 'English Country Garden', 'King of the Fairies/Bel table Waltz'. They verged into the irrepressible 'Octopus' Garden' then the bright 'You are My Sunshine' and more modern classics: 'Blowin' in the Wind' and 'El Condor Pasa'. The Irish drum then presaged 'Little Donkey' from the indelible Christmas tale Bing Crosby has delighted so many with down the decades. The small crowd applauded long and hard. The storm's entrails meantime had blown themselves out at last. And Jennifer and David had arrived, after being 'that close' to turning back.

From somewhat halting beginnings (I reflected on my first meeting JM thru the poem 'Centaur' circa 1974, and the latest, 'Rich Men's Houses', with its meditation on the Luna Park fire), Jennifer Maiden's voice grew strongly as her material delved deeply into body politic. 'Kevin Berry' flowed into 'Positional Asphyxia' and 'My Heart has an Embassy' (ref Julian Assange). There was then a consideration of Dorothy Hewett's work and talk of Jennifer's set of three novels called 'The Knife'. 'Lily' then emerged and 'Potted Palm in the Al Rashid Hotel Foyer', thence 'Princip in the City (Sarajevo, 1914)'. We were deferred then to later productions: the 'To End All Wars' piece and, after talk about the mother and daughter syndrome, an all but mesmeric 'Menopause as a Bee Freed from a Fairy Floss Machine'. We went to supper in a calmer courtyard with David and Jennifer vividly catching up with the convenor and the band still rosy from their efforts.

In the Open Section, Catherine Jones delighted with her '90 Not Out' and 'Sea Change', set outside the new North Shore Hospital. Douglas Nichols was back to tender Philip

Larkins's 'Arundel's Tomb' and Seamus Heaney's 'Digging'. Mark lent a sobering tone with 'Death Trap' (ref the Grenfell London housing tower disaster).

It was left then to announce the Un-Darwin Awards and the other categories of distinction. Short Fiction Cup (Jill Carter-Hansen – 'Harry's Unfortunate Eating Habits'), Monologue Challenge (Michael Cowdred), Open Section Poem of the Year (Charles Freyberg with '2014'). The Orange Wig Award for outstanding performance in a poetry-related show was shared between Alan Gannaway and Bee Perusco (for 'Fixin' to Die Rag').

It had been quite another year to savour.

I had a crazy idea to descend into the sewers

I came down to
these dark dripping tunnels

For the answers
I couldn't find above ground

I wanted to know

How can we save this world?
What's wrong with humans?
Does the love I'm looking for exist?
and
Why do all my ankle socks
have such short-lived partnerships?

I'm not sure yet

but yesterday I counted
520 plastic bags
443 plastic cups
440 plastic straws

I saw tampons
swollen with rage
and bloodied pads
floating past
like miniature life rafts

I saw torn-up food wrappers
empty beer bottles
and newspaper covers
crazy with grief
for the pages
that used to be inside them

I can't sing
but I've started singing

to meet the noises
that echo so clear and loud down here

The eager gush of human waste

The grinding of anonymous machines
The trains screeching
to a violent standstill on the tracks

I wish I was in a musical
Like *Stomp* or *Cats*

But it's just the world
going on as it is

and how can I even
express the horrors of it

when I'm also
scurrying into corners
and drawing up borders

shutting out the stars
buying and discarding
quick quick quick

I wanted to 'dig deep'
live with rats
without sunlight
and my smart phone

I wanted to know
that amongst
the mess and stench and noise
I will find what I need
to make the most
beautiful song I can

Ember Flame

Intercultural Communication

At the end of the year
snow-chained buses ploughing the slush of Sendai streets
my Japanese students, graduating women,
took me to dinner at a fashionable downtown restaurant.
Would not let me pay. Plied me politely with
sashimi, nabe, crab claws, practised their English.

To reciprocate the compliment, I powered into
my recently-learned idiom for 'elegant sufficiency'
when I could manage not another mouthful.
Onaka ippai desu.
Forgive me for mentioning my stomach. It is full.
But I mixed up the vowels,
uttered an international malapropism:
Inaka oppai desu.

The room was suddenly silent after my optimistically
delivered words.
What did I say? I asked one of the top girls. She grinned.
They'd all enjoyed the joke
barely concealing their mirth behind fingers
parted over their modest lips.
Sensei, she said, you said,
I have the breasts of a country woman.

David Gilbey

Teeth and Passport Photos

Our civil liberties have taken a punch in the guts.
We are no longer allowed to smile in our passport photos.
Travelling has become a serious business.
In response to terrorism is this our brave face?

Not everyone's resting facial expression
presents a closed mouth.
Many relaxed mouths if not gaping
are at least ajar. One of those mouths is mine.

When you have an overbite that frightens
rock-climbers, pursed lips are a bit of a stretch
and when I look at my passport photo
I see an unnatural act.

I see opposing sides forced together
like the north ends of two magnets.
I see an unhappy sight.

I see discontent where there should be laughter.
I see downward trends where they should be rising.
I see the proverbial upside-down smile.

I do not recognise the man, and I ask you –
is that the purpose of the passport photo?

Clark Gormley

These Are a Few of My Least Favourite Words

(with apologies to Rodgers & Hammerstein, from the song 'My Favourite Things' in *The Sound of Music*)

EXcesses, EXposes and downright XEnophobia, EXpressed for
to incite Far Right Dystopia, Frown Dividing Rampages, lined-up
Rant Herds, These Are A Few of My Least Favourite Words.

EXplicit SEXting with X-Rated TEXtualising, EXtolled & sold to
tabloids so stigmatising, EXiled from all EX-sightings & Extant
Gaslightings, These Are A Few of My Least Favourite Words.

When this world fights, yet this life clings, though I'm reeling, mad,
I simply EXtract My Least Favourite Words by not ever saying or
writing them in / on my Ipad.

I simply EXclude My Least Favourite Words so our tongues can meet
instead in silent dyad.

Hamish Danks Brown

Couch Adrift

That painting you did of the old sofa
tilted slightly at an angle upon loose, strewn,
screwed-up pages of old newspapers and girlie magazines –
'Couch Adrift off a Lee Shore' –
made me think of the vague lilt of humour,
the not quite upright seriousness
of good artistic method which spills over
from your life. Something more telling
always there to mock those who presume.
As when, peering at the rough water,
we notice the pink, naked nymphs
asplay in the crimps of the sea,
and point them out to unsuspecting
others come to look for more
littoral truth. I think this is the model
for the many ironies that lurk
unassumingly in life and art:
to show what is, through what might also be.

The couch leans to leeward
and the water nymphs play beside.

Be always before me, brother,
looking back knowingly from your kingdom of paint.

Philip Radmall

Jacky Gallipoli

Jacky Gallipoli, who has killed two wives –
one by accident, one by law – when he speaks
the men beneath the melaleucas listen.
He can tell what it is to take a ritual spear
in the meat of the thigh; or to walk alone
from Howard Springs to Hooker Creek
in the dry season, to pay a ten dollar debt.

Of all this he thinks very little, and shrugs –
debts must be paid, money-debts, blood-debts:
and anyway, he knows that country, he says,
as a man might know his own shadow
cast among many shadows; knows the places
of ghosts and spirits, and hidden waters
more secret even than a woman's thoughts.

Grey bearded, serene, Jacky Gallipoli
politely borrows Drum and rolls a cigarette
with the hands that killed an unfaithful woman.
I will write him in a song, I say, and he smiles,
shaking his head: each man has one song,
he says, and his has already been sung:
he will sit in this place, he knows, until he dies.

Anthony Scanlon

Writer's Block

The brooding pen,
like the hen that's stopped laying,
produces no chickens –
it scratches at an empty nest.
Yesterday, my mind was elsewhere,
my hand improvising on the page
while the paper, subservient as always,
just lay there, waiting – waiting like a bored
housewife coupled on a Saturday night
with a drunken husband – waiting,
waiting for the union of two inert forces
to spring to life with the aid of a little
imagination.

Yesterday, my mind was elsewhere
when the pen prematurely ejaculated.
The paper's a whore.

Dulcie Meddows

The Weather Always Wins

Stormy weather in the lead-up to the elections – then the sun
just when I thought the rain would never end.
I'm in my garden walking my dog with the early birds
celebrating worms amongst the dock and dandelions,
the lawn out of hand, paspalum tangling with ivy,
jasmine and honeysuckle fighting over camellias,
wisteria scrambling up the plum…

I won't go beyond the four stone steps.
Bamboo is on the move, roses rambling wild
bougainvillea guarding the crazy paving
with drawn thorns… Turning
I catch a flash of colour within a mess of privet
a huge hibiscus canvassing red…

In Hawaii
young, brown skin in tight sarong, bold
flower behind my ear – I invite a passing lover…

In Springwood
the dog chafes at her leash. But I'm cold
in my old dressing gown and slippers.
It's raining…

On the breakfast table that red tart,
pistil at the ready, disrupts
my marmalade and toast – I open up
the Herald. Results are still coming in.
Looks like another hung parliament
again.

Maureen Maguire

Float, Ophelia, float

Float, Ophelia, by narrow channel in fallen leaves.
Here the foliage is not taken away
not like up the road under the trees
on the left side of the rivulet.
Float girl, the water is old
wrinkles run in its depth
and on its surface, there are wet leaves
of linden maple rowan
a woman in a raspberry coat rakes them away
she removes them all.
Once she turns her back
they cover the soil again without breeze.
So float Ophelia, by a channel curved in a broken dogleg
if ever a dog was here it disappeared.
Float Ophelia, just don't look at wild ducks
at a young couple wandering by a park holding hands.
Don't look at fallen foliage covering your way
at rosehip still blooming by the sides
with a burgundy scream into the sky
at children playing in the park
at fat ducks fumbling on the shore
at a man walking a terrier
at an apple stub hardly seen among leaves
at sunny paths among the shadows
from pines in knots along the trunks rising to the sky.
Don't look at the sky
and at a cat running by a path catching a mouse or a lizard.
Don't ask him
Ophelia, you float, over the water
in a crevice between the shores.

Then inside one
inside concrete pipes laid under dunes
it's dark and stuffy there
for so long it's all the same
still better than in a coffin.
Float underground Ophelia
under water under sand under concrete.
Float more
then
mosaic of stones over gray sand
then float Ophelia
ahead
you will see the ocean.

Tatiana Bonch-Osmolovskaya

Michael on Darlinghurst Road

I move through ever changing light
as jumping pig and pussycat
cast an alluring red
tinged with green
over clusters of searching faces
but I cannot settle on anyone
as shoes jostle, swerving on asphalt.
A seagull squawks at chips in the gutter.
Love songs intertwine
from each new door
in blue and purple balls of light
glowing in the bubble of schooners.
Drinkers pulsate, gesturing and dancing.
Faces jump out from the rev of cars honking.

I'm here for myself
not trapped in a tightening, unloving knot of men
with clenched arms and ogling faces.
The checks in the starch of my shirt
are circling, jumping
so far away from my room's dull truth
of static white light.
I'm revolted, I'm electric
I want to run home
but I open my arms
and let it all shake me,
as a handsome drunk
knocks me off my feet
and smiles as he scuttles away.
I look up from dodging boots and stilettos.

Tree leaves flutter with pinkness
as the cat's purple tongue licks its green whiskers.
It stretches and jumps, then gives me a wink.
I'm here, I'm alone
as love twists high in guitar and song
boy fights with girl as engines screech.
I'm alone with all this
not the reproach of dark voices
and my eiderdown in baby blue
embroidered with cars.

Charles Freyberg

You Stole My Childhood

You stole my childhood from me
I cannot open the curtains again
I look in fear from the parting window
There is smell of smoke
I don't know if it's day or night
My mum and dad, they cannot hear my voice
Where are my brothers and sisters?
Where is everybody?
I look around in fear
I'm afraid of these sounds I do not understand
I don't want food or water
I want my mom and dad
I want to see my brothers and sisters
Where are they?
Where am I?
This does not look like my home
I want my nice home and my nice garden
You stole my childhood from me
You said War-War
And you stole my childhood from me
You all STOLE my childhood from me
You took my toys from me
You left me orphaned
I have nobody now
You stole my sun
The curtains and the windows
I cannot open any more
I cannot see my friends
I cannot go out to the street
I cannot even eat a sweet any more

You said War-War
And you stole my childhood from me
I cannot walk and I cannot run
I cannot see anything any more
I just wait by the door
I forget tea and the water doesn't taste the same
Aunty neighbour doesn't even come out any more
I'm afraid there is nobody around
You said War-War
You took my childhood from me
I don't have a toy car or a doll
I don't have stories or a school
I don't even have a ball
You said War-War
And you stole my childhood.

Seher Aydinlik

I was going to go to Dorothea Lasky's book party in Brooklyn, but instead I stayed on the couch with my depression, not crying

I was excited and I was going to go with another writer I'd met at another book reading
a few days earlier and I clicked *Going* on the facebook event and I felt good about this.

that morning I went on a chocolate factory tour in Bushwick and I coped with
leaving the apartment and getting on the subway and finding the factory and being
around people and I chatted over hot chocolates and croissants with hazelnut butter
and I was excited about going to the book party that night and I felt okay.

I went back to the apartment so that I wouldn't get too worn out before the book party
and Neha messaged to say she was worn out and couldn't make it and I was disappointed
but still felt okay and I ate lunch and had a little nap and looked at the clock and read emails
and looked at the clock and wrote a poem and looked at the clock.

at 4.58 I checked how long it would take me to get to the book party and it would take
47 minutes and that was okay because all I had to do was brush my teeth
and put on my shoes and I checked the route again in case there was a different way

and it was still okay because all I had to do was brush my
teeth and put on
my shoes and I looked at a different map to check the route
and it was okay because
all I had to do was brush my teeth and put on my shoes and I
looked at a video of
Dorothea reading one of her poems and it was okay because
all I had to do was brush
my teeth and put on my shoes but I couldn't face brushing
my teeth or putting on my
shoes or leaving the apartment or seeing other people – even
if I didn't interact
with them, just seeing them – and getting on the subway and
finding the venue
and being around more people and I didn't cry because even
though often there's
no actual reason when I cry uncontrollably during the day or
at 2 a.m., right then
I didn't need to cry. I couldn't cry. I just couldn't leave. I couldn't.

Paula Harris

How Do You Tame an African Eagle?

The African eagle
soaring high
gliding with grace
claiming the African skies
hunting in silence
yellow eyes penetrating the jungles below
scanning the vast savannah plains.

The African eagle
predatory in nature
vast wings obscure the sun
casting shadow over the rugged, drought ridden hillsides
large and small prey scamper.
The eagle swoops in savage attack
talons grip prey in death's embrace
oblivious of the constricted anguished cry
shreds flesh and snaps bone
to satisfy a gluttonous quest.

Indeed, how do you tame the ego
sitting on your shoulder
embracing you like a royal mantle
wings obscuring eternity's light
talons gripping your heart
mighty beak devouring your beingness
to become one with its predatory nature.

How do you tame the ego
when it is a part of your beingness?
When it is universal?

Dorothy Makasa

My Heart Has an Embassy

Written the night Julian Assange went into the Ecuadorian embassy

My heart has an Embassy
for Ecuador where I will seek
asylum. Earthquakes
and aftershocks undermine
my hope and my means to work
and the Americans
have wormed into my psyche
with their black knack at fear.
My heart has an Embassy
for Ecuador as rare in air
and sumptuous as the Andes,
as clear as the Equator. There
will be in it waterfalls
and jungles like salvation.
There will be friends
whom I owe nothing, no
famed bail, no knotty
knowing sexualities. My heart
has an Embassy for Ecuador
where there will be no secrets
and the truth falls down like water
from giant granites of despair.

Jennifer Maiden

The First Publishing Decade

Poetry publishing by established companies in Australia, often seen by the major players as a 'loss leader' to their novels and other works, started contracting as the 1980s rolled into the 1990s. It became increasingly harder for new talent to find a print outlet for their work, apart from the very competitive specialist magazines. Small publishers have always flourished in the poetry world. Another one entered the fray to give poets heard (and seen) at the fledgling Live Poets' Society, North Sydney, opportunities to see their work in print. Live Poets' Press (LPP) was born in a Cremorne flat in late 1990, when I excitedly lobbied for the idea – and became founding editor and general dogsbody (of that organ!).

Litmus Suite, our first anthology, went to press in 1991, featuring forty-six poets who had read in Open Sections or had guest spots at Café L'Orangerie and later, Don Bank Museum, North Sydney.

A few years earlier, I had edited a history book by James Ruse's descendant Janet Ruse Israel: *My Mother Reared Me Tenderley* (yes!). I worked full-time as a newspaper journalist and had also worked on computing and photographic magazines, so I had some knowledge of publishing in Australia. I had also edited a roneoed (who remembers that?) *London Poetry News* before I moved to Australia from London. My partner Danny Gardner, who worked in a library as well as doing freelance travel and sports reporting, had self-published and promoted two chapbooks of his poetry in London in the early 80s. He agreed to help with proofreading and general assistance, and we were off!

It was exciting and mad! We both had full-time jobs and I

worked many evenings reviewing arts events and reporting on council meetings in Sydney as well as being a journalist during the day.

Danny worked freelance as well as a day job. Maddest of all – we didn't own a computer! (Yes – it was that long ago!)

Friends and Live Poets regulars came to the rescue, letting me use their computer kit to type in poems, design pages and so on. Danny and I designed the first book's cover (which looks far too much like a newspaper headline shouting out!). We improved with the help of artistic friends. Poet Simon Lenthen and his lovely father, Paul, were particularly generous with their time and technical knowledge. They and others – Tony Scanlon, Jorie Manefield, Karen and Mel Williams, the late Ian Thomas and Nolan Project Services, run by then North Sydney Mayor, Gerry Nolan, in particular – gave generous hours to LPP projects. Danny and I were effectively doing volunteer work. (We only ever wanted to break even, financially – and did not pay ourselves a cent!) Other people offered help with food and drink at our launches. One time, an anonymous businessman donated $400 for wine – while an a cappella choir sang for free at the launch of our book that raised money for refugees, *Open Boat – Barbed Wire Sky*.

But the help didn't stop there! The incredibly supportive North Sydney Council allowed us to use their Hutley Hall for many launches and local artist Peter Kingston offered artwork for the cover of *Open Boat*. Meantime, Carol Dettman, of Neutral Bay-based publisher Chapter and Verse, stepped in to design that book. The printer gave us charity rates for that project and advertising colleagues on the *Mosman Daily* helped with earlier book covers. We even won a competition run by Wild and Woolley of Balmain. The prize? Free printing of our next book. As I said, we were blessed.

After the first two anthologies – *Litmus Suite* and *Live at Don Bank* (with sixty-six poets, published in 1993) – the difficulties of people having collections of poetry published in the shrinking opportunity pool seemed even more acute. So I decided to change tack. I offered five poets thirty pages each – mini-books within one volume. *Five Live* was first in that format. *Live n Kicking* followed suit, showcasing another five poets.

Launches varied greatly. Sometimes there was live classical music accompanying, once the afore-mentioned a cappella; sometimes Elizabeth Webby launched a book – sometimes another well-known poet (Martin Langford did the honours for *Five Live*).

From just Danny and I sitting at our dining room table triple checking spellings and spacing, layout and typeface, by the time *Open Boat* was birthing, a team of writer and reader friends – including North Sydney Council's then Director of Libraries, Martin Ellis – turned up to help proofread. It was a supportive, dynamic, caring cocoon, a fabulous community of talent.

I received some quizzical looks at the first book's title: *Litmus Suite*. I meant litmus in the scientific sense of testing, suite in the sense of a collection. So it was a collection of poems, a cultural 'sounding out' of our area; a testing of what was going on in the local arts world. I soon learnt, though. All the later books had much simpler, more accessible titles (generally with the word 'live' featuring!).

But *Open Boat* broke the mould in so many ways.

Litmus Suite had a packed launch where the late novelist and poet Amy Witting 'broke the bottle against the ship's side', as it were, at North Sydney's Stanton Library. And the book sold like hot cakes!

And why not? Among its pages were established writers and poets like Heather Cam, Anna Couani, Jack Healy, Tony Scanlon, Jennifer Maiden, Vera Newsom, Edwin Wilson. Yvette Christianse, Jerry Beans, Olive Lawson and Billy Marshall Stoneking, Peter Skrzynecki and Marjorie Pizer. Crowding in, too, were people who had turned up at our readings to be part of our often giant Open Sections. And those who came to listen, happily mingling in the Don Bank cottage courtyard in the interval.

That set the template of so much of what was to follow,

Sue Hicks
Lea, Preston, Lancashire, UK

A Momentum Was Created…

Time flew after that rain-shadowed evening in the full café at L'Orangerie that got things buzzing! Before we knew it, we were thinking and talking about the first anthology. There's only one thing to do after you've had some success: make it accessible in physical form. So there it was: *Litmus Suite*. Oh, not everybody knew what it meant straight off. And boy, you couldn't unread the headers! But what was really different about it? You don't get brass rubbings on Australian-made anthology covers very often!

1993 and the second Live Poets tome, *Live at Don Bank*. This cover was impressive – professional. Those guys know where and how to arrange the elements! David Fairburn did it. We were going through some old doorstoppers at his second-hand bookshop in Crows Nest one dull afternoon and we came across this picture of Jesus and I thought, you know, we've got to have that. The fire coming out of his mouth. On the cover! And Victor Ramos, who'd brought flamenco and fiery verse to Don Bank, was soon seen walking around, saying, 'Syllables are bullets! Words are bombs! The man of passion speaks!' And we even had sweatshirts and mugs made with this image on it!

A few books with a different focus – on the individual rather than the collective – came out next. *Five Live* with DG, Joan Aronsten, Richard Miller. Jim Provencher and Tony Scanlon between covers. Then *Live n Kicking* – same deal with Simon Lenthen, Sue Wildman, Maureen Maguire, Barry Donlon and Daphne Baldry inside. Covers by Dulcie Meddows. And poet pics by *Mosman Daily* cameramen. The vibe was definitely different!

In 1997, we had some electricity – *Live Wires!* Only twenty-two poets and they had a bit more space to sprawl – four or five poems and more. It was actually financed by us winning a competition run by Pat Woolley of Fast Books, who had been our printer up to then. Who designed that cover? Was it Bev Partridge? They made a mistake drawing lines – and bingo!

2001, a milestone to celebrate: *Ten Years Live: Ironic, Satiric, Sardonic – but not Moronic – Humorous Verse.* One wag suggested we should have called it Evil Pesto – that's Live Poets backwards. But first we had to say, folks, we don't want reams of rhyming doggerel! The masks on the cover were a clue – emphasising that poetry is a form of theatre, the poet being somebody else as well as themselves! And then Julie Cordner added another dimension on the backside.

Again it was made possible through 'other financing' – a Federation project grant – and a nice launch at Hutley Hall next to the Council Chambers. What role did it play in Sue and myself being awarded a Centenary Medal each? And it (the book) had a commercial side – featuring ads inside (OK, the company logos on one page). One of those companies produced Live Poets' first non-writing guest – Joe Mellis of Poets Corner. By the way, do you know that Merlot is 'finished' with the addition of two important fruits: cherries and blackberries. That may not seem important now – but bear it in mind for later!

Only two years after that, *Open Boat* was on the horizon. Enough was enough for the plight of refugees and asylum-seekers in Australia's detention centre gulags! Modern Australia has always been a nation of migrants!

What a rush that was getting that book done! From poets far and wide hitting bullseyes with incisive, biting material; Peter Kingston in his studio showing us a painting he said we could use for the cover; everyone pitching in to help from typesetting to proofreading to social commentary notables being quoted on the back cover, as if poetry was mainstream... To friends pouring the champagne at Hutley Hall yet again. To the cheque winging its way to the House of Welcome in Carramar. The first of many.

But this doesn't tell you about the cow bell, the bellydancer, the violinist, the Shakespeare-speak in harbourside mansions, the Valentine's Day in a bookshop, the Daylight Saving Day readings in the Balmoral Rotunda, the birthday candles at the Castlecrag amphitheatre, the poets' kids, the singing mayor, the good wishes postcards authorised by Ita Buttrose, the notes in the green sign-in book.

But by gum, we've started something!

Danny Gardner
Wentworthville, NSW

2019

The February meeting began with sadness. Notices of and tributes to the passing of long-time Live Poets stalwart, poet and illustrator, Sue Bacsi (her artwork graced the cover of the venue's twenty-fifth anniversary anthology, *Can I Tell You a Secret?*), and author, ethnographer of Aboriginal people, Deborah Bird Rose. There was also the incidence of calamitous floods in pastoral Queensland which had led to a *cri de coeur* from a resident on national radio, from which the convenor concocted a poem that he read before the meeting got started. He also called for similar responses from other poets to be celebrated at Don Bank within a regular feature, Homage to Country.

Optimistically, there was also this note: 'More young people are reading poetry than ever before', according to latest US and UK figures. It was stated that this is happening as identities are increasingly fractured by a disparate world controlled by corporations and leaders desperately seeking to hold onto diminishing empires under the looming shadow of climate change.

Specifically, February for Live Poets was a busy evening with special guest Tug Dumbly and the launch of the venue's Short Fiction Cup Chapbook (SFC), featuring the best stories from the comp's first five years. There would also be a Greenwich Village Time Capsule – famous and infamous residents' views on the small area of infamy in Manhattan – read by a selection of Live Poets attendees.

Tug's set was designed to promote his new chapbook of poems from Flying Island Press, *Sun Songs*. Hence items like 'Black Elephant', 'Irony Age', 'Life Advice' and a 'Poem for George Pell' ('I prefer God's funny old stuff!'). There was the paean 'Children – Unplug' then 'Love Poem for Dad', '(Dance) Like No One's Watching', 'Hate Wave' about pack mentality. There was an elegy, 'Black Sea', in English and Romanian, for a lost friend.

There was little of the interview we normally engage in when Tug visits. It all started and carried on rather straight up and noble (save for the Pell piece, maybe), but the audience bayed for a notch-up. Tug obliged with 'I Love a Stunted Country!' ('The lucky country lie, Dorothea!'). There was an observation called 'Plenty'. There was a 'poem for my son', 'Peeling'. A bit of a snarling rave about coincidences, 'What Could This Possibly Mean?' There was more baying and Tug swung into 'Nursing Home Playlists' (re songs on permanent replay which residents could nominate) which, invoked by Tug, simply raised the roof! The applause and hilarity was what you should always hear as a sign-out! There would be lots of signing of merchandise at interval.

With the SFC launch that preceded Tug, George Clark and Marie Mcmillan read their pieces 'Average Sex Life' and 'Tweetin' the Ashes' respectively and the convenor read Susan Sleepwriter's 'Boil a Billy', with its singular devilish menace inherent that I hadn't noticed previously. There were twenty-three books given out, including one that would be sent to Olga in Adelaide and two I would later deliver to Susan Weddell. Kerry bought nine for her friends and family.

After supper, the following people – Megan, Cathy, Emilia, Caroline, Lindy, Charles, Phil and Graham – read from the Greenwich Village Time Capsule with testimonies from such residents as Nat Hentoff, Larry Fagin, Patricia Clarkson, Lenny Kaye, Amanda Foreman, Matt Umanov, Raymond Sokolov,

Wynton Marsalis and Lou Reed. The convenor led things off with Dave Hill's 'The Village – Will we Ever Understand It?'

In the Open Section, Lynda Lovechild got us started with 'Three Steps to Miles Davis', 'Bag Lady' and a riotous Skyhooks parody, 'Livin' in My Seventies'. George read 'Angels', and Jenny Thurstun (back after a long absence) 'Bread and Peanut Butter'. Emilia Leonetti was a new face. Clark hit us up with some music including the eruptive 'Elephant in the Room' and I read a Max Jacob translation in honour of Peter Boyle, Deborah Bird Rose's partner.

March was a sell-out with Geoff Yule Smith appearing in a special show with his daughter Jade Yee-Smith (see 'Other Shows Featuring Music and Art chapter) and Mary Tang reading from her latest book, translations of famous Chinese poems entitled *Not Perfect*.

There was a quote to open the night from the (then still surviving) Clive James on the mystery of poetry: 'While reading about despair you might be suddenly visited by the music of elation.'

There was a tribute to American poetry icon, Lawrence Ferlinghetti – 100 years young this month. The convenor read LF's 'In Goya's Greatest Scenes We Seem to see…' and 'Don't Let that Horse (Eat that Violin!)'. Graham Cameron read the long, rushing, emblematic 'I am Waiting' and Phil Radmall stepped up with 'Constantly Risking Absurdity.' There were two more passings-on to celebrate and honour: that of American poet and translator W.S. Merwin (twice named a US Poet Laureate and twice winner of the Pulitzer Prize) and Australia's own Rudi Krausman, long-time editor of the art and poetry journal *Aspect*, a late flowering of the Australian Modernist Movement.

The convenor read Merwin's 'For the Anniversary of My Death' and this enigmatic piece by Krausman: 'PNG' – 'You stare at me and I look back (where the butterflies sleep) / black and white / is no more soda club / instead a new mask / with patches of colonial ice.'

In the Open Section, Phil read a new poem about his childhood, 'Harbinger'. Emilia Leonetti was back for another go with 'When They Ask Me'. Willem read 'Ray Charles, 1963' and (the cheeky) Des Maddalena shared 'Having a Coffee with Lulu'. Kerry read a short story, 'The Book', in a sort of promo for the SFC chapbook, more copies of which went out the door this night (authors bought them at cost price!). It was good to see Ava Banerjee back after a long time!

Mary Tang had been a guest in 2011 at Don Bank on the same bill as Omar Musa. There was a warm but brief interview with the convenor where she reflected at what had happened to her in the interim. The sixty poems in her book *Not Perfect*, written by famous poets from the Han to the Qing dynasties (206 BCE to 1912 CE), were short and poignant, the English translation following the Chinese. The convenor left Mary to provide background and context to her endeavour. Indeed, Mary's publishing team – editor, cover artist and calligraphist– were all present and we were taken on something of a tour of the book's impulses and generation; the circumstances in Mary's life that prompted the poems she read; and the wiles of translating grammar – 'easy Mandarin into long-line English!' Generally, as Ross Macleay says in his intro to *Not Perfect*, 'abundance of meaning is carried by brief expression in this book'. It's instructive to think of Mary's selection method: 'she would be moved to translate a poem by a change of season or the weather, by everyday experiences and the departure of friends ('Song of the Three Islets' by Chen Zi Long), an echo of a poem by Robert Frost ('Mountain Path' by Du Mu) or the recollection of a poem sung as a schoolgirl ('Flower not Flower' by Bai Ju Yi). Similarly, this evening the background to 'Egrets' (Du Mu), 'Occasional Poem on Returning Home' (Hi Zhi Zhang) and 'Autumn Reverie' (Zhang Ji) (that season ensuing in late August in China) were set in particular tableaux that resonated poignantly. An ironic twist lay in the fact the Mandarin character (now much simplified in modern times) was often intoned in Mary's Cantonese. Overall, a somewhat mystical but humorous and lyrical thirty minutes for the audience.

'Autumn Reverie' is a nice example: 'I see the autumn breeze in Luo Yang city / stirring in me much yearning to write home / fearing that I had left things unsaid as I hurried / I unseal my letter yet again ahead of the courier.'

Mary was a clear, polished performer and no word was wasted. Several people came forward to secure the merchandise.

April was our birthday month – again! There were amusing snippets from Live Poets' History Bits and Blobs and Questions from the Venerable Riddle Barrel for the raffle prizes.

The special guest was Tricia Dearborn reading from her latest book, *Autobiochemistry*. There was also going to be a major sing-off entitled Being Van Morrison for Five Minutes, where all and sundry could attempt the daunting task: do a song a cappella, like The Man! Several people had promised to give it a good crack – but there were not enough contestants as it turned out. (Only the convenor!) OK, I shrugged,- that's another idea that didn't come off!

We began with Rules for Writerers, a gag that's done the

rounds before. Bee and Alan had piked the VM contest but rattled our cages with some pearler songs: 'Don't Tell the Truth', 'Ain't Talkin' to You' and a version of 'Ode to Billy Joe' which did really bring the house down (yes, I remember Choctaw Ridge!). Jill did a song ('Eva') and Michael reminded us of an 'Anzac Day Hero' (it was tomorrow after all!). Mark offered up an untried rhyming couplet such as the Facebook group Eclectic Creators tease members with.

Tricia Dearborn last read at the Bank many moons ago (from 'Frankenstein's Bathtub' in 2005) and after a nostalgic session with the convenor read a set of poems from *Autobiochemistry* with a link to elements in the periodic table: 'Chlorine', 'Calcium', 'Tin', 'Covalent Bond'. There were reflections on relationships: 'Everything Including the Obvious'. And, after reading Virginia Woolf's memoirs, 'Vita (1925)'. There was 'Freud's Narcissus', a piece entitled 'Certain Kind of Silent' and the rather surreal, even creepy, 'Therapist Dreamt' and 'Scar Massage'. ('Unpack that!' as Tricia challenged the audience!) 'Change and Notes from the Field' warranted further investigation. 'Perimenopause as a ticket to KL' was a chance to get a few things off her chest, smouldering and incisive too. And we wrapped up with 'A Chalk Outline of a Soul'.

A most generous reading, everyone agreed with applause!

Literary Cities: Cairo (Words from Night's Tomb) saw Graham, Caroline, Jill, Michael, Danny and Emilia tender their services. Caroline did a piece by Rudyard Kipling and later, Artemis Cooper (from her book about Patrick Leigh-Fermor). Michael offered an impression by William Burroughs (drugs and maybe guns). Graham read Michael Palin's piece and we waited for the humour to start. Danny read his own 'Mistaken

Identity' from *Brains in My Feet*. Jill read Jennifer Maiden's poem 'George Jeffries Woke Up in Cairo' and Emilia emanated a timeless impression from Lawrence of Arabia, which Caroline captured in a vivid photograph. Jill also did more of her own pieces after supper – 'Awakening' and 'Identity One' – along with contributions from Remy and Stephanie. I asked myself at the end, should I have done an a cappella of Van's anyway – 'Ballerina' or 'Slim Slow Slider'? I think now I should have. I contented myself with more Live Poets, Don Bank history bits and blobs.

In May, it was time for several somethings different (see chapter Other Shows Featuring Music and Art on James Griffin, Ali Whitelock and Lynda Lovechild).

There was another tribute this night following the death of Les Murray. The convenor offered up an anecdote. Mr Murray was a guest one evening at a Sappho Bookshop reading in Glebe, run by Roberta Lowing. Afterwards, Les was invited to judge the Open Section. In that session, this convenor half-read, half-sang a Burkino Faso song (the original artist escapes me) in the 'original' dialect I'd perfected from several audio replays. A clearly bemused Les granted him the gong.

The convenor then read out two poems of Les's – 'Bat's Ultrasound' and 'Hearing Impairment' – which indulged Murray's delight in sounds suggesting matter.

To honour May traditionally being Live Poets' travel number, the convenor read out 'Trials Beyond Trail', which reflected on a recent book by ecologist Robert Moor, *On Trails* – how/why tracks through abject wilderness originally were formed and survived to be used/abused by modern civilisation.

There were two stand-outs in the Open Section. Beth

O'Driscoll's moving poem for her deceased son (which went on to win the Open Section Poem of the Year award) and Ian Hamilton's guitar and vocal 'Soldier Liberatore' (based on a Henry Lawson poem).

The annual Monologue Challenge was again enthusiastically embraced with seven contenders inhabiting speeches drawn from the hat. Marie Mcmillan got the most votes from the audience with 'I Saw a Woman Murdered' by a clear margin from Graham Cameron's 'Blind Date' – while Stephanie, Caroline and Mark also polled well with their efforts.

The Live Poets Players again featured in June with The Art of Modern Love (see chapter on Live Poets Players).

Anna Couani did a special guest reading, mostly from her book *thinking process*. Anna has been a leading figure of the Sydney art and cultural scene for decades. She's had several solo exhibitions and sundry collaborations with other artists. She's written seven books of poetry, was an art teacher and currently runs the Shop Gallery in Glebe, lately the scene of numerous exhibitions and book launches. She is currently working on a book of the suburb's rich history. Her artwork was personified for me by her PR photo for the Live Poet's leaflet – her face gazing past what appears to be rope (or the bar of a cage) to the wider world outside. It's a simple image with all sorts of connotations. Her cover art for the startling anthology *To End All Wars*, produced to signal 100 years since the 1918 Armistice, combines beauty and ash-like vacuity in a striking montage, again with a rope running down the middle.

thinking process is basically about 'making art'. Anna read several poems from it this night, including 'To Do List', 'About White' and 'Bitter', which reflected on the mind steps you go through in realising an image in another form and the layers of motivation behind our unconscious pattern-making. It also spoke of teaching art and Anna's relief that that 'trial' was no longer necessary!

The elements are laid out in the air in Couani's poems as we speak them. She also read 'Arc de Triumph', composed using a series of lines from the writers Remarque and Antigone Kefala to fashion a compelling harmony. In one poem, Anna asks, 'is it ekphrasis / if the poet also made the picture?' As Mark Roberts says in his intro to *thinking process*, 'the connection between the visual and the literary has always been at the centre of Anna's work'.

In the Open Section, it was a pleasure to welcome back Avalon from many years ago. After supper, there were some beautiful moments when Kari McKern, with only a couple of people yet come back from a necessarily late supper, presented, or rather emanated, a sort of physical essay in movement and word on identity with the haunting 'Discursive ID: four stages of She'. It produced a consummate presence that lingered vividly in the mind.

July was lit up with My Sauce Good (Dirk Kruithof, Laura Brodsky and Tim Bradley) and the question 'How Art is Good for the Brain (see chapter Other Shows that feature Art and Music). It also saw a visit from Jennifer Compton from Melbourne, who read from a couple of books, including *Now You Shall Know*, material from which won Jennifer the Newcastle Poetry Prize in 2013.

Jennifer's pieces ranged from 'After the Wake' and 'Sorrowful', which nevertheless 'instructs', 'do what is needful to make new', to quirky tones: 'Life is a Movie', 'Like a Butterfly' and

'Free Books'. Not to mention sociality with 'Frankston Massage' (with quixotic incursions from a Norfolk Island hostelry that 'just won't shut up!'). Jennifer took free rein on a question – what is the best strategy re a poet's approach to winning 'the Newk'? (according to her considerable experience). 'Something about the death of a parent – that's a clue!'

In the Open Section, newcomer Dorian had people engrossed with a couple of poems. Cathy Jones read a funny piece about the Archibald and then announced, 'I've just heard from my daughter overseas that I've become a grandmother!' George Clark ('Heaven and Earth' and 'Angels') and Kerry Jamieson ('The Last Time') read.

August saw a healthy crowd for the visit of Adam Aitken reading from several of his books and the latest edition of the Short Fiction Cup.

Adam related his scholastic connection to North Sydney (he still lives in a nearby suburb) before he reflected on that with his poem 'Class Photo'. There were several poems about his time travelling and living in South East Asia – 'Aubade' and 'S21' – and, most movingly yet also cryptically, 'Mon Agual'. From his time in Europe, Adam read, 'Walking in the South of France'. 'Hunters Song' freely engaged, whereas 'Hostage Video' took the reader/viewer into precarious perceptions. The audience responded to Adam's entreaties and his warnings.

There was another bumper field for the Short Fiction Cup, followed up by a promo for the chapbook on the first five years of the comp released in February. Will Tibben's entry was called 'Had She Been Back'. Bee Perusco read 'Murphy's Day'. Graham Cameron intrigued with 'The Turning of Mr King' and Marie Mcmillan revived her piece 'Vivid'. George Clark's story was called 'Renewal' and Charles Freyberg tendered the personal 'Terrania Creek Fantasia'. Kerry Jamieson, a past winner like George, presented 'Married to Jessica'. Wil Roach read his 'Fence' and Mark Marusic rounded proceedings off with the company-solidarity farce 'You Should Have Jumped Off that Train!'

As has happened a couple of times before, there was a dead-heat after the audience tendered their votes on the performances. In fact, three people had scored nine votes each. Lynda had not voted originally and now had the casting nomination. She voted for Mark. I have rarely seen him so happy as he accepted the specially decorated cup in triumph. Commiserations to Messrs Roach and Cameron!

In the Open Section, Will Tibben read 'Shark' from *Suburban Veneer* and Alastair Spate offered up some limericks. George Clark presented 'Harvest and Heartbeat' from *Crossing the Divide*, while Lynda did a rendition of the Aeroplane Jelly ode and song. Marie took us inside 'My Sensuality' and Charles offered up 'User Pays'.

In September, there was a presentation of the special, News – What Is It For? (see chapter Other Major Shows Featuring Art and Music), and special guest Alastair Spate. People from the floor would also read from the UK collection *News That Stays News* (a common description of poetry). Andrew Vial would also have a special treat for us.

Alastair read from his recent book *Lindt Café and other poems*. His work has a frequent relationship with current affairs and he stated as a preface, 'So many momentous events have happened in recent years – often you can only grasp them through isolating one's personal experience of them – such as I talk about here. It's often too difficult to approach them in any other way.'

He started with recorded music to which he sang 'Land of Hopeless Tories' (to the tune of 'Land of Hope and Glory'), a Brexit reflection, and produced a hat full of bits of paper: 'In case I need some more jokes!'

Aside from the quickly notorious Lindt café hostage drama of 2014 there were poems about a 'Road Kill' (near Phoenix, Arizona), 'Immigration' (of Africans to Europe by boat – tragically topical). There was the story of Jake Biliardi (from a Victorian small town to ISIS). A poem about the killing of Justine Damond, 'Mohammed in Minnesota', and a piece in memory of 'Little Philip Hughes' – 'so summer itself has gone in a mere game'. There was the Thai schoolboys cave rescue in 'Boys in the Earth'. In adroit alignment to the night's theme, Alastair seemingly proved there's a miniseries in every news item.

In the Open Section, there was 'What Bird Is That?' from Willem. Geoff offered pieces on George Pell and the scam of the original GST by John Howard and Tim Fischer. Kerry gave us the ominous family drama 'Glass is a Verb'. One of the 'original' Live Poets, Simon Lenthen, materialised with 'Old Man Talketh'. Jill performed 'Dark Horse' and a song, 'Woman's Tale.'

After supper, Andrew Vial, with help from Keith Heys and Graham Cameron, performed the playlet *The Seagulls* by Fran Bowick. This was an often hilarious portrait of the birds' relationship to humans and how they (arguably) mirror human characteristics to best survive. It had the audience falling around in mirth. Well done to those helpers who hadn't seen the script before. Maybe this piece should have been reported on in the Live Poets Players section. Thank you, Andrew.

Roll on to October and our Literary City tribute to Venice, with Bee and Alan providing Songs From Italia in their spectacular costumes (describe Alan's festival mask, people!), and the Masked Bard Ball Game et cetera (see chapter Other Major Shows featuring Art and Music).

This night also saw the interview of Wil Roach by Andrew Bukenya about Wil's (recently released) London memoir *Black, Gay and Under-Age*. Bukenya, born and raised in London, graduated with a BA at UAE before postgrad studies at Tokyo University of Music and Fine Arts. His presenting and hosting skills were honed in *Weekend Japonology*, syndicated to over 180 countries. In Sydney, he is a presenter of the *Sydney Symphony Hour* on Fine Music 102.5 FM. Early in the interview, Andrew reflects on the 'background music styles' in Wil's manuscript seemingly echoing his unobtrusive but insightful voice as the narrator of his young life. Wil: 'It was porous in my notebooks – the Little voice against Big voice – the necessity of not being heard in the small rooms so pivotal in my world in Ladbroke Grove. You couldn't get accommodation if you were black and had children and in a combined-family household of ten, the emphasis was on silence and an accepted, adroit separation of tasks.' It was a world of adult control. Wil: 'But as you made yourself smaller, you sharpened observation skills. I didn't miss anything – and this hyper-vigilance helped later with my talking to people. It was a dull existence – dull, grey and slow.' The young child resolved, 'When I'm adult, I'll be able to do things beyond "don'ts".'

From the book: 'So many inhibiting conditions had an effect on me as I grew. I would speak in my head rather than to adults. I don't think I trusted them at all. I turned to a nonverbal activity: cutting out paper soldiers. I conjured up my battle scenes and arranged the soldiers on the floor in our room – silent again at last. Our inner sanctum.'

Meantime, the parents worked or were at home – they didn't go out and didn't have holidays. Their power structure was established 'in the eighteenth century! But there was my mother's feminism – they had a shared bank account. I thought my father was a frustrated storyteller. The memories were so sharp – I didn't keep a journal! I put all the salacious things in code in adolescence. I was sweet to her but I was a boy and mother would snoop around.' There is an uproarious scene when the young author 'outs himself' to his mother. 'I loved high-heeled shoes and made some for myself – from wood blocks and some sticky tape!' (Of course, mother found them!)

Wil: 'Looking back on my adolescence, I see myself then as a teenage boy alone… I look in the mirror and think, 'I'm ugly. Why can't I disguise myself with white paint?'

This was before the blatant racism the family faced when his parents wanted to get Wil to a better school. The teachers seemingly marked him down from the first lesson. Wil admitted, 'My heart went with craft subjects.' But his father was impatient of his people crowing about being sportsmen and good at manual work: 'If [they] were going to progress they had to get better education.' His mother was never included in these discussions about scholastic matters and as Wil says (in another excerpt from the book): 'I didn't have the verbal skills to counter Dad's arguments…nor could I draw on my friends. Dad didn't know them. I couldn't invite them to my home.' He had invited one but then it was cancelled because Wil was embarrassed about him. 'I realised I would just have to wait until I left school to live my life the way I wanted, and have whatever friends around – including gay men. I decided twenty would be the suitable age to act – to leave or fake it with happy, smiling parents… The only alternative to avoid that fate was dying.'

In November, the guests were Rozanna Lilley and Raghid Nahhas. There was a 50-60s Sing-sing in the courtyard to farewell the year (see chapter Other Major Shows featuring Music and Art).

Rozanne would be presenting her book *Do Oysters Get Bored?* detailing her life with an autistic son. I built the interview with her, before her reading, around sundry questions 'Oscar' would ask her, which seemed to me to make the reader look at reality with new eyes. For instance, 'Who am I today – Mr Greedy or Mr Messy?' This was in reference to the Mr Men series Roz would buy for Oscar – they were good for enabling autistic kids to understand different emotions and personalities. Roz: 'I became various "Miss" people!'

'What's Bing Lee?' 'What is an hour?' 'What is an avatar?' 'What is a verse?' 'What does unversed mean?' Roz to me: 'Oscar has only one mood – the imperative!' Oscar has a frequent anxiety about the moon staring at him. Roz: 'Oscar was periodically hyper-anxious about going outside.'

'So, Mum, how did Cave Men discover fire?' 'I wish I was an invertebrate.' 'Do aliens have ancestors?'

'There's no need to be Australian. You can just be yourself,' Oscar says, looking at Australia Day celebrations at the beach. Seeing an Australia Post satchel a postman has over his shoulder as he passes, Oscar exclaims, 'It must be hard to be delivering mail to the whole of Australia!'

There are complaints while Roz is reading comics to him: 'If you're Spongebob – sound happy! Squidward is the one that's always miserable!'

Then there are the statements like 'Even though it's my birthday, I still care about you.' But 'What would you do if you were the most intelligent person in the world?' 'Do oysters get bored? If you were an oyster, would this entire place be unknown universe?'

Rozanna Lilley grew up in South Perth the youngest of five children. Her parents, the poet and playwright Dorothy Hewett and writer Merv Lilley, were both left-wing radicals. The family moved to Sydney in Rozanna's last year of primary school. After school, she attended drama school and as a teenager found herself in two feature films: *Journey Among Women* and *The Chant of Jimmy Blacksmith*.

Rozanna has worked as a social anthropologist at universities in Australia and Hong Kong – she returned home to Australia when her second child Oscar was born. She then completed a second PhD in Early Childhood at Macquarie. She's published a lot of creative non-fiction and poetry in newspapers and journals. *Oysters* was shortlisted for the National Biography Prize this year.

Rozanne's evocation of a seaside holiday in Berrara early in the book makes the normal fresh and vivid, super-real – it has a sort of *Under Milkwood* feel. Inevitably, the interactions with father Merv take on a remorseless and revelatory poignancy, a cycle of timeless overlapping, of the past acting on the present. These parts could not have been easy to write. Roz: 'Merv has been asking me for thirty years if I would like to go with him to Queensland or WA – anywhere that smells of his younger days and frontier adventures. He is certain he will go cane-cutting again and punch out men in their prime. All this while he is in a nursing home!' There are unsettling passages where Roz sees women and thinks, Are you my mother?' There are inevitable questions about Roz having to 'grow up in public' in her mother's permissive social scene. Roz: 'My mother didn't intentionally hurt me – but neither did she protect me.'

The convenor: 'The relationship between your parents – they seem such opposites at times. I recall one scene where Dorothy is upstairs with someone else and Merv is cooking dinner for you and suddenly starts crying.' I asked Roz how she navigated those times. What has been the hardest thing to accept about your parents' legacy?

The reply is really in the poems – at the back of *Oysters*, which she now read out. 'Soap Opera', 'Come Here, Child', 'Town Hall Café', 'Mickey Mouse Romance', 'Coming of Age', 'Dream Mother' and 'Love Poem to My Husband'. Neil was in the audience.

Raghid Nahhas, when he originally set up his guest appearance at Live Poets (when his latest book was launched at Gleebooks last April) planned to have his good friend Ghassan there to read his poems and back some of Raghid's verse with his oud-playing. But sadly Ghassan lost his life before then – a bolt out of the blue.

Nahhas was born to a Syrian father and a Lebanese mother. He graduated from the American University in Beirut – completing his PhD in Hull, UK. He published his first article on literature at sixteen. He founded and edited *Kalimat*, an English-Arabic quarterly, in Sydney from 2000 to 2006 and has translated many other writers for publication.

This night, he opened with an English version of his poem 'Temptation' followed by a recorded singing of the poem in Arabic by Ghassan Alameddine as he played his oud. Raghid then read from *Cities*, a book by Ghassan published earlier this year and, *No one Knows My Name*, a bilingual collection by Khalid Al-Hilli. Raghid concluded with 'My Damascene Lover' verse by verse in English and Arabic – enlightening our attention in both languages.

The convenor had opened what was a very busy night with his poem 'Haze', written in response to the imprisoning smog from bushfires impacting the city. Robert Kennelly did not have any of his own poems but cheerfully read 'Postcard from Guantanamo' by John Carey from *Light on Don Bank*, our fifteenth anniversary antho. Lou Steer, back after some time away, presented 'Flutter', and Kevin Heys in 'I Black' commented on racism in a young boy's schooldays. Les Wicks had an announcement re Poetry on the Path to Peace, an annual event staged by the World Poetry Movement online from Paraguay, originated as a novel response to crime and gang violence in that country. They now apparently hold poetry festivals before thousands of people!

After supper, there was a response to the attacks on the offices of Charlie Hebdo newspaper cartoonists by Marie Mcmillan. Lynne Lovechild sang a question, 'Have You Seen my Budgie Smugglers?' Charles Freyberg presented 'Terrania Creek Revisited'. His partner in a recent show organised by Ang Stretch in a Surry Hills church, Tug Dumbly, reverted to the wiles of Andrew Marvell with a sly ode 'To Her Coy Master'. Beth Jessop (O'Driscoll) read a telling 'I Am the River', while Phillip Radmall offered 'Repton Warrior' from his last collection. Thirty-six attendees meant this night was another sell-out and the voices kept coming: Cathy Jones with 'Words Fail', some more extemporations by Kari McKern, George Clark with 'De-Stocking' from life on his farm, and Marc Marusic took us out with 'Perfect Codes'.

An announcement of the Un-Darwin Awards (the year's special guests basically) and the general Don Bank Awards followed: the Monologue Challenge (Marie Mcmillan), Short Fiction Cup (Mark Marusic), Open Section Poem of the Year (Beth Jessop) and the Orange Wig for outstanding performance in a show – Alan Gannaway got that gong this year with his plague-mask and costume of frills as a Venetian 'carnivalist' in October.

The traditional raffle was held in the courtyard before the onset of the 50s Sing-sing (see chapter Other Major Shows). Yet again proving we know how to say goodbye to the night!

We could scarcely know – as no one did – what was on the horizon.

1937

A five-year-old child
gazes at the walls of her lonely cell.
With one tiny finger
she traces the names of her brothers and sisters
into the brick wall.
The bumps and cracks feed into her tender skin
the way she imagines her new teeth sink into rich, juicy tomatoes.
She only wanted some tomatoes.
The grown-ups in tricorns say she stole them.
She was hungry
and her mother always said to her:
'*Mi vida*, when you are hungry
you eat.'
The young child sits in the corner
visualising a feast
fit for ten.
Patatas allo pobre
arroz con pollo
washed down with a glass of full-cream *leche*.
Her fantasies pause
as they become punctuated
with the sound of sweeping gunshots
over Andalusia.
At home, her teddy waits patiently
spread-eagled on the duvet
pining for the warmth of her chest
and the steady time of her heartbeat.
A five-year-old child
sits and waits
for her feast.

Emilia Lionetti

For Detainees

The Statue of Liberty says,
send us your outcasts – or something like that.
It stands at the entrance to New York harbour,
an encouragement
for the rejected of the world,
holding high the ideals of
charity and compassion…

Here, in Australia, we say,
send us your outcasts
but not in leaky boats.
Send us your tortured and downtrodden
but not through the back door.
Send us those wanting a better day, another way
but, not without papers.
With the desert at our doorstep
we are afraid of empty spaces
to breathe, live in, turn into a garden.
We are afraid we will lose our way.
But isn't it lost already
when we throw away pity, lock up charity,
turn men's hearts away from the sun?
We, a sports-loving country,
remembering the rules
forgot the game.

Hearts like stone don't produce flowers
or a garden after rain.
A shoot grew from a rod
when other wanderers were looking for a home.
From stone
nothing grows.

Susan Bacsi

Bamboo

Shoots for stir fries and spring roll stuffings
winter ones stew in slow cooking crocks
split sticks for creating kites in summer
while kids cool in its shelter where

poets and lovers left their vows
on those proud and upright trunks.
Symbol of an enduring spirit.
Symbol of an upright scholar.

Now my brothers are wielding bamboo
poles that break the backs of brothers.
The rush and whoosh between the poles
once bound now torn at the roots.

Mary Tang

I wrote this poem after pro-democracy demonstrators were viciously attacked by thugs with bamboo poles.

Marcus's Song

The music's gone,
the turntables don't turn.
The keyboard's silent,
your pen and paper don't stir.
The bag's on a hook in the hallway
waiting for your return.

The poems I have in his book,
his story he told on CD.
I cry gentle tears in the morning,
for the beautiful man who loved me.
But I know where you are my son,
I know your mind's now free,
to wander in far-flung places,
to dimensions way beyond me.

Like those who have gone before you
the courage you showed on Earth
went unnoticed by ordinary people
and filtered away into mirth.

But you'll always be young in my eyes,
always be loved and near
I feel you in the breeze sometimes
and hear your words so clear:
Don't give up Ma, keep on trying
and tell them what I say.
It's not what happens to you in life
it's what you do with what happens.
That's the way.

He fought so hard for his sanity,
for all like him to be cured.
Of that we dare not speak of,
schizophrenia's a very big word.
Twenty he was, when it happened,
he dabbled in drugs and then
his mind took a flight to the heavens,
leaving paranoia and terror instead.

You fought the big fight my son,
I've never known braver than you.
The years you tramped hills in darkness,
craving the sleep you once knew.

He searched the internet daily
in the hope of finding a cure
dreaming for himself and others,
their minds and brilliance restored.

For the drugs they give you are numbing,
they play with body and brain
and leave but a trace of the person,
their spirit dies slowly in pain.

He took his life one November
on a hot, blistering day.
He gave me a necklace that morning,
with a smile that would melt you away.

But love's what he came here to teach us
and love is what he left behind
his beautiful gentle nature
and gifted talented mind.

And his ashes were thrown in green sanctuary
near the railway tunnel he'd slept.
Flowers were strewn on the river,
round a painting of memories we'd kept.
I wondered who'd see that flotilla,
what idea would they possibly make
of the soul of my son drifting softly,
beyond storms to the calm of a lake.

Beth O'Driscoll

No Friend But the Mountain

Dedicated to Behrouz Boochani – for all the men in Manus prison – and sung to the tune of 'God on My Side' by Bob Dylan

My name it means nothing
my age it means less,
the country I come from
is anyone's guess.
I was taught and brought up there,
it's laws to abide,
but the one thing I don't have, is the Libs on my side.

From over the ocean
I come seeking peace.
From my war-torn country
I ask for release.
But you put me in prison
and torture my soul,
but do I deserve to
live in this hole?
For many long years,
I've thought upon this.
That writing's my saviour
it gives me my peace.
To let you in Australia
know what's going on,
I put ink to paper
to sing you my song.

No friend but the mountain
to witness my pain,
to relive my trauma
again and again.
All I want is a homeland
I'm asking you please,
to live in Australia
where I can be free.

My name it means nothing
my age it means less.
The country I come from
is anyone's guess.
I've lost everything but
my will to survive
and I certainly don't have
the Libs on my side.

Lynne Fairy

and my heart crumples like a coke can

you never ate fusilli nor farfalle nor spaghettini. you did not like all that italian shite. you liked chocolate eclairs penguin biscuits beef with string in gravy and custard with steamed pudding which is like a fruit cake. a long time ago we wished you would die. you loved tractors and bobcats. a bobcat is the australian name for a digger. one winter you dug a hole in a field with your bobcat cut off the electricity supply to the entire village burst the mains water pipe. the water froze children skated on it wayward cars skidded into badgers and lambs born in unseasonal snow. your father was a farmer. he gave you your love of tractors. and potatoes. he skimped on other sorts of love. once you gifted a plough to mum. and a socket set. another time a cement mixer. you smoked and drank. grouse mostly. embassy regals. one time you moved a washing machine for a neighbour. you bought old tractors and renovated them sold them in the classifieds. although you could not spell it you were an entrepreneur. your legs went thin. the nutritionist said all you had to do was drink complan. you used to wash your car a lot. the celebrant at your funeral said you would be on your way to heaven in a gleaming vehicle. nobody laughed. you were not religious. i do not believe in heaven. your brother in canada rings me a lot since you died. he told me you were coeliac. it is unrelated to motor neurone disease. you were seventy fucking two. david bowie sixty nine. alan rickman the same. your adam's apple stopped moving. i realise i too will stop breathing one day. at your funeral your sort-of-wife asked for donations to the disease you didn't know you had. i don't know if anyone donated. nine days before you died i visited you at your pebble-dashed house, sat beside you on your tan leather couch, watched upside-down chaffinches feed on the bird nuts hanging from the hills hoist in your front garden. a hills hoist is australian. in scotland it is a whirly jig. i have been away too long. you tried to make your way to the bathroom on your zimmer frame. you fell in the hallway. i didn't know how to get you up. i lay beside you on the carpet. you kept apologising. there was nothing to apologise for. the nutritionist was wrong. you died the tuesday after valentine's day. valentine's day was on the friday. stephen hawking had motor neurone disease too. his is different to the kind you had. there are four different kinds. yours was diagnosed the day you died. you were already dead. stephen hawkins liked cosmological stuff and the big bang. you liked tractors. when i think of how much you liked tractors, my heart crumples like a coke can.

Ali Whitelock

Feline Frolics

Pixie perched upon the Pixie ladder
what other feline could feel gladder?
I'd safely say that Audrey would.
Perched upon a car's warm engine hood
soaking up the loving strokes
and patting from the passing folk.
You'd scarce believe this pint-sized puss so cute
could be a bully and a brute
to her feline neighbour Maud
in territorial discord
for a former dunny service lane,
and she might even be the one to blame
for heavy sprays inside the home
of her feline rival's servant Simone.
She's a boofhead with all other cats
except with Pixie, happy sharing household mats.
She gets on well with humans, doggies too
more to canine traits than feline she seems true.
A doggy in the body of a cat
she's not been known to catch a mouse or rat,
whereas Pixie has caught heaps
with miaowing loud to wake me from my sleep.
And waking Audrey too, beside me on my bed.
A night time stay at home cat, movements not widespread
unlike Pixie, night-time rambler, roamer
spurning company, glad to be a loner.
The Pixie ladder is her exit
from her home life to her wilder orbit
in Sydney's hipster inner west.

The ladder is bespoke, built to be her nest
after hours roaming she returns
to the edges of her home, framed in nocturne,
perched upon the highest rung.
I may be their servant, but they'll never get my tongue!

Mark Marusic

To Do List

find starch to use as glue
old type in box
add colour to artwork
use plate oil to change
viscosity of ink
print as monoprint
note
colour print on reverse side of rice paper
use pigment in glue
press book
post on Facebook
take book out of press
take close up of poppies
upload photos
write list of instructions
before forgetting
transfer list to other book
scan textbook for lists
of instructions
create lists from YouTube tutorials
remember to write list
find small saw

Anna Couani

The Goddess of Forever

Who earned great renown by blunting mad attacks.
She, who healed the living dead with holy heat.
She, Embracer of lovers and of just cause, ferocity,
knowing her body well.
She, who story spreads across cultures of the folk
and slips through the tick of time.
She, Goddess of the pearl palace.
She, who is as was and does as did;
woman, scent-laden, fleshy-full, as was written
and lo, shall be always rendered.
She, Who Rises whenever we journey inward
to the heart, the truth and the core.
Fullness of great duration, is now
and ever shall be.

Kari McKern

Wildlife Park, Gold Coast

Aged forty-five and famous as
the last to photograph a live thylacine
the first to breed a platypus in captivity
the only one to fly three plats to Bronx Zoo –
this Australian put animals first.
David Fleay left the south
to counter the ethos of the Fifties in the north.
He preached: learn from nature, preserve!
If it moves, DON'T shoot it.
Wife, kids and a carload of creatures
settled in.
Mary sold lollies, the kids did the cleaning
locals donated roadkill to feed the eagles.
To help the people care, he gave the fauna *names*:
Dudley the Lungfish and Wombat Keith.
Fame came. Her Majesty the Queen cuddled the koalas
and Ringo became a Dingo.
People liked the milker of taipans
who would offer them baby plats in cupped hands.

Fleay could have bulldozed Kombumeri middens
could have made his descendants millionaires –
but instead…*in the fifties*…he put animals first.

Lesley Synge

I Might as well Be from Mars

I stand patiently
waiting to be served.
Others come from behind
they get their orders filled.

I move places,
perhaps I am standing in the wrong place.
Others come, get served and go.
I stand patiently.

Am I not saying the right thing?
Am I invisible? Am I see through?
Am I different colour? Am I green?

They fail to make eye contact.
How could they not see me?
But I stand patiently.
Waiting to be served.

The clocks tick away.
I have somewhere else to be.
Surely there is something wrong!
I should speak up.
Stand up for my right.
Mustering up courage
I say 'Excuse me.'
They are also deaf, not just sightless.

I stand in sorrow.
Many have stood in lines
waiting for recognition,
waiting for food, water, shelter from the storms raging:
man-made or by an angry abused Mother Nature.
Waiting for months and years for a safe haven,
mercy, relief, a place in the sun.

My need for toothpaste is in comparison small.

Taking a deep breath,
exhaling in a slow meditative release.
Hard to not get stressed.
I wait some more,
give up, move to another counter.
Hoping for better results.

I might as well be from Mars.

Nur Alam

I Met a Teacher Who Returned from Mars

I met a teacher who returned from Mars.
He said that planet not for the learned.
Never, he saw a school or students.
Probably Martians never craved for knowledge.

I met a physician who returned from Mars.
He said that planet not for medical practitioners.
Never, he saw a hospital nor any sick.
Probably Martians never worried about health!

I met an undertaker just returned from Mars.
There he felt like a square peg in a round hole.
Never, he spotted neither a coffin or a corpse.
Probably, Martians never believed in death.

I met a lawyer who returned from Mars.
He appeared dejected and crest-fallen.
That's not a place for litigation or court house.
Probably, Martians remained law-abiding citizens.

Finally, I met a priest just returned from Mars.
He let slip the Holy Book from his grip.
None of the parables in the book referred to that planet.
Martians asked him to return – after making some interpolations!

Bhagavadas Sriskanthadas

The Little Boy Knocked Off His Bike

The urge to look is so powerful
that I express it with a sidelong glance.

Between one step and another step
I know that the knot of urgent people

standing tall around what I took to be
a bundle of old clothes and a horizontal bike

– I can see the mobile phones aloft –

that is the way we stand
when one of us is down.

The urge to rush and kneel beside him
– touch him, smell him –

is so powerful I have to clench my will
to keep on walking down to Aldi.

Jennifer Compton

Mont Aigual

In the crumbling church
there's a bone of a saint
the Romans boiled in olive oil.

A coat hanger is a deformed cross
that has outlived the golden vestments
of the priests.

In her office on the hill
the virgin's ears intact in fake fur.
She will stare forever
at the very same stars that wheel above
the world of the true night.

A forgotten swamp's refilled
to the level of the recalled banks
and the swifts return each dusk
to the paper map spread out
candlelit, and illumined as their valley.

Adam Aitken

Mohammed in Minnesota

the death of Justine Damond

Mohammed came to the state of a thousand lakes
to run from the slums, the tribes and the drought.
He left many kinfolk behind there
but never his angers and doubt.

The river folk had been borne out of traders,
raised in the habits of trust,
that a man becomes less of a stranger
when his price is fair and his word is just.

Their winters were long, and their God was hard,
his bounty seemed never enough.
Such souls can fall to the habit of guilt,
like payment for receipt of God's love.

Thus they too easily loved the Mohammed.
Oh, he could laugh and shine like the sun.
They gave as much of themselves as they could
– like a house, a badge, and his gun.

Justine, like them, was blue-eyed and fair,
and gathered the river folk all about her.
She'd come from a land where birds joke in the trees
whose songs fill cities with laughter!
One night, out the back in her laneway,
she heard danger in a woman's scream.
Went to help, rushed back to call the police,
their instructions she was right to believe.

Then she ran to meet the patrol car,
at the window to make her report.
Mohammed simply shot as she stood there,
her body bled out on the walk.

While her corpse in the morgue lay cold,
death-white in a metal drawer,
the judge gave the sheriff his warrant
to break through her front door.

They took strands of her hair just as fair
as that of the river folk had been;
the scraps of her skin, her fingerprints,
the fluids of her secret seas.

And the river folk mourned and wept
as they stood at her lover's side;
she'd lived by the light of the best and by trust.
But it's also by trust that she died.

Alastair Spate

September 11

I hear the sound of marching boots
It's hard to hear and far away
But clear to me above the breeze
On a warm and balmy new spring day

It's on the screen, spin doctors spinning
Tales you half believe are true
The task? To catch FREEDOM'S thief
What WON'T they do to bring it back to you?

I hear it in the voices of those
Who want to right the wrong
Prejudice is on the rise
A new world order helps it along

I hear it when the boots are stomping
Hard on faces who disagree
Why can't we just respect each other's rights?
And leave each other be?

As empires fall, minions watch
Revenge and hatred is not the way
What happened to turn the other cheek,
As eyeless, toothless, we face the new day?

Our little ones learn by watching us
What do they make of the sights they see?
They've sure learnt fear and hatred now
Is this how we want the world to be?

From my view on this precipice
I hear the thudding beat of boots
Our thoughts have made what I now see
I see a tide, a sea of marching boots

Bee Perusco

Coming of age

At 16, so sophisticated
smoking cocktail sobranies for the colour
Mum offered money for a party dress
        it glitters darkly

An occasional lover drops by early
His gift is LSD
Last time it was a steep hillside a dark park
He said it wouldn't happen again
invoked some serious girlfriend

Today we take a tab together
and use my bed
        It feels like victory
It's my first time on acid

My boyfriend senses duplicity   attacks
I step between   my skirt is rent

We are all caught
in the silver net of the night sky
tangled in my billowing broken girlhood

Rozanna Lilley

Fatima

Have you heard my name?
I am the Syrian moon goddess
The Source of the Sun
The Fate Maker and
The Controller of Time
I am al-Uzza, al-Lat and Manat
I am The Creatress
The Tree of Paradise
The virgin Queen of Heaven
I am Astarte
I am Mary
The Leader of the Worlds' Women
I am Hypatia
Murdered by a Christian mob in Alexandria.
I am Fatimah The Immaculate,
The Sinless, The Gracious,
The Chaste, The Pure, The Infallible
The Honest, The Blessed, The Clean,
The Bright, The Shining,
The Mistress of the Day of Judgement.
I submit to the will of God
who is always satisfied with me
I am the water carrier
I sweep the floor, no servants to help me
I grind corn, knead the dough and bake the bread
I take care of my parents and husband
I care for the injured in conflicts
I am the Mother of Imams
Umm al-Hasanayn:

Mother of Hasan, Mother of Husayn.
I am the sister of Zaynab, Umm-Kulthum and Ruqayyah.
I am the Mother of Her Father –
I belong to the prophet's household.
My land was confiscated
and I was deprived of my inheritance.
I am Fatimah az-Zahra'
Stand witness to my glory and purity.
I am the mother of the two martyrs.
I am reborn with the
mothers in the occupied land:
I am today all the women of Gaza
where every hour a Hasan is killed,
a Husayn is slaughtered,
Jesus is crucified in Jerusalem every day.
And one thousand times
my father is killed among the Arab tribes.

My weeping continues…

Raghid Nahhas

So Sleeps the Deer

Standing in the gap,
not knowing how to keep out
not knowing how to come near.
Time advances, lingers,
does not advance, does not linger.
All I remember is that I slept
without fully closing my eyes.
I woke up without fully opening them either.

'So sleeps the deer,' my mother says.
As if I were not asleep or awake,
not sleepless or slumberous,
a feeling between caution and fear,
concern and apprehension,
indulgence and anxiety
as if ants were crawling on my eyelashes.
As if an old desire is splitting my life.
As if life cannot be lived
except by turning a blind eye.

Ghassan Alameddine

Icons of Live Poets

Four Views of Dulcie (The Dulcie Meddows Tribute)

1

Dulcie is an old-fashioned name. And in many ways Dulcie Meddows had old-fashioned values. She represented the best of an Australia that is passing. She was forthright, upright, but left-leaning and defensive of workers' rights, but non-defensive in her personality and was vulnerable, honest and direct. She'd tell you to your face exactly what she thought. She liked people. And people liked her. Friendship was an art form.

Dulcie was a non-believer and opined that religion, like much of what passes for culture, was indulgent. We became friends immediately and the friendship lasted. I visited her and she came to our house for meals. Dulcie had a distinctive style of reading verse. 'I'm not going to posh it up for anybody.' She engaged an audience.

When I offered to publish her first book (through Gavemeer Press) she was grateful but not too grateful, as I wanted to eliminate some of the worst Australian narrative verses with 'dee dumpty dum' rhythms. 'I'm a package deal ' she said. 'You either take all of me as you find me, or none of me.'

The editor was paid but none of her suggestions for corrections were accepted. So the book ended up with a wide range of quality – from fine nuanced verses to ones in which the last word on a line had to find a rhyme later, no matter what. But it was published and our friendship remained intact. The book was launched with a letter of invitation signed by Dulcie Meddows, Published Author.

It was a success. How many poetry books have reruns?

But poetic success can be judged by other means. People learned her verses by heart. Her verse became an essential part of the international Eisteddfod movement. She gave permission for photocopying. 'I get letters from Indian kiddies who have dressed up to recite my verses in their eisteddfods. And from proud Mums in Wales.' Her best friend, Tina Colagiuri, had used Dulcie's book to teach speech and, through her, it became the first of Dulcie's *many* books.

Dulcie was a poet who gave deep thoughts in forms that could be remembered by people who weren't used to verse.

David Wansbrough

2

I first met Dulcie at a very early Live Poets meeting at Café L'Orangerie in Neutral Bay. It may even have been our inaugural event. Dulcie was sitting next to me and asked me to hold her hand before she read her work – she was very nervous and said it was the first time she had read to an audience. We all know she went from strength to strength, reading at many, many venues and always taking her heart with her. She even entertained three young children at my flat with her poems when she visited one day. Now in their late twenties and early thirties they have never forgotten that reading. Dulcie knew how to have simple fun and we laughed a lot as well as discussing poetry.

When I worked at a primary school here in Preston, Lancashire, teaching creative writing to years 3 and 6, Dulcie wrote to some of the children, putting comments on their poems as well as smiley faces. It was a poor area. They had never had letters from Australia or from an adult poet. They were thrilled –

and some wrote back to dear Dulcie, who also offered some art work for our one-off poetry magazines, faxing her drawings to our secretary. Dulcie Meddows was a very good friend.

Sue Hicks

3

The poet Dulcie Meddows is strong! The nuns advised me to visit her sooner rather than later and warned that she would not recognise me. Her friend Tina took me there.

Dulcie roused, looked intently, and clearly said, 'David.'

I spoke about Live Poets at Don Bank and she said, 'Danny.' (Danny Gardner) Her eyes sparkled and she smiled and said, 'Sue.' (Sue Hicks)

Always a down-to-earth free-thinker, apparently she now enjoys being taken to the chapel. And a kind priest reads to her in the evening from her purple-coloured poetry book. She is physically on this side of the divide but you can perhaps see her spiritual attainment.

Those who love Dulcie know that she left an abusive marriage in her late fifties and started writing while recovering from a fall into the hold of a riverboat.

People with Alzheimers can experience terrible panic but are somehow aware of our thoughts.

So, poets and friends, please focus thoughts on Dulcie – now.

She'll know.

David Wansbrough

4

Another to grace the anthology *Litmus Suite* when Live Poets' Society first got started, Dulcie was a writer/illustrator who used to present a current poem each Friday on 2NBC FM. Later she ran her own radio program, *Australian-made Poetry* (our venue was a good source for her guests). Dulcie's poems, often frank, funny and earthy, certainly struck a chord with audiences at Don Bank. She even composed a 'rap' song (Dinosaur Rap) so she could 'get with' a modern trend and stay youth-relevant. She also did the odd caricatured drawing of LP management!

At her memoriam at Live Poets at Don Bank in 2018, there was not a dry eye in the house.

Joan Aronsten

Joan Aronsten was a fellow of the Fellowship of Australian Writers. She wrote many stories for children, contributing to Kindergarten of the Air and scripts for television. She was published regularly in *School Magazine*. Joan became a copywriter and scriptwriter for adult listeners, doing a variety of jobs in radio during the war. She and her musician husband Max used to compose advertising jingles for everyday products on radio. She came to concentrate on fiction and poetry and was published in several anthologies, including *The Oxford Book of Australian Verse*, Poetry Australia, Women's Redress Press, New Zealand Poetry Society, along with *The Oxford Companion to Australian Children's Literature* earlier. She had several stories in *Australian Women's Weekly*. Joan became one of the first regulars at Live Poets when she was a member of the Willoughby Arts Workshop. She was chosen to be one of the five poets in *Five Live*, Live Poets' Society's third anthology of verse. She was a continuous and instructive delight to our audiences for many years. Joan left us in October 2013. She was ninety-eight.

Hilarie Lindsay

Hilarie Lindsay received the Grenfell Henry Lawson Statuette for prose in 1966 and 1967, the Queen's Jubilee Medal in 1967, an MBE in 1974 and an OAM for services to literature in 2006. A past president of the Society of Women Writers, Hilarie was also a toy manufacturer. Hilarie was an early convert to Live Poets' Society at Don Bank. Her poems always had a telling, often satiric edge. She caused a stir one night as she detailed being instructed by a doctor to 'just keep admiring the Jackson Pollock *Blue Poles* print' as she lay on her stomach while he conducted an inspection of her private parts. She and her husband Phil used to sit up the front of the Don Bank sitting room, with Phil's hearing aid oft-times giving off a keen wheezing sound. Hilarie always made sure the two took their chairs back to the shed outside and she often offered to help with the washing up. After a long time of middling commercial success as a writer, Hilarie hit the jackpot with her book *The Washerwoman's Dream*. It featured the extraordinary life of Winifred Steger, who left her bullying husband and her four children in the north Queensland country, went to the outback to work in a pub and fell in love with Ali, an Indian trader. One critic described the biography as 'a tale of such fascinating scope it could pass as a novel'. That was all down to Hilarie's craftsmanship. The book was a major seller for Simon & Schuster in 2002. In 2016, Hilarie was still coming to Live Poets, attending the fifteenth birthday celebration of Live Poets at Don Bank and making us grin with her observations. She passed away in May 2021.

Maureen Maguire

Another who featured early in Live Poets' story, Maureen was one of five poets in *Live n Kicking* (LPP book number 4) she was finally able to have her first collection, *Sometimes Smiling*, published in 2019. The poems therein convey the ups and downs, highs and lows of a life well-lived from post-war England as a child to being a new citizen in Australia and settling in the Blue Mountains. Her book has an honest, down-to-earth style, poems leading to observations unexpected in their endings. And now three generations of Maureen's family have read at Live Poets – grandson Nick at the age of nine was the latest.

Tony Scanlon

Another 'Live Poets original', Tony had poetry and prose published from the mid-1960s and his poems won the Jesse Litchfield Award and the Red Earth Poetry Prize (twice) in the Northern Territory, where he taught in the 1980s. That success led to his first collection of verse, *Rain at Gunn Point*. Tony had a PhD in Early English. He had been a poetry reviewer for a number of Australian journals and was published widely in Australia and also England and the United States. Tony's subjects moved to more broadly based themes in later years, although human relationships and the impact of man on nature – as well as tributes to his beloved Bears rugby team and memories of 'Brandivino days' and key family experiences – still featured.

Ed Wilson

As others have stood by the spotlights, Ed has been assiduous as Live Poets' artist in residence, with first poems, then sketches and oils of his previous lives in Mullumbimby and at the Sydney Botanic Gardens, to launches of his latest books of distinctive verse. In 2017 he presented riotous memoirs of his infamous uncle Frank, who claimed descent from Horatio Nelson and was an important mentor for the young Ed. His anecdotes are legion any season and have added richly to Live Poets' lore. The night we 'invited' the poets of the 1890s to Don Bank, Ed was in his element channelling Henry Lawson. He has imitated a didgeridoo on occasion. As one observer noted, 'He's fearless!' He even took Tom Gleason to task the night he won the big brass Hard Quiz mug on the ABC!

Willem Tibben

Bill has published four books of poetry, the last, *Suburban Veneer*, in 2017. In Live Poets' *Litmus Suite*, he asked the question, 'Does Bill Shakespeare (with whom he shares a birthday!) do the dishes?' Willem actually 'came back' to us in the mid-2000s to be the convenor's right-hand man on the door and collecting money from latecomers. He even made a video of the venue's twentieth birthday party and (sh!) its after-party. He also Re-Heated the Beats in 2015 and partnered Danny and Maureen in the combo Running Order, at this and several other venues. He was inveigled into re-enacting the moon landing in 2009, portrayed Guillaume Appollinaire and Aristide Bruant (but not at the same time!) for the Live Poets Players at Le Lapin Agil, and co-performed a late-60s Chain blues song with the convenor. But he has not, as yet, played his beloved guitar and sung Van Morrison for us. There's still time!

Kate Maclurcan

An experienced professional singer/guitarist, Kate has often formed the backbone of the music of a Live Poets' evening, both at the venue and other events off-base. Her range of songs – originals and covers from John Prine, Eric Bogle, Bob Dylan and Kris Kristofferson and many others – is wide. Her local choir sessions and North Sydney Leisure Centre activities were renowned. She has relocated to Victoria now but she is constantly in touch on our progress.

George Clark

George has been a Live Poets stalwart for decades. He can quote Slessor and Lawson on cue and has been a mainstay of the Live Poets Players, from playing a drunk spouting Belle Epoque verse in a Paris café to singing 'Mack the Knife' in the Weimar Cabaret. His stories have twice won our Short Fiction Cup. His brightly labelled red wine is a fixture of our suppers. He believes meditation and silence to be a form of prayer, particularly after a day of hard yakka on his farm near Oberon gazing up at the stars.

Geoff Yule Smith

Geoff is a pianist with a keen eye and a ready turn of phrase and some of his short stories can have you in fits. Around Homebush Olympics time, he entered a comp to write a new national anthem. As a Live Poets Player, his stature grew, from channelling Patti Smith doing 'Gloria' to making an ear worm of the Beatles' 'For the Benefit of Mr Kite' in a flashy coat and glitzy top hat. His greatest joy was doing a show with his daughter Jade (sublime with a pop ballad) in 2019 which. on a night that also featured Mary Tang. was the sell-out of the year amongst some stiff competition

Bee and Alan

Bee Perusco and Alan Gannaway have formed the Live Poets house band for over a decade with their versatility, from Piaf plaintive to Spanish café cantar to 'Ode to Billy Joe', Songs of Old Italia, the hit songs of 1968, and songs they've writ themselves. Their costumes have been something to behold (witness Alan's plague nose and ruffles in Venice and Bee's headdress in Homeless: A Sea Creature Speaks). The duo's lights and mikes have also made many other Live Poets shows look their theatrical atmo best. They have been excellent Live Poets' Players too – as in Ballad of Frida and Diego and The Art of Modern Love – sharing Orange Wig awards. Bee has won the Monologue Challenge with her Puck portrayal. Son Remy used to just photograph his parents but now he's threatening to complete the performing trio!

Dianne Schultz-Tesmar

Another early adherent to Don Bank, inveterate traveller Dianne was long content to watch. But her enlistment in Live Poets' Literature Olympics persuaded her to present. Soon she was reading some of her student-day favourites and her uncle's war letters. In 2021, in our quest for Australian Travel Poems, she took us on a 'Trip to Fairyland'.

Barvara Hush

One of our longest-standing supporters, Barvara lives closer to Don Bank than any other regular – particularly handy in checking local conditions in these Covid times! She has rich experiences of artistic milieus like Manhattan and the Greek islands. Her 2018 show of her time in the Big Apple opened many eyes. Barvara remains a keen protester against injustice in all its forms. She shines in the heady buzz in the courtyard after a performance.

Andrew Vial

AV told me flippantly the other day, 'I've been coming to Don Bank for thirty years!' He's a film producer of three decades plus and has acted in too many films to mention. He's always keen at Don Bank to encourage people to enact a sketch from a famous movie or TV show here and there, even one-act plays. His monologues can be confronting to the uninitiated. His poems can be surprisingly gentle. There's always another situation to demonstrate a point and Andrew sees no end to that part of the human experience.

Marie Mcmillan

Marie's versatility in presenting other people's as much as her own work, was demonstrated at the Live Poets show The Literature Olympics in 2012. Seamlessly, she portrayed the wiles of Dr Seuss's 'Cat in the Hat' as, at the other end of the show, she inhabited James Joyce's Molly Bloom monologue – the finale of 'Ulysses'. That was something of a foretaste of Marie's Slam Poetry career, which made her something of a household name in Sydney poetry circles in various open mike sessions from Glebe to Marrickville and Woollahra – even Nimbin and the Tasmanian Poetry Festival. Her guest spot at Don Bank in

2018 was SRO and crane-in-at-the window if you please! The throng were then treated to a retinue of Marie's greatest hits from her archly comic impersonation of eccentria to her more serious approaches to the reality of the Irish potato famine and the tentacles of terrorism. Other people wondered what had become of the lady who wanted to tango with Clive James. Or remembered reading her short story of 'tweet' messages between Shagger Shane Warne and Instagram porn, Liz Hurley.

2020 – The Year We Had to Forget

The bushfire crisis had inevitably ramped up communal anxiety levels over summer. For our February meeting, we would have two outstanding guests: Anne Casey (originally from Ireland) and Heather Bourbeau. Out here on a nostalgic revisit from California, Heather had come to school in Sydney on an exchange program in her teens.

The convenor began with an address of what Live Poets celebrates as it enters its thirtieth year of life.

Anne read from her latest book, *Out of Empty Cups*, from Salmon Publishing. In her pre-reading interview, she was asked, 'Does writing help you get a suitable distance from intimate subjects?' She replied, 'I think it helps you, rather, to embrace even confront them – get closer to what they mean to you.' A particular appeal to the listener is Anne's range of phrasing and facial expressions promoting an intimate connection. 'Between Ebb and Flow' garnered such attention as she played the observer of her past and home in the emerald isle. Similarly, the link to her mother and her way with words – how memory's 'light and dark define us'. There was the charm too of the protest poem posited a certain way such as in 'Recipe for a Giant Pickle'. Or the eco-poem where 'into the big big black hole…14,000 species of indigenous flora' informs the telling; 'Singularity' with its 'end result – the fate of the blue globe'. There is the humour too of 'Unconventional Love Poem' and 'Wildness' with its breathy confession: 'I have nothing on…and there's nothing I would change…but wrap myself in your shed skin.' One could have heard a pin drop at that. We were taken out with 'You'll Never Walk Alone' and 'Somewhere in the out there'.

Heather Bourbeau had been billed as reading from *Daily Palm Castings and other poems* but she had a confession: 'Unfortunately, I attended an event in LA on the way here and sold them all! But I'm getting together a new collection I have about half done and looking for a publisher. You can access *Palm* online.' I cast the audio of a video Heather had made of her reading out a poem, backed by a Syrian musician playing the tambour, as a general introduction. Her work had strong references to ecology and the human interaction with the animal. There was 'Grasslands of the Arctic', a 100-word story from a comp a couple of years ago. A paean to the 'Last Californian Grizzly' and the offbeat 'Maid of Nevada' ('watching an atomic testing demo with dancing girls'). There was 'Birdman of Istanbul' with its cafés of caged birds calling to invisible mates, with its concurrent comic side. She told of a game she and her writer friends play where they have to 'vomit write' on a theme under a strict time limit. There was the poem inspired by Aretha Franklin's hit song 'Respect' called 'My Song' with a wry anecdote – 'you put on any Motown record at my place and I'm back with my mother again!' Heather ended her set by calling up Anne for a photo with her before we went to supper.

There was a subtitle for the Open Section, How Do You Write a Poem?, with performers invited to explain how their verses get writ. A couple of people complied. Dexter Dumphy, once a LP regular, was back after some time and proffered two poems: 'Kite-song' and 'Waverley Clifftop Walk'. George Clark read a drought poem and explained some of the difficulties of assembling images. Amory Hill revisited 'Angry Ocean'. Typically, Bob Howe came forward with a piece, 'Writing a Poem', which starts with the protagonist noticing a spiderweb in the corner of the ceiling as he is taking a shower. Des Maddalena performed a rollicking 'Nimby' ('written some time ago now' as he sheepishly explained). Phil was on point again with 'Many a True Word'. Live Poets debutant Wil Boag read a sonnet he had concocted 'to help combat the effects of Parkinson's'.

It had been a pleasure to get another year started. The convenor wrapped things up with two items: the poem 'Before You Go Out Today' from an upcoming chapbook about climate change, *We've got 30 Years*, and 'Ship of Doubt', a story involving a country couple who'd spent the summer fighting fires to save their cottage in southern NSW. To celebrate, they decided to go on a cruise. But it failed to leave Yokohama and they eventually discovered why they were being held on board and the boat was restricted to port. People were being tested for a malady – a virus that had originated in Wuhan, China, according to rumour.

We would not be going 'live' at Don Bank in March. Or for the rest of the year, in fact.

Others had plans for us, though. Ange Stretch was curating a poetry festival in Darlinghurst which would see me interviewed by Brook Emery as part of the Live Poets is 30 rag. I had quickly outlined in my mind my most significant experiences at the venue, but the fest was canned. I went to the launch night of the 2020 Sydney Writers Festival, where Auburn Poets & Writers would be performing '2020 on the Human Experiment' but a pandemic was now performing an act on us! It too was shelved. Slammed into a coma like the rest of the city's activities.

Our actual thirtieth anniversary date arrived at the end of April and the 'show' was on the Facebook page with people tendering best wishes and messages. Mark Marusic recommended 'its enjoyable mix of featured acts and open mike. The affable host.' Later, he expanded. 'A hearty congrats to Live Poets for thirty wonderful years of entertainment and creativity. A hearty thanks to Danny and Helen, also Willem and Graham as steadfast helpers. I've been a fairly frequent attender for ten to fifteen years. A wonderful community. I always look forward to catching up with people I know there and meeting new people – so many memories…special place in my heart as this is where I met my beloved partner, Stephanie.'

Bee and Alan irrepressibly did a couple of songs in French on a video. There was this from Olga Kulanowska: 'Hi, everyone. This is a big hello from a strawberry that migrated to Adelaide! Missing you all. So many wonderful memories and friends. The other strawberry named Megan is keeping me updated.'

There was this from Wadih, who was one of Three Arabic Poets on a program from many years ago: 'My honour to be with you dear Danny in Live Poets at Don Bank.'

And Catherine Jones: 'Happy thirtieth anniversary, Don Banks Live Poets! Thank you, Danny, for all the fun and interesting nights you have organised for our entertainment. Guest artists and great open sections where people like me can read their poetry. Thank you, Helen, for preparing all the suppers and your delicious soups. I can't wait for Covid 19 isolation to be over so we can get our lives back and see you again.' She then read a poem called 'Beware the Air'.

People dropped in and out with salutations.

Geoff Yule Smith (+ Belinda + Jade). 'Hi, folks! Congrats for thirty years of Live Poets – and supper! The Geoff and Jade mini-show was devised especially for Live Poets! But here's something I've just written! 'While trying to survive Covid virus / Sco Mo's got us all acting so pious. / With no parties and pubs / And only hand-washing and scrubs / We're hoping the boss won't fire us!'

Mary Tang sent a poem translated from the Tang dynasty: 'Song of autumn wind' by Li Bai (701–762) – with this enduring double couplet: 'Who knows how long we will be apart / Love is a torment tonight at this hour / Long we miss each other long we reminisce / The shortest absence seems to last forever'. The poem came with an image: 'Tonight my living Matisse in flower'

In the week following, there were lots of articles and images from Live Poets' Society's first year – on Facebook – and succeeding frames of book launches and gatherings up to the 2000s.

Reviews of Live Poets Players' performances from the last eight years would be mounted on FB later in the year to remind people what the venue was about. A plan was hatched to produce a book to honour the anniversary of our thirty years at Don Bank (in April 2021). The public liability insurance for our Don Bank nights was paid even though we didn't know if we would be able to use the venue again in a 'live' sense.

In August, Auburn Poets & Writers celebrated fifteen years as an entity outside the Peacock Gallery in Auburn. Their FB page was suffused with memories of the multicultural group's early times and all their SWF shows since 2006.

Live Poets management toyed with the idea of doing meetings on Zoom, each month hoping that Covid's grip would lessen sufficiently for us to make it unnecessary. In November, on the date that would have been our last show of the year, we caved in. The 'event page' was heralded with harbour fireworks exploding over yachts in b+w. A goodly crowd turned up. There was lots of punchy wit and elegies and edgy music.

Bee and Alan got the ball rolling with 'Crazy Blues'. Kerry Jamieson read 'Fruitball'. George Clark the poignant 'My Tears are Locked Up'. Mark Marusic revealed an 'Unearthly Visit', and Bob Howe 'became' the (inevitable) 'President'. Andrew gave us the politician's non-answer, 'It is What it Is!', while Willem took us rural with 'Fence Post'. Bee and Alan came back with 'Got to be Goin Free' and 'Last Song'. Helen Wren reminded us of the 'Old Tree', while the convenor lent irony with 'Long Weekend at Long Reef'. As this was about half-time, the convenor called virtual supper and gave us the latest news. Marie Mcmillan came on to wish us all the best but was on her way out!

In the restart, Lynne Fairy couldn't resist 'Today's the Day the Teddy Bears Have Their Picnic!' and Barvara recited the curious 'Mask'. Kerry J came back with 'Spring' and Mark read 'Iconoclasm'. Bob then offered a haiku about Edgar Allan Poe – or was it Philip Larkin – at Halloween (can you imagine those guys as parents?). Andrew Vial re-confronted with 'Army Guys' ('Someone who just wants to SLOT someone!'). Helen Wren was there again with 'All My Christmases'. Bee did a piece about being on Zoom (!). Barvara waxed once more with the expansive 'Harvest Moon': 'think of all the full moons you've missed'. Willem gave a report from 'Sick Country' (uranium in the NT). Danny was supposed to finish with 'Crocodile Day' (still in NT) but someone said, 'Where's Helen?' and somehow we all knew it was time to sing 'Happy Birthday' to Andrew!

A more uncoordinated version I have yet to hear. He had the grace to blush.

And that was it – from the year we had to forget!

In a Sunburnt Country

Here where men are busily at work,
carving out new
deserts where wild
boronia once grew,
rivers running rapidly
dry, wallum frogs croaking by
their thousands, koalas choked
out of their ancestral grounds,
as sag-skinned cattle
carcasses graze on empty acres,
fenced against an inland sea–
one more migrant tide
repelled, kangaroo shot through
at sunset – their sorry hides
blanching over bleaching
bones for
daring to outrun
the culling gun
on
this new battlefront
where parched and starving natives
are run
aground, swarming from
new deserts carved out
by men
busily at work where wild
boronia once grew
rivers running rapidly through
and wallum frogs once croaked
in their thousands.

Anne Casey

Untitled

It's the extrovert that has to have its say
exhuberant, excitement unconstrained.
It's not the taste alone that marks the day
the sounds and sights are also unashamed.
Was born in northern France, a bubbly child
it's childhood in Champagne it grew up fast,
with many friends and parties very wild.
It gained a reputation and a past.
Now with its sense of place that is terroir
it knows the ground that guarantees survival,
it knows its base no longer just bourgeois
an adult now, completed its revival.
This drink of celebration and for sorrows
will never die, there'll always be tomorrows.

Wil Boag

Ode to Nimbyism

No – not in my backyard

I have lived a quiet life in the city
and have a tree-hugger neighbour that's a bit strange.
He is worried about the black-throated finch
living in the Great Dividing Range.
He is worried about the effects of coal mining
on lizards and bats at Maules Creek.
He is concerned about endangered species
at the Pilliga – he said he can hardly sleep.
He said we need to protect them
their lives and homes are as important as mine.
I thought his ideas were a bit simple
although his intentions were quite fine.
I said: they don't live in my backyard.
No, they're not in my backyard.

My other neighbour has a flash car and boat
and is an important commercial banker.
He likes to flaunt his wealth, his pedigreed dog
and is a bit of a loud-mouthed wanker.
He's only concerned about the stock exchange
and how it's continually changing.
He said the market is down and Aussie debt was up
and it really needs re-arranging.
He said the Yanks are making fortunes from fracking,
a type of unconventional gas mining.
We could do it all over Australia, if the locals
and greenies would just stop whining.
He said – but I don't want it in my backyard, mate.
No, not in my backyard.

This year the grain farmers are all smiling,
there was good rain and they've just finished sowing.
The weather is warm, the soil moisture is right
and a bumper wheat crop is growing.
The beef farmers are happy too, life is great it seems,
their pastures are lush and green.
The milkers and calves are fattening nicely
and the market prices the highest they've been.

They read about these new gas mines
and the greenies protesting, while downing another beer.
Those dole-bludging tree-huggers are a nuisance
they should be arrested and gaoled for a year.
They said: we don't want them in our backyard, mate.
No, not in our backyard.

The mining director was really happy, he's secured another good deal.
The foreign shareholders would all agree
to the payment of his bonuses with great zeal.
He was going to build hundreds of coal seam gas mines
in the middle of prime agricultural land.
He was going to flood the world with gas
if the prices stayed as high as planned.
He wasn't worried about the water needed
there was plenty deep underground.
He'd paid all the pollies quite well, but he was still
worried about greenies hanging around.
He thought, I don't want them in my backyard, mate.
No, not in my backyard.

The Pilliga farmer was unhappy, he's just found out
what the local council had planned.
They had agreed to a coal seam gas mining lease
on the block adjacent to his land.
In panic he went to see his local MP,
a fine, country-bred National party man.
His MP said, there's money to be made, we need to
build CSG mines as fast as we can.
With Global Warming coming, there'll be drought
and your farm's as good as dead.
I can't help you at all, I've quit farming
and welcomed the miners to my land instead.
The farmer replied, But I don't want them in my backyard, mate.
No, not in my backyard.

The farmer studied up on coal seam gas mining
and it soon became crystal clear.
It would pollute the underground water and poison the air
for animals and people living near.
It would ruin the farming land for generations
and speed up global warming as well.
It was invented for foreign investors for profit
but make the environment as toxic as Hell.
The farmer cried for help, the pollies and farm unions
were deaf, but the greenies heard of his plight.
They rallied the city-slickers and tree-huggers
across the land – and they all came to help him fight.
This is our land…we don't want gas mining in our backyard
mate. No, not in my backyard.

The moral of this story is quite clear. When you see a greenie
give him or her a hug and a smile.
Say, thanks for your help in caring for our great land;
I couldn't understand you for a while.
Now I realise your intentions were pure.
I listened to the pollies and got the message quite wrong.
Those political bastards have sold us all out for their own gain,
there'll be nothing left before long.
I think I've changed my mind, all of us in the cities
and all on the land must unite while we can.

We need to fight this together, vote out all the corrupt pollies
and create a national gas mining ban.
Australia is my backyard and I don't want it in my backyard, mate.
No, not in my backyard.
I think I'll come out and join you
And I might even vote Greens next election…what about you?

Des Maddalena

Untitled (Ibis)

An ibis
is poised on the edge of a bin
balance precarious
like a wind farm
on a cliff-edge tilted.

It takes off
energy-sufficient
wings pushing off the hard air
of politics

its bone middens
settling in for the millenia.

Robert Howe

I am – i am (trilogy)

Who am I
to tell you who you are

Who are you
not to know who you are

*

I am 'i am'
and nothing more
birthed by infinity
within my core

*

It is not about…
who I am
who I was
or who will I become

It is about…
the deeper i am
that is, was and will remain the same

Olga Kulanowska

The Burn

Smoke travels free –
no papers needed at open borders
where branched-elbows bend
dropping black to a groundsheet of ash,
bark skinned from each limb – a passage-free transition
to every pore of skin it travels through
depositing dark promises in streams and cavities
of lungs…hearts – hidden places –
nowhere is immune.

Those seeking shelter wait in libraries, cinemas, hospitals
escaping to the cool of enclosed spaces
hiding from the haze, a mist of compounds
the minutiae from destroyed forests,
terrorised creatures, insects, implements and houses,
the residue from bodies once unscathed and unafraid
become a fresh dough rising
before that final oven, seals the crust.

Each morning I watch winds bearing
the night's torment of smoke – stealing city features
locations now veiled…invisible
while ashes pose as falling snow
forest trees arriving piece by burning piece.
Gum-tree leaves – drop pewter-black,
buildings lost – turbaned in smoke
while McDonald's sign disappears –
a conspiracy of Nature – logged out from recognition
the once familiar no longer existing –

with smoke insisting under doorways…through fine cracks –
ash resting on whatever it encounters
every shelf, tin, jar, apple or egg…every utensil
dulled in its existence
each surface finely-textured to the touch.

And what of the Water?

A thickened sun mocks shadows-falling red,
posing blood-bold in the evening sky
ash drizzling soundlessly.
No birds sing: no wings carve through the airways.
Lungs panic – threatening foreclosure
hosting the fine drifts of the unknown
in a closing account with low interest rates,
as bits of trees and kangaroos, bees and cattle too,
settle at the doors of Insurance Companies and City Banks.
Killing all hope of returns – unlike the ash as it lands
still burns.

Jill Carter-Hansen

Authorities found in his possession a 'Literary Device' capable of disrupting perception over a wide area

I believe a poem
Is what you say it is
Whether or not
It's in time
Or rhyme
Is my biz
I believe a poem
Is a pile of sounds
Arranged like a
Painting for the ears
and for the heart
and whether or not
you do or don't
get it
doesn't mean it is
or isn't
Art.

Alan Gannaway

August 2020

When you sleep
The day breaks
In the afternoon as the city beats on
Comes the nightmare

Deaths. Explosions
Children crying
It's the aftermath
Of a Beirut afternoon

They are heavy with heart
Was it chemicals?
Or
Was it another bomb?
That they heard for mile sand miles and miles

They are saddened
As the grains are scarce
Oh Beirut
Oh Beirut

We do not walk along the water's edge
We are starving in the afternoon light
There is no water
No electricity
Yet we cry over spilt milk

When you sleep
Another day dawns
The clouds are not clouding they
The musket of chemical warfare
When dusk happens
A child dies. A mother dies. A father dies

There are only tears for Beirut
Only tears

Ann Jarjoura

The Lovely Rituals

The lovely mysteries are served by gentle rituals.
Reverential is the buttering of toast;
the slow preparation of coffee also has its order.
The placing of the cups and plates
on the table is somehow holy.
The jam spoon is an unread augury.
If dawn words are spoken with awareness
of their weight and lightness,
then our day will be truly blessed.
Touch your lips with love to the cup.

David Wansbrough

Adam

The sky is my song
Each note holds

Beholding him as he awoke, dumbfounded was I:
the exquisite rounds of his fingertips as he
touched the more sensational organ of his mouth.
No words yet had he with which to name the taste
of this most aromatic and beguiling of enterprises,
now unquestionably his: life.

When he arose – compliant, rapt, eager –
turning toward me,
I knew I would give him the world (and, in time, the word too);
I would sacrifice my own command
that he might stand without visible support.

What remains to be conjured
is that when he looks straight at me
      with the warmth of his engaged, engaging gaze,
    he sees me not: I vanish. Neither sees he
the luminous worlds bedazzled even in their efficacy.
He sees only this imagined ground where he,
now resigned and oddly enthused, resides.

Ten Ch'in Ü

Is It Really 2021?

With the Covid protocols still making a 'live' performance inside impossible for any more than ten people we were determined to have an open mike session in the open air over summer. We did a lot of talking about it with Auburn Poets. On the third Saturday in January, Live Poets gathered in the garden outside Don Bank cottage.

As the grey skies gradually ebbed away, quite a crowd had answered the call. We had a performance table set up, the local café was open to get coffee and even a meal takeaway, and those garden seats were starting to fill.

After a brief 'new year' from the convenor, Andrew got the proceedings started with 'Why Didn't Anyone Tell Me? and the politician's favourite reply, 'It Is What it Is!' Helen Wren followed with 'Back in Our Own Backyard' (a lockdown poem). George Clark had come up from his home in Blues Point Road with Sappho the dog and he read a poem about the letter 'C'.

Leigh and Lynne did a presentation about an exhibit they had in the Newtown Art Seat outside the Neighbourhood Centre in Australia Street. It featured Leigh's photos supported by some street-laced poetry from Lynne.

Mark did a poem from his book, 'Iconoclastic Journeys'. Cath Jones did a witty piece about where can we travel – why not try outer space? – reflecting on how the billionaires Musk, Bezos and Branson want to get us free of the contagion's realm. It just takes a very very well-heeled pocket to apply! The piece which features in the 'newest travel mag' was made very attractive by Miss Jones!

Barvara told of us a trip to Ettalong Beach in her childhood and later showed us her book with its pictures of Matala, some caves in Hydra (Crete) where she summered as a young lady. Caroline read us some haikus.

Andrew was keen then for us to have a break and give the local café some custom.

When we resumed, Mr Vial got us going again with 'Guts', followed by a scene from the money market. Helen W had us 'Remembering Mother'. George read us a poem reinterpreting the Mahabharata written by a young Indian lady. Cath Jones told us how writing in partnership with an artist in a book production had opened her eyes anew to her craft. Mark read another Australian piece from his book.

The convenor then read some poems from his recently released chapbook *We Have 30 Years!*

Anne Forsythe had wandered off but now Janet arrived and gave us just four lines uttered by a man who died after being caught under rocks in a kayak trip on the Colo river. People wondered how she had got that information.

We were almost wrapped up by then but Helen Wren had a song for us. It was based on the Scottish ballad 'Loch Lomond' but the lines in this chorus ran that tune thus: 'You take the high road and I'll take the low road – but I'll be in Scotland before yew! For me and my true love will surely meet again on the bonny danny don banks of Loch Lomond!'

When it came to the normal start of the Live Poets' season – Wednesday, 24 February – we were on Zoom once again for a truncated session. There was news to impart about the Sawmiller Sculpture Prize, and people wondered whether there would be a poetry prize for 2021 too. People reported back on seeing Edwin Wilson's latest exhibition at the Artarmon Galleries.

Only a few people had signed in. But Olga was online from Adelaide with a poem in French and a piece about the hour between the dark and the wood. Helen Wren read a poem, 'Night of the Storm', in her childhood. Andrew offered up two pieces about relationships: 'Ikuko Dreaming', about his ex-wife in Japan, and 'Journey of Life', which was about his mother. George offered a piece on Isaac Newtown in Latin – and a Carl Philips image-study called 'Archery'.

The convenor said he was negotiating with North Sydney Council and was hoping to have a 'live' meeting in March. Meantime, there would be an exhibition re Live Poets' Thirty Years at Don Bank at Stanton Library but the details were sketchy.

Preparations for the Live Poets' Thirty Years at Don Bank anniversary swung into full gear despite the lingering of Covid. The anthology, offered to Ginninderra Press as an idea with North Sydney Council support, was in prep. Invitations were sent out to anyone who had been a special guest or had read in the Open Section since 2015 to offer poems. There would be background chapters on the role of author and musician interviews, the annual competitions, the first publishing decade and so on.

There were conversations with Ian Hoskins, the Heritage Director at North Sydney Council, about the display in Stanton Library. Originally, he had asked for members' books to be tendered but during our meeting at Stanton we went into so much else that he was after: manuscripts in various stages of composition, physical things we used at the cottage to promote ourselves – ephemera like PR leaflets and theme night links, how program ideas were generated, and so on.

Several Live Poets regulars immediately sent their books. I had to organise and present the other items from Live Poets' 'impeccably arranged' archives.

Wednesday 24 March was billed as a welcome back to Don Bank 'live'. It would be all Open Section – no entry charge, no supper, no special guests and we would finish by nine thirty p.m. It became our new template for the winter months. There were a half dozen of us by the time we began. Mark Marusic offered up 'Reflections on a Distant Past', which was being workshopped for the Auburn Poets & Writers Sydney Writers Festival event on 23 April. Kerry Jamieson did two pieces, 'Shelter' and 'Down' – a confronting take on domestic violence. Marie Mcmillan was eruptive in 'Flunking Parenting' – what could one say after all? Stephanie read a poem about Mark's cat, 'Pixie', and *The Lost Book*, won in a raffle on a poetry visit to Melbourne, written by Timothy Train, basically a little tome inscribed in Tim's exquisite handwriting detailing how God had writ the world. Anna Forsythe read 'San Carlo Bliss' and 'The Conductor' – part said, part sung with lines from 'Old Man River'.

In the night's second part, Mark presented 'Pictures from the Past', another item from the aforementioned SWF show How Distance Can Keep Us Together. Marie read 'Invisibility' (how people get noticed, I don't!). Anna returned with 'Secret Body of Acoustics' and 'Woman in a Flannel Pyjama'.

In the evening's third section, Danny introduced the book *Republic of Conscience*, a 2002 anthology produced for Amnesty International of poems that 'tell of what should be challenged and changed in our world'. The convenor opened up with the poem 'Hamra Night' from Sa'di Yusuf (Lebanon), which implied there was a candle for everything in the world, which devolved to 'a candle in my hands'. The other people then called out a number between one and a hundred and read the poem on that page in the anthology. Thus Kerry read page 17, 'If Death' by Miguel Huezo Mixco (El Salvador). Stephanie read 37, 'The Messenger' by Zbigniew Herbert (Poland). Mark read 44 – 'Massacre Sandhill' by Grandfather Koori (Australia). Anna read 54, 'Weapon' by Judith Wright. Marie read 61, 'The Twenty-First Century' by Kevin Hart (Australia). Danny read 68, 'Sentence' by Saul Yurkievich (Argentina). Kerry read 'Beirut' by Ahmad Faraz (Pakistan). Stephanie – on a tangent – read an Australian rhyming poem, 'To Pee', composed while musing on the convenience 'available' on a bushwalk (!). Mark read 102, 'The Stalin Epigram' by Osip Mandelstam (USSR). Anna read, 'No Speech from the Scaffold' by Thom Gunn (UK). Marie read 'Internment' by Vincent Buckley (Australia). Danny read the first couple of paragraphs of the book's intro, which explained the premise behind it: 'Yes, I will describe it! This nightmare!' He then read 'The Slaughterhouse' by Jana Stroblova (Czechoslovakia) and metaphorically asked, 'What do you expect from a poem with this title? How can we be encouraged to believe there is something beyond the perceived horror – what the beaten prisoner feels/thinks when he opens his eyes again, how anyone hopes beyond an interval of dark which might be endless but, somehow – there is an interval of light again!

We wrapped up with some anecdotes from Live Poets' past and consideration of the creativity and so on of a TV program like *Would I Lie to You?*

The official thirtieth birthday at Don Bank was the next

item on the agenda on Wednesday 28 April (see story The Party).

The Stanton Library display was late getting mounted and its three panels of items would remain in the library until the end of May. Apart from the creatively arranged books and photographs, the highlight was the promotional T-shirt for *Live at Don Bank*, the group's second anthology, mounted around a female body, and a mug with a crowing cock urging, 'Five Live!'

Wednesday 26 May we welcomed Martin Langford, who would read from and talk about his new book *Eardrum*. As May is normally our travel number, we were conducting a search for the Australian Travel Poem (since we couldn't fly off to anywhere else under Covid!). People were asked to tender what you have found on this matter!

The roll-up was reasonable – it would properly test our new format. A wildcard was the eclipse of the 'super-moon', which had been gathering anticipation as a distraction – supposedly at its peak about nine p.m.!

There was a great response to our unofficial competition. Simon Lenthen read 'Great Ocean Road 'and followed up with 'How to Cry in Outer Space'. Beth Jessop broke people up with her 'My Orstralia!' Kevin Heys was off subject regardless with his poem 'The Tragedy and the Paradox of Greek Civilisation' by Vincent Kavaloski and he also talked about the 'philosophy' behind it. Helen Wren gave us 'Earth Mothers', which was based in the Northern Territory. John Carey, back after another long time absent, tendered his new book as an idea for our next feature and read 'Festival Up North' about the Byron Bay Bluesfest. Devina Bedford, who had made her Live Poets debut at our birthday party in April, rendered 'Poem from the Hume', a blues rag, a catalogue of our contemporary sins half-said half-sung as bushfire devastation was visited from a moving vehicle.

Andrew Vial started the second part of the Open Section with 'Visuals' and then invited Mr Langford to enact with him the 'coin-tossing scene' from the film *No Country for Old Men*. Marie Mcmillan offered 'Underground', which involved Lewis Carroll and the White Rabbit. Phillip Radmall bade us look down 'At Empress Falls'. Dianne Schultz-Tesmar invited us on a 'Trip to Fairylands' at Lane Cove National Park. And the convenor swept us cross-country in 'Drought and Beyond'.

In his prefatory comments to *Eardrum* (subtitled 'poems and ideas about music'), Martin lamented briefly that this should have been released last year but for the obvious. 'I didn't set out to write a book about music – it grew slowly. All poets are generally attracted to another art form – there's the musicality of notes vs that of words. And thinking about music can be another way of thinking about poetry.' He reflected on the classical music contention in its pomp and sense of celebration. 'Can we take this art, music, to heaven? Can we rediscover paradise…or just find the words for it?' We wanted to answer that question too. 'What is genuine emotion? There's lots of the other kind in theatre and rock music – with its three minutes to make an impact.' Martin wanted to write about more than one sort of music: 'Music is everywhere – almost a sixth dimension…we live calculated lives these days and we are losing something in that.' Like reading poetry, we are rewarded by really taking the time to listen to music. He read 'Jack', where a working class lad finds magic, 'The Symphonists', 'The Country Where Nobody Sings' – and Australia with its birds is a natural place for songs. In 'Uses of Music', the different way music is employed is made instructive. As light relief, there was the occasion of the unveiling of the Hornsby Fountain to finish.

I set up the drinks in the courtyard while Martin was still inside getting books sold – but because we had so efficiently finished ahead of time, most of the audience had decamped to get their peak moon eclipse shots. They did come back as I was sampling the Merlot and proffered disposable paper cups to take their fill! This new regime might work after all – especially in the winter months.

We only had one more meeting 'live' as of October. That was when we were visited by David Falcon with his new collection, *Hidden in Plain Sight*, in June.

Wednesday 23 June we were also being treated to a discussion on Dylan vs the Poets posited by an English literary critic who had some novel ideas about His Bobness's place in the literary firmament.

We were a small but cosy band in attendance as the Open Section began. Andrew Vial read Rudyard Kipling's famous 'If' and two personal poems – one to his ex-wife, 'Ikuko', and 'Images of Love', dedicated to his mother. It's a side of Andrew we don't often hear. Clark Gormley was there with his brother Graham to suss the set-up of the room for the fringe show he had concocted with Robert Edmonds, Failure to Launch, which those guys would be bringing to the Bank in July. He lobbed a couple of verbal grenades in 'Too Hard Basket' and 'Coel' – the nest-robber from the north! Kerri Jamieson was brave, deciding to read 'The Man from Snowy River' from her iPhone!

David then stepped forward with an intriguing promotion for his book. Instead of listening to him read and then people would be able to 'purchase the merch', David turned this on his head by saying, 'I'm giving this book out to you free of charge so you can follow my reading.' He proceeded to dispense *Hidden* to all and sundry, 'and you can take one for a friend who might be interested too, if you like.' This was a bonus for the likes of Wendy, who had never been to Live Poets before and had travelled from some way off to attend after 'booking a seat' over the phone.

In conversation with David, we discussed how he had been writing and presenting for years with some very fine material. What had finally persuaded him that a book should come out? He mentioned that he was the only reader in his family but he was so grateful his parents let him pursue further education. He spoke of how poems arrive out of a matrix of behavioural traits and trust in people, in the life around you. The 'quotidian' as Martin Langford said in a back cover comment re *Hidden* – the little events that make poems real – add a third dimension. David looked back on ironic phases of his life 'like where this line came from: "life is subtraction after 50"!' I remarked how I was so impressed by David's poem 'The Bridge', 'and those pieces where you are travelling in the country ('Crossing the Hay Plain at Sunrise', say) or the honouring of time past and outlining a family history from pivotal gestures rendered. He obliged by doing all his favourites and chatting with his 'followers' over this aspect or that. It was a reading with a 'fireside chat' feel to it. And those who did not make the trip really missed out!

I aimed to keep the momentum humming with the Dylan discussion. His place in the Parthenon – sorry, pantheon! – has been in vigorous contention since he was granted the Nobel Prize, in 2016, was it? Christopher Butler's essay, which I read out sections from, mention critics' wish to encourage connections of Robert Zimmerman's work with higher literary traditions and 'make it more acceptable to educated elites'. For instance, likening Dylan's approach to those pursued by Elizabethan troubadours (in 'It Ain't Me, Babe') or the metaphysical poets like John Donne and William Blake ('Love vs Zero/No Limit' vs 'Oh Rose, thou Art Sick!'). Dylan's work is prone to express abnormally elevated states of mind – can 'Desolation Row' be a tilt at the work of T.S. Eliot or Ezra Pound?

When Dylan was asked about his reaction to these theories he is a 'poet', he replied, 'My "poems" obey the conventions of the song lyric first of all. Allen Ginsberg is the only writer I know. The rest of them I don't have much respect for.' And he cites a 'middlebrow' lot, both past and present.

Butler maintains a songwriter in modern times has to come to terms with ideas in a way that is unique to himself and not as a matter of 'dutiful allusion'. Dylan, in Robert Christgau's opinion, is someone who has 'berserked himself into a genius – his surrealism owes as much to Chuck Berry as to Andre Breton – or even Gregory Corso (his contemporary).' Dylan's imagery is seated in epigrams which songwriters call 'good lines – some already quickly clichés!' Dylan may not be as 'good' to read as the poets but his revivified cliché, wit, rhythm, rhyme and everyday speech are far better than most of his contemporaries to listen to, Butler avers. It is a matter of the conflict between the socialised self and those drives of personality that exceed rational formation and definition. Dylan, like others in his postmodernist milieu, have all perpetuated their revulsion against a preceding stasis, the conformist squares that would pigeonhole them. Dylan's lyrics have done far more than anyone to develop receptiveness in a mass audience to things imaginative and non-trivial. Dylan: 'popular song is the space where the people hang out'. But which role models are those new discoverers offered – beyond the American dream again of self-fashioning and self-transformation to make anew? All judgements carry with them a number of potentially offensive social values. That surely is the price of individuality. The reality, Butler maintains, is that Dylan can be an extraordinarily complex, witty, self-aware and dramatic user of language and he preserves a difference by his singing that people can't emulate. His texts are not poetry, designed to be read autonomously but in service to the song, and they are not obligated to aim at and join the 'poem' in its autonomy. When we hear these lyrics, the music they are carried by is an inescapable part. But are there hymns hovering around in the background of Larkin's 'Churchgoing'? Or real organ music to accompany Milton, for instance? There are no tunes in Mallarmé, though there are plenty of vital, articulating rhythms.

Despite the Nobel's best efforts, Butler's contention remains: it's horses for courses. And I'm sure His Bobness is happier really that he decided to, after all, fulfil his Nobel obligations and respond to the commitments thrust upon him.

The discussion in our little group afterwards buzzed to some disorder.

Good to have a musician on hand too to discuss the nuts and bolts to a deeper extent, as Clark Gormley was so ready to do.

Matala

Crete, 1968

In Matala, life is lived by young travellers,
in caves by the sea, once tombs of yesterday.
All nationalities, today's peace lovers,
many long-haired, and some confused
searching for Utopia in this small community,
to the bewilderment of local Greeks.
Dreamers meet by the one and only water pump.
The well of yester years, communal of course.
At magic time, travellers assemble on the sculptured rocks,
applaud a sunset, or sing a song to the African wind.
From a distance ant-like activity scales the face of cliffs,
eroded with time, yellow pink at sunset the caves.
Black silhouettes, mostly women, wash dishes,
bending and standing in the lavender sea of Zeus.
Invited to a fire and another smoke, solve world problems,
itinerant thoughts and philosophies, writers and films.
At night, guitar strings slide over the ivory beach, the dotted lights
embedded in cliffs – time for a rice pudding or ouzo at the Mermaid.
Later, I sleep on stone now a softened bed, look around and wonder
of past dwellers, a tomb – perhaps a leper colony?

The sea sounds sometimes pelt the rocks.
Sometimes laughs hang and then angry sounds.
Even in this small world now so tranquil and free,
some 'beautiful' people cannot agree.

Barvara Hush

Down

When Dad used to come home after the pub
we kids would always know to keep out of his way
or he would yell at us, and box our ears.
He used to hit Mum
I assume, more because she screamed than because I
heard any thumps.
She used to come into our room and lock the door
to protect herself, and us.
I used to cry into my down pillow
until he went away.
And in the morning
he was always contrite, and would
bring her flowers, and say
I love you.

Kerry Jamieson

How to Cry in Outer Space

'In space, astronauts cannot cry properly, because there is no gravity, so the tears can't flow down their faces!' – Strange Facts.com

A piece of grit may cause an irritation,
(A grain of sand or some such dust)
The eye will generate self-irrigation
Without gravity, the attempt goes bust
You'll wink and blink with frustration
Leave the eye alone, what you must
Do is look dejected, and wear a frown
Until your rocket ship's touched down.

As you journey through outer-space
a void outside, and one within
You have a frown upon your face
that extends down onto your chin
Maybe you could try some mace
so that the outpour can begin.
But tears are hard without the pull
so your ducts must remain full.

An eye-dropper applied beneath the eye
can simulate a tear,
but without gravity to help you cry,
the drop you cannot steer.
The best that you can do is heave a sigh
Maintain a sad veneer,
Refrain from partaking in astronautic mirth
You can cry when you return to earth.

Simon Lenthen

King Charles

Oh I do love a King Charles Spaniel,
with their darling button noses and big ears.
They just want to love you inside and out
and trot around trying to please.

They are so soft and fluffy,
and are perfectly easy to control,
they're not at all unkempt or scruffy
come on command, no need to cajole.

Perhaps a little dalliance on the way,
but with royalty that is quite okay,
and the mistresses must simply obey.
They smell the roses as they clip clop by,
and water the plants with a cock of the eye.

They talk to them too with their yappy little bark,
knowing full well they'd rather sleep after dark,
and in the morning they're on the Fox hunt,
they don't want to be called a little runt.

So they allow their coats to be smoothed,
and they like to keep their ladies amused,
as they really have little else to offer
other than contribute to the Royal coffer.

They're playful, affectionate, and sociable,
fearless, patient, and adaptable.
But above all else they prefer luxury to poverty,
and to be treated like one of Mummy's corgis.

But on a more serious note, I really must say
that the importance of the Royal Family today
is becoming less and less significant
with farcical incident after incident.

One barely needs a good imagination
to come up with the ridiculous situations
and all the various machinations,
from affairs to fires to possible murders,
staff betrayals and palace intruders.

We've had accusations of Edward being gay,
Diana's love child from Hewitt on the way,
Charles wishing Camilla was a tampon inside him,
and a thousand other stories just as grim.

What about Andrew and his inappropriate behaviour?
He's been holed up in Royal Lodge waiting for a saviour
to get him back on deck and out of trouble.
He feels much safer hiding near his Windsor bubble.
He's even talking to his ex, rather than sex trafficking,
games he nearly got away with, never to be King.

Fergie's toe sucking escapades seem trite now
when compared to the current brouhaha.
And as for Harry winding back the clock
to give us yet another one out of the book,
reminding us of the constitutional crisis
when the Duke of Windsor abdicated in 1936.

He has nearly brought the monarchy down
with the antics with his American dream.
The actress Megan got under Harry's skin,
so he married her, and to many it was a sin
that her background was from an African nation,
prompting accusations of racial discrimination.

She like Wallis Simpson was also a divorcee,
but after two years of marriage who could foresee
that her prince would be stripped of his military honours
and would retire to a life with all the commoners.

As for Charles, the first in line to the throne,
while he still talks to his plants his future is unknown.
For it could be William who gets in first
to beat him to rule Britain's universe.

And with Prince Philip now gone to his maker,
his departure could well be the deal breaker.
That makes us question the monarchy debate again,
and I know what I would recommend,
that we do not need all that caper
on our side of the equator.

We have enough buffoons here,
so hopefully this will be the year
that Australia becomes a republic,
with a focus on its own indigenous public.
So no, we do not need a King Charles here,
Nor do we want spoons of him as a souvenir.

Devina Bedford

Ghost Town

We live in a ghost town.
Look, there are ghosts roaming the streets.
You can't see them, but can almost feel their presence.
Yes, masked people, carrying their dull eyes in their bewildered heads,
rushing somewhere, in a hurry, to return, from wherever they had come out,
to walk, to get food, to give food, or care, to run to the shop, or to the doctor's,
trying to avoid touching anything, scared of others they find on their streets.
Looking through my window, at this sunny winter afternoon, when the sun is just right on your back
I put my mask on, too, and get out just for a short walk,
joining the invisible others and also trying to avoid them.
Yes, I'm a ghost too, one of many, scared of those walking on my street.

Neera Handa

Friendship

A single thread of silk runs between us.
So strong, delicate and thin, unseen.
It transports our friendship
around the globe as it spreads.
And yet a single word said wrong
a word not said
can cut it, shear the thread
frayed too much it will break.
We can come across these floating threads
and choose to grab them
tie it back together.
Others are left to dissipate
it is impossible to hold on to them all
we can become tied in knots,
and yet others have very few
joined to the fingertips.
These strands protect us
cocoon us against the storms.
I hold on
pleased that you hold the other end.

Michaela Simoni

The Unwelcome Permanency of Implausibility

Three times today
I saw a man that could have been you.
One had your crossed legs and brown shoes.
Another, the company
I think you'd keep in the city.
The third almost had your luminosity,
the intrinsic brightness not always
given leave
tied to your own crowing cock.
But whose denial is it
and does it change
the plausibility that it was you?

If you denied yourself it couldn't have been you.

Three times today
I found a voice that could have been yours.
One had your narrative caught – paper bound
another, the silence
I think you'd hold on the ferry.
The third had your manner of speech and
rumpled rapidity of words when laughing.
The wind colludes to try and whip away
the speaking, steaming
sounds of your industry.
Denying that it could be you?

If you were denied, it couldn't have been you.

Three times today
I missed a man that could have been you.
One had your wings on his body
tattooed, arched, reaching.
Another, the subjection
I think you'd clothe in holey armour.
The third stood at your train station
held his body almost like yours but
he had no wounds
and story-less steps.
I am at a station of the cross,
an impractical reverie.
Wanting it to be you?

If I denied you, it couldn't have been you.

Trish Jean

A Virus Has Escaped!

Hear Ye Hear Ye
Media spread the word
There is a virus on the loose
Attention Attention!
My lovelies,
a virus has escaped and it is making its way to you!
Warning warning!
Go home lock your doors and stay clean
the boogie man is carrying a virus
and it can get
you, you, you.
Stay home!
Don't go outside.
We will deliver your food!
We will inform you!
We will update your news as it happens.
just stay Home
Twitter, facebook, Instagram, whats app, tik tok
Keep your people informed
The virus is spreading, people are dying
Keep them entertained
Keep them at home
Stay home people, the new world order is happening
5g towers are going up
Chemtrails flying overtop
Cashless society is on its way
Vaccines compulsory, your consent is not needed
Hand sanitisers, social distancing, mask your new norm
You can leave the country *only* when we tell you
So many dramatic conspirators

(scrolling social media)
'classic literature club' *join*
'Russian Literature club' *join*
'History' *join*
'Turks around the world' *join*
'Sydney nightlife back in the day' *join*
'Gardening Australia' *join*
found all my new tribes, all with similar interest
Stay home! Sure!
New friends, new groups, new clubs
Isolate? Sure!
Stay home? Sure!
New friend request – Hmmm who that?
Oh yes Peter from 12 years ago! yes Add!
Virus smirus
New world order, I welcome you!

Yasemin Dolcel

Ties

the shell an odd name for something so soft
cut on a splay to prevent twisting
contains tailors' secrets
of webbing interlining blades and slip stitches

the first ties i held were my father's
silken in shades of tan and gold
they lived in his wardrobe
with collar boxes felt hats tie bars and cufflinks

they were so redolent of him
part of the mysterious terrain
of adulthood i had not entered
when i received my own ties

they were double blue stripes
school kit
never a hook into the world of grown-ups
in the late 50s i spent saturday afternoons

shining my shoes laying out clothes
ready to go to the pictures that night
sinatra red and mitchell blue with matching socks
bobtail with no phallic arrowhead to signify manhood

when potential employment demanded their wearing
i borrowed my father's until savings allowed
and growing independence
demanded my own

open neck shirts now proclaim my life
in terrain no longer mysterious
now i don't wear ties
not even to funerals

David L Falcon

Against the Glass

Transantarctic Mountains, 2039

We run into the ice tunnel.
The light is pewter, the air flint;
our breath bruises the walls.

The sulphur fires hunting us
reveal a thousand-roomed museum:
a canoe with fossil ferns in the bark,

the stilled hands of the bearded man
in the blue dark; his dog, ears forever
pricked, in a vault down the hall.

We run and as we run
we wonder. What did we know, what
did we know, obsessed as we were

with lighting our northern caverns?
We thought we could always escape
with sleight of hand: the doubled joint,

the key in the mouth.
But we were a carnival
applauding itself.

As the air grows a fiery crown,
we run through the last ice tunnel
to the underworld, where even Houdini
beats his hands against the glass.

Roberta Lowing

You Get One At Every Meeting...

A foghorn of the forum   a saviour of the quorum
a standing orders-suspender   an agenda-bender
a pointer-of-order   a white-boarder
a sorry-I'm-later   an inter-school debater
an outgoing chairman   a projector-repairman
a carping complainer   a total abstainer
an offence-taker   a coffee-maker
a keeper-of-the-flamer   a let's-change-the-namer
a floating voter   a pass-the-silly-noter
an on-a-curve-learner   a move-we-adjourner
a resolution-drafter   a possum in the rafters
a hoverer by the door   a cockroach on the floor
a minutes-keeper   a grim reaper

a sound of crows squabbling on a blasted heath
a clock ticking like the slow grinding of teeth.

John Carey

Some Sort of Reason

We, apparently, have some sort of reason,
to dam the rivers and rape the forests,
to dig up the ground and concrete the grass,
to cage all the wild animals and fish out the seas,
to pollute the air and poison the water,
to reconcile our actions in half-truths to each other,
to build massive weaponry to protect ourselves
from each other.
Don't you think instead we need some sort of valid reason
to live in nature's universe?
To really honour and protect our fellow-participants
the animals – their lands and territories,
as part of nature's miracle;
it's delicate balance,
that pivotal interconnectedness
we alone could never make –
before it's too late?

Danny Gardner

The Party

The stage was set. The storyboards dressed the stage area and the classical music wove once more among the excited chatters of people greeting each other…the thirtieth anniversary of Live Poets at Don Bank cottage was about to go off!

We began with some history. How Live Poets got its name. When did it move from the Neutral Bay café? When did the first anthology come out? What else was published in that first decade? Open Boat was the highlight, raising almost $10,000 dollars for the House of Welcome, Carramar.

The Open Section was started by long-time supporter Di-anne Schultz-Tesmar, with her piece 'The Dancer'. Roberta Lowing followed with 'Pachyderm' from her forthcoming collection. Poets had been asked to nominate their best and worst experiences at Don Bank. Roberta always remembers reading from her book *Ruin*, based on the war against Iraq, with Baghdad refugee now Australian citizen, Nashaa, in a headscarf, apparently eyeballing her from the front row.

Simon Lenthen (one of the Live Poets originals) was next up and read 'Spider Web at Dawn' before reflecting on the poets and musicians of those early years of Live Poets – the atmosphere of those times when poetry was so new and vital to him.

Bob Howe then read some limericks – 'The Occasion', 'The Convenor' and 'The Partner', a bit close to home with some lines – in his inimitable style.

More history then, remembering Live Poets icon Dulcie Meddows and her cartoon caricatures of Sue Hicks and Danny Gardner. Her book covers and her down-to-earth verse. Ed Wilson – our artist in residence, scholar of Paterson and Lawson, with his propensity for anecdote. Willem Tibben and the help he lent the convenor with all manner of projects as well as collecting money from patrons on the door. Unfortunately, Bill could not be here tonight.

A newcomer to Live Poets, Devina Bedford, was next up with her poem about the Royal Family in the wake of Phil's demise, 'King Charles.' Then there was Charles himself – that is, Charles Freyberg – who took us inside the mystery of his grandfather from the Great War in '2014' when his grandson had that question answered. Mark Marusic did a piece from the Auburn Poets & Writers Sydney Writers' Festival show How Distance Can Keep Us Together. That show was on tomorrow night in Auburn!

Mark didn't mention it but when he won the Short Fiction Cup one year, I've never seen a guy so delighted!

It was then time for Marie Mcmillan. She recalled her most difficult reading – a poem about doing the tango with Clive James, with all his admirers owlishly eyeing her off. Best experience? The Weimar Cabaret here in 2015. She let out a few more 'secrets' about that night before launching into her opus 'Assimilation'. Never short of an attention span when she's around!

More history now. How Live Poets discovered the poet interview with all kinds of characters swelling that archive – from Robert Adamson to Omar Musa. Marie had reminded everyone of the Live Poets Players phenom which had rather directed traffic at the joint since the Literature Olympics in 2012. Lynda Lovechild presented her song for Behrouz Bouchani (who wrote *No Friends but the Mountains* by text from Manus). Lynda's piece was 'sung' to the tune of Bob Dylan's 'With God on My Side' and entitled 'No Libs on My Side'. It was this night's poignant highpoint.

George Clark followed with 'The Farmer's Hat' and an extract from Lawson. Best memory? Doing pieces from Kenneth Slessor's 'Darlinghurst Nights' at the Homage to Darlo evening. His worst? Doing 'Mack the Knife' in the Weimar Cabaret – in German! Danny G read a note on George's enduring 'living treasure' status at the Bank – and then there was his wine from the farm!

Catherine Jones is always up for whatever surprise Live Poets has in store – 'but it ends too late when you have to work at seven a.m.!' (We're often still here at eleven thirty p.m., that's true!) Her piece this night was 'Covid to the tune of Good King Wenceslas!'.

Phil Radmall then brought the house down with his poem 'If Poetry Were Soccer', with its immortal lines like 'He had so much potential as a poet / but he had such a vulnerability to injury!' And 'You're only as good as your last poem' and other hyperbole sports stars and their coaches and commentators come out with. And Phil is normally such a serious chap – couple of times he's been on the podium for the prestigious Newcastle Prize. World records were in the air when Garry Macdougall jogged in to top the score – even without Guinness on hand to record them! Garry's 'Town of the Dordognes' had to be completed within a certain number of seconds – so Leigh became his timekeeper! This was set up after a 'stripdown' by Garry that had the ladies trilling. There was another race against the Bard's clock. Then a sort of ditty, with a drinking song chorus – moronic but hypnotic if you please! – saluting each verse of 'The Hero of Our Time'.

Helen Wren kept the music coming with 'The Bonny bonny bones of Don Bank' to the tune of Loch Lomond (you take the high road and I'll take the low road, and so on) followed by her poem 'Gum Tree'. And there was this heartfelt take on Don Bank: 'It's so warm and you're so welcoming and unaffected that we feel free to make complete fools of ourselves and no one will judge us!'

More icons now, speaking of Bee and Alan and their shows and lights and mikes, Geoff Yule Smith, and other people who have passed on, like Maureen Maguire and Tony Scanlon – 'His last reading here was "the best I've done!" he decided.' And there is Caroline, who's taken so many photos of the drama and music and acting here!

Poet and actor and film-maker Andrew Vial was the last person up before we went outside. He read passages from *Cyrano de Bergerac* and the pollie's cliché response to questions: 'It IS what it IS!'

There was just time to talk about sell-outs at the Bank and Kaveh, the Unlikely Poet who made us a nightclub, and our perennial comps: the Monologue Challenge, the Short Fiction Cup and that Fifties Sing-sing in November 2019. But folks, 'There will be supper and drinks responsibly served outside and then the Riddle Barrel will be wheeled out for the – ahem! – Literary Quiz Snizzo! Please have your entry tickets handy for the call! There are books, books, books to win!'

And what were the questions proffered for the gifts of renown?

Who did Ernest Hemingway counsel in the loo of a Paris café with the following comforting fact? 'See? Compare that to those Greek statues in the Louvre! The way you're hung is fine!'

Who said the following? 'One cannot review a bad book without showing off.'

What famous Greek philosopher was Thomas Babington Macaulay talking about? when he said, 'The more I read him, the less I wonder why they poisoned him.'

Which English author once claimed, 'My main motivation to write came from my urge to annoy my readers'?

What English literary wit said, 'George Moore wrote excellent poetry until he discovered grammar'?

What English female author said this? 'He was a queasy undergraduate scratching his pimples!'

What Irish author was she talking about? (Clue: so many people have not read his more lengthy books but talk about how great they are, incessantly!)

The birthday card Helen Wren had kindly supplied was now doing the rounds and we'd just all said an almighty THANK YOU to Helen for her soups!

Graham's friend Angela noted again the sameness of each track from the Greek peasant singer Lu had on the soundbar. 'I can see that you like this music.' Graham was asked, what's been your best experience here at Don Bank? 'When you had the Brazilian singer on and there were only about six people watching!' Worst exp? Was that when you had your over-trousers halfway on – or off as she saw them – at the back of the room that stopped Marie in her tracks that night?

Passing the Baton On

So what happens to Live Poets at Don Bank from here? When will it be able to have 'live' shows again? (That was the question when the text of this book was originally being concluded!) It's formally confirmed its agreement with North Sydney Council until July 2023. It has this book to launch. It will be mounting some of its interviews on MP3 podcasts to Facebook. It will continue its social media forum regardless. I will have properly started organising the Live Poets archive once the podcasts have been completed from the audiotape originals. Our current publications before this one will still be for sale. But there will be no more books after this one. Covid has started the process of withdrawal through the first pause for it – but has not defined it. There are other projects I will move on to. There will be other people starting up poetry venues and I hope if they've seen how ours work(ed) they have had some questions answered and mission statements sharpened.

I – we all, I would hope – wish them well and lots of luck. But it's always taken more than luck. A certain type of hunger. A certain nerdy application to detail. You can never have too many ideas and practical solutions on how to execute them.

You need good people who support you. And you don't know what you've got till you're properly started.

Acknowledgements

Beth Spencer, Advice for Van-dwellers, Vagabondage
John Egan, The Mariner, The Long Way Home
Kit Kelen, fantasy here at home, Scavengers' Season
Martin Langford, Early Questions, Ground
Richard James Allen, Prologue, Fixing the Broken Nightingale
Audrey Molloy, The Spindle Shell (response to a poem by Anthony Lawrence in Ordinary Time)
Lou Steer, Frida – the Red Flag, Frida: Obsidian Butterfly
Les Wicks, Ho Ho Heil, Getting By – Not Fitting In
Mark Roberts, letter to frank, Concrete Flamingoes
Philip Hammial, Grand Theft Auto, Marooned with Pork Jinn
Garry McDougall, Crave Love, French Pilgrimage
Willem Tibben, hume and hovell monument, Suburban Veneer
Dona Samson Zappone, Tiger behind those rubber trees, New Straits Times
Katherine Gallagher, Year of the Tree, Circus Apprentice
Mark Mahemmof, Monumental Care, Urban Gleanings
David Gilbey, Intercultural Communication, Pachinko Sunset
Rob Kennedy, the other thing, Diverse Poets' Tribute to Brett Whiteley
Hamish Danks Brown, These are a Few of My Least Favourite Words, The Broken Candle
Philip Radmall, Couch Adrift, Earthworks
Tony Scanlon, Jacky Gallipoli, Flying Blind
Dulcie Meddows, Writers Block, Ten Years Live
Maureen Maguire, The Weather Always Wins, Sometimes Smiling
Charles Freyberg, Michael on Darlinghurst Road, Dining at the Edge
Seher Aydinlik, You Stole My Childhood, To End All Wars
Jennifer Maiden, My Heart Has an Embassy, Liquid Nitrogen
Sue Bacsi, For Detainees, Open Boat – Barbed Wire Sky
Tricia Dearborn, Therapist, Dreamt, Autobiochemistry
Ali Whitelock, And My Heart Crumples like a Coke Can
Anna Couani, To Do List, thinking process

Nur Alam, I Might as Well be From Mars, from the SWF show of the same name by Auburn Poets & Writers
Baghavadas Srsikanthadas, I Met a Teacher Come Back from Mars, from the SWF show I Might as Well Be From Mars by Auburn Poets & Writers
Jennifer Compton, The Little Boy Knocked Off His Bike, Now You Shall Know
Adam Aitken, Mont Aigual, Meanjin
Alastair Spate, Mohammed from Minnesota, Lindt Café and other poems
Bee Perusco, September 11, from her presentation Homeless – A Sea Creature Speaks
Rozanna Lilley, Coming of Age, Do Oysters Get Bored?
Raghid Nahhas, Fatima, In Italics
Ghassan Allemeddine, So Sleeps the Deer, The City
Anne Casey, In a Sunburnt Country, Out of Empty Cups
Ten Chi'n Ü, Adam, Mosaic (Auburn Poets & Writers)
Michaela Simoni, Friendship, from the SWF show How Distance Can Keep Us Together by Auburn Poets & Writers
Trish Jean, The Unwelcome Permanency of Possibility, from the SWF show How Distance Can Keep Us Together by Auburn Poets & Writers
Yasemin Dolcel, A Virus Has Escaped! from the SWF show How Distance Can Keep us Together by Auburn Poets & Writers
David Falcon, Ties, Hidden in Plain View
Roberta Lowing, Against the Glass, Transantarctic Mountains, 2039
John Carey, You Get One At Every Meeting, Quadrant
Danny Gardner, Some Sort of Reason, I Protest; We've got 30 Years

The reviews of the Live Poets meetings are the personal recollections of the convenor.

Thanks

North Sydney Council for their generous, unstinting support of our presence at Don Bank cottage.

Helen Lu for her hot suppers, and still images and videos of the monthly proceedings for our Facebook page.

Willem Tibben for his perennial unstinting assistance.

George Clark for his special liquid refreshments at supper.

The media, particularly Kate Crawford at Cumberland Newspapers, the Spectrum crew at the *Sydney Morning Herald*, the *Northside Courier* and 2RPH – Radio for the Print Handicapped, for their stories and publicity.

The Blues Point Bookshop, Antique Bookshop and Half-Back Exchange at Crows Nest, the North Sydney and Crows Nest Community Centres and Stanton, Mosman and Manly Libraries and the North Sydney Council Marketplace Notice-board for displaying our leaflets and notices.

The various and evolving membership of the Live Poets Players who've followed up every performance request made to them so adroitly and for the general Open Section for their help in mounting themes for our meetings.

Special mention to Bee Perusco, and Alan and Remy Gannaway, who've so often provided lights, mikes and atmosphere to their and the venue's general presentations.

Special thanks to Caroline Turner for her photographs of Live Poets performances.

Our regulars – we would be inadequate without your persistent patronage.

Those people who help put the chairs back in the shed at the end of the night.

All the poets and musicians who have read or played at Live Poets at Don Bank and all those people who have come to listen and 'discuss over supper in the courtyard' over so many years. You are the reason we open the door.

David Wansbrough

It would seem, on the surface, that David's involvement with Live Poets was initiated when he agreed through Gavemeer Press to publish the work of Dulcie Meddows, in the early 1990s the convenor of *Australian Made Poetry* on the radio. But who's to say he would not have found his way to Don Bank anyway? That he would not have discovered a camaraderie there and people who wanted to discuss art and poetry. A glance through his work in *Live Wires*, the Live Poets anthology of 1997 with its increased scope for individual voices, soon indicates the power of his words to convey his feelings and purpose as a counsellor of the spirit. Russia had already witnessed that power. He was a visiting poet at Moscow State University in 1993 and became a poet in residence at the Faculty of Foreign Languages at Lomomosov University from 1997. He still makes yearly visits. Then you discover David's 1988 book *Pillar of Salt* won the Albert Einstein Academy Medal. And tonight, you hear his voice boom

(Photo by Catalin Ovidiu Anastase)

out in the Open Section, inveigling you into a street scene far away with compelling motivations; brushing you against strangers you will need to make friends of, and there is no mystery about any of this. This is how the world works and, in David, you have the perfect guide to negotiate it.

Sue Hicks

(Photo by Danny Gardner)

We are only here of course because Sue Hicks's mother, Margaret, loved poetry and passed on the entrancing quality of words and spoken rhythms to her daughter at an early age. That is likely what led Sue to edit a poetry magazine at the University of Birmingham, England, in 1973, after performing with a poetry and music group called Black Columbus in the English Midlands in the early 1970s. She realised of course she had to use words in another way to earn a living and she became a journalist – a craft she was still practising when she linked up with a young bloke awash in his own poetic adventure in London in the 1980s. By the time the couple were living in Cremorne and Sue was writing for Cumberland Newspapers, her drive to get a new venue for poetry on the North Shore established was growing. Ultimately, it – and the many wonderful, determined poets, musicians and artists in its train – could not be stopped.

www.ingramcontent.com/pod-product-compliance
Lightning Source LLC
Chambersburg PA
CBHW070459120526
44590CB00013B/697